THE PRICE OF A FREE LUNCH

THE PRICE
OF A FREE LUNCH

The perverse relationship
between Economists and Politicians

ALEX RUBNER

WILDWOOD HOUSE LONDON
BOOKWISE (AUSTRALIA)

First published in Great Britain 1979

Wildwood House Limited
1 Prince of Wales Passage
117 Hampstead Road
London NW1 3EE

In Australia by Bookwise Australia Pty Limited
104 Sussex Street, Sydney 2000

ISBN 0 7045 3019 8

Typeset by Saildean Ltd, Kingston
Printed and bound in Great Britain by
Redwood Burn Ltd, Trowbridge and Esher

CONTENTS

INTRODUCTION   7

I   HOW ECONOMISTS HAVE CHANGED   12
*Is television to blame? Columbia did not like
Barbara Ward. They want to be men-of-action.*

II   THE LUCKY SEWAGE ENGINEERS   18
*Four unsatisfactory assumptions. The glory of
being a scientist. The sterilization of Wigan's sludge.*

III   SCIENTIFIC SOOTHSAYERS   25
*The aptitude to forecast. The Beckerman game.
The morality of false forecasting.
Cowardly or meaningless.*

IV   LIFE IS CLEAN AND HONEST   42
*Do illegalities matter?. Tax evasion. Bribes.
Smuggling. Breaches of exchange regulations.
In the Fatherland of Socialism.
Why illegalities are swept under the carpet.*

V   THE EXPORT MYTHOLOGY   76
*The wickedness of Marks and Spencer. Some imports
are marvellous. Not all exports are wonderful.
Two uncomfortable surmises.*

VI   THE IGNORANT PUBLIC   93
*Honeydew. A pot-pourri of irrationalities.
Garlic and metrication.*

VII   IT IS POLITICS THAT MATTERS   105
*Harold Laski and General Motors. Externalities.
What motivates politicians? Galbraith sneers.*

VIII   THOSE KNAVISH TAX-GATHERERS   124
      Patriotism is not enough.
      Seven techniques.
      Foreigners can help.

IX   THE RECTITUDE OF INVESTMENTS   141
      Investing is noble.
      State investments are even more meritorious.
      Dictatorship is good for investments.
      The moral argument.

X   TIME IS OF THE ESSENCE   154
      Ambiguous percentages.
      Spell out the time scale!
      Five time preferences.
      Roy Harrod and the stupid public.
      The politicians have their way.

XI   THE WEAKNESSES OF STRONG
    CORPORATIONS   171
      The selfless corporate autocrats. Big is best.
      Big is bad. The time devil.

XII   THE DREADED DREADFUL MULTIS   193
      Righteous or evil? Workers of the multis – unite!
      A world conspiracy. Ten debilitating handicaps.
      Coca-Cola leads the way.

XIII   354,000 HOUSES MADE MACMILLAN
    PRIME MINISTER   220
      Down with the private landlord!
      The bill of damages. On the political sidelines.
      Bevan and Macmillan.

XIV   SOME SOMBRE CONCLUSIONS   235
      Their numbers rise. Jobs for economists.
      There are free lunches. The future of economics.

    BIBLIOGRAPHY OF CITED SOURCES   247

    INDEX   254

INTRODUCTION

*Look, Maisie, when I'm doing business, don't waste my time
with economics.*

Expresso Bongo, *Wolf Mankowitz*

Roy Harrod's hagiography of John Maynard Keynes [64] was not
meant to deal exclusively with economics: the book was 'to bring
together all the varied aspects of his character and interests'.
Although the author says explicitly that he was not 'conscious of
any suppression', he nevertheless did not refer to his hero's
homosexuality. One must note with sympathetic respect why
Harrod is said to have penned deliberately an incomplete story of
Keynes's life – he wanted to spare the feelings of living friends and
relatives. Davenport, an intimate of both Harrod and Keynes,
offers however another explanation: 'I once asked Harrod why, in
his biography of Keynes, he failed to mention or even to hint at the
homosexual background of his early Cambridge days. He told me
that he thought it might lessen Keynes's influence upon economic
thought if he had done so.' [63] What does 'influence' mean in this
context? Harrod could not seriously have considered it necessary to
suppress seemingly unpleasant personal details in order to sway
professional evaluations of Keynes's theories. If Davenport's eluci-
dation is correct, Harrod must have had in mind Keynes's putative
influence upon the thinking of the man-in-the-street. It is certainly
true that the average elector looks unkindly on the unorthodox
sexual proclivities of public figures – but does this really matter in
relation to prominent academic economists? Nowadays, a surprisingly large number of economists behave as if it did matter. They
want to be regarded as men-of-action. Consequently, they are more
concerned to sell their wares to the readers of tabloids than to

earn plaudits from professional colleagues. I shall be arguing that the direct impact of economists upon political and business decision-making is feeble. It is therefore irrelevant whether they are homosexuals or not and what the public knows about their private habits.

Economists need not play by the rules of the game which candidates for elective offices are advised to obey. Politicians must sell themselves in the market place where their warts are screened and their personal righteousness extolled. Hence, aspiring and incumbent presidents of the United States have a vested interest in keeping their extra-marital relations a secret. John F. Kennedy may have enjoyed his peccadilloes but he had to make sure that they did not become known to his Catholic supporters. British prime ministers have not been averse to keeping a mistress, though none was as devious as Lloyd George who managed to pass himself off as Simon Pure to his nonconformist chapel-going constituents. These deceptions were and are necessary if one wishes to be simultaneously a sinner and a politician.

In 1961 Governor Nelson Rockefeller was the front-runner amongst the Republicans who sought their party's nomination for the 1964 presidential race; he had an overwhelming lead in the public opinion polls over his nearest rival Barry Goldwater. [145] Rockefeller, however, was not prepared to camouflage his private life and showed a public disdain for the prejudices of the masses. In 1962 he announced his divorce followed by the marriage to a woman he had loved for several years. When he returned from his publicised honeymoon, he trailed behind Goldwater. Nevertheless, by the time he contested the primaries in 1964 he had recovered somewhat and in the week before the polling in the decisive California primary, he was actually again in the lead. Three days before the voting came the bombshell: the media broke the news that his new wife had entered hospital and given birth to a son. Overnight, he lost his regained popular standing and was defeated in California, thereby losing the nomination and the chance to become president.

The capacity of individuals to serve the common good, and the soundness of their programmes, are of no avail if the electorate does not select them for public office. The sex life of politicians is politically significant because it may influence the voters. This is why politicians must be packaged and marketed as attractive personalities who are both God-fearing and maritally faithful. (Economists, engineers and writers of detective stories can afford to have deplorable personal habits without this detracting from their occupational successes.) Politicians learn at the beginning of their career how important it is to gauge what the public thinks of their non-political habits. If this is an unfortunate fact of life, it is not surprising that when they attain positions of power, they frequently feel impelled to apply this criterion to their political behaviour. Consequently, they tend to judge legislative proposals not only by their intrinsic merits but also, and often mainly, by whether the general public esteems them meritorious.

The translation of original socio-economic thought into action depends largely upon the transmission-belt operated by the politicians. It works in devious ways. Economists either do not understand this or, when they do, become impatient and angry. Having a prescription for sale, and having succeeded in persuading the decision-makers of its inherent soundness, economists are frustrated when it is not immediately taken up. What the vendors of economic advice fail to take into account is that a politician cannot set into motion a policy just because he is convinced of its intellectual merit; he must make certain that the electorate will be prepared to take the medicine. However, as the following story indicates, there are apparently some naive economists who believe that experienced politicians are easily overawed by the learned pronouncements of illustrious scholars. Balogh was invited by the Swedish sponsors to nominate a candidate for the 1977 Nobel Prize in Economics. He wrote back indignantly that, on principle, he opposed this exercise since he did not regard economics as a discipline suitable for the awarding of such prizes. Balogh further expressed his displeasure that awards had recently been made to people – the reference was to Hayek and Milton Friedman – of whose views he disapproved strongly. The *pièce de résistance* of Balogh's protest is his assertion that this conferment of the Nobel Prize upon unworthy economists had helped 'to mislead a number of non-economists in positions of great power – like the present West German Chancellor – into policies which will ... lower the living standard of those least capable of sustaining such pressure'.[146] What fatuousness to attribute to Chancellor Schmidt that he is likely to adopt an economic strategy just because it is recommended by economists who have gained the Nobel Prize! Economists fancy themselves if they imagine that this is what makes politicians run.

Samuelson long ago recognized the relative unimportance of economists; he described them as being 'like highly trained athletes, who never run a race'. [117]   Of course, there are individuals with a background of economics who have become successful politicians but they only did so after first burying their economic erudition in a concealed pigeonhole. There are also people, trained as economists, who have become prosperous businessmen; they achieved this not because of but despite their handicap of having studied economic theory.

*   *   *

Though this book deals mainly with economic subjects, economists are not meant to read it. My aim is to enlighten (and perhaps also to entertain a little) the intelligent layman, a task that may end in two pitfalls. On the one hand, professional economists will be able to point to deficiencies which unavoidably creep into any non-technical presentation of technical matters. On the other hand, the non-economist audience to which I address myself may after all find it too boring and difficult. Others will pass judgment on whether I have fallen between two stools. Galbraith has drawn on his extensive experience when he warned fellow-writers: 'It is a terrible and sobering fact that the first part of any book, and especially one on economics, is likely to be better read than the last.' [16] Let me therefore comfort potential readers that whilst the first few chapters may contain more abstractions than they care for, things become more concrete as the story proceeds. Indeed, the prosaic chapter on housing, at the end, epitomizes the 'message' of the book.

I hope that my concluding chapter (XIV) will demonstrate that the separate, and apparently unrelated, themes treated in chapters I to XIII are all blocks which fit together to form one solid structure. Whatever else critics will have reason to accuse me of, it will not be the sin of preaching a sermon. The aim has been to describe and not to prescribe. One of my chief propositions is that economic life proceeds by a momentum that is not directly impelled by the brilliance of contemporary economic theorists or the ingenuity of living Treasury officials. I believe that hard work, saving, ingenious inventions, managerial acumen, and other such noble features, have a more limited impact on the standard of living and the attainment of corporate profits than is usually ascribed to them in the speeches which some American businessmen deliver to captive audiences at Rotary Clubs. If I am right in my analysis, then it follows that much of economic forecasting – except perhaps that which is disseminated with evil design – is sterile. It is in the political powerhouses, of democracies and dictatorships alike, that the important decisions affecting economic life are made. Politicians, however vociferously they deny it, are much guided in their actions by the knowledge that most of the public is highly irrational in its comprehension of economic phenomena. This in turn makes politicians obsessed with short-term strategies.

Many of the book's illustrations are drawn from North America. Most of the examples, appertaining to absurd or wicked state-interventionism, have been taken from the thick portfolio of iniquitous policies by successive British governments. Practically all have their replicas in other countries. The perverse relationship between politics and economics abounds everywhere – on both sides of the Iron Curtain.

Chapter I

HOW ECONOMISTS HAVE CHANGED!

It is very tempting to turn one's back on the whole mess that economics has become and turn to pottery or subsistence farming as a more sensible way of passing the time ...

Anthony Harris

IS TELEVISION TO BLAME?

G. C. Allen waited 45 years before publishing his fascinating encounters with the 'most distinguished professional economists of the time'.[1] He had been instructed by Lloyd George to pick their brains and ascertain whether they knew of practical remedies to stave off the impending world crisis. It proved a 'disillusioning experience'. The *majority* of the 1930 luminaries at British universities chose to proffer no concrete ideas for an action programme. Some were diffident about their ability to make practical suggestions – and actually said so. Some thought that economics was unequal to this task. Some did not think it worthwhile to formulate recommendations because they were sceptical about the competence of governments to apply them. With humility the majority preferred to remain silent. Only a minority (which included Keynes) of the leading pre-war British economists 'showed the confidence in offering prescriptions for our ills that the world now associates with the practitioners of this science'. Allen reveals how shocked he had been by Lloyd George's pathetic reaction to the detailed proposals of those economists who had not been too shy to speak out. The great man just could not have cared less about the worthiness of their economic prognoses: 'his concern seemed limited to their political expediency or feasibility'.

Since those days the disposition of economists, particularly of the academic ones, has undergone a profound metamorphosis. Nowadays, almost all economists insist that they have the competence to tender practical solutions to national – essentially political – problems. Professors claim that their vocation calls them to write for learned journals and beckons them to become missionaries who preach to the ignorant man-in-the-street. Most economists also assert that they are better equipped than others to predict future events.

The advent of television has accentuated this new role of the economic 'scientist'. The vanity that grips dustmen and politicians alike, when they are honoured to appear on 'the box', has also affected economists and their families. Of course, Adam Smith and Irving Fisher, Karl Marx and Maynard Keynes, were never given the opportunity to preach from an interview-chair in a television studio. One wonders whether they would have changed their style of presentation had they lived in the second half of the twentieth century. Would they have remained intellectual snobs whose writings were intended only for an élite? Or would they have attempted to communicate directly and effectively with the broad masses? The modern professor of econometrics does not question that it is within his professional sphere to tell tired and mentally unprepared television viewers why the drought in Canada had an adverse impact on industrial output in Mexico. He is respected by his children and pupils for having been found worthy to appear on television – and his peers are green with envy.

In American studios stronger libation is often available, but in the reception lounge of the British Broadcasting Corporation invited economists usually have to be satisfied with Spanish sherry. When appearing for the first time, they may be told gently not to make blasphemous, vulgar or libellous comments. As if professors of economics would ever entertain using proscribed language! They also will be admonished to speak in simple language. If they mention the term 'GNP', the moderator of the programme is instructed to interrupt: 'You mean Gross National Product, do you not?' (Television producers on both sides of the Atlantic dislike technical abbreviations. They seem to think that viewers, who are unversed in economics, will be the wiser when the acronym 'GNP' is deciphered.) The most important injunction to the performing economist is that he has but three minutes in which to develop his theme. Has anyone ever walked out at this stage protesting that the difference between demand-pull and cost-push inflation cannot be elucidated in such a short span of time, particularly as the speaker is also enjoined to put forward a remedy for the current ills of society? Perhaps there have been such cases, though there is no record of any. For most economists – and I confess to my sinful membership of the club – the accolade of appearing before millions of invisible viewers is too great a temptation to be resisted. There is always the prospect of meeting next day the neighbourhood barber who will accost one to say: 'My wife saw you last night and she thought you were marvellous!'

In September 1974 President Ford put a glamorous seal on the link between television and modern economists when he arranged the televising of his summit meeting with America's leading economists. His guests were allowed to hold forth on the measures which they advocated the President should adopt to cure the ailing US economy. The cameras were focused on these poor deluded creatures. No doubt their views were seriously held and their prescriptions thoroughly researched. Glued to my television set, I listened to many of their discourses but cannot recall that even one made mention of the presidential elections that were due in November 1976. Yet, I suspect, the President probably thought more about that forthcoming event than about the counselling of the televised economists.

COLUMBIA DID NOT LIKE BARBARA WARD

In the summer of 1967 Columbia University proposed to appoint Barbara Ward as an Albert Schweitzer Professor of International Economic Development and allocated supporting funds of $100,000 per year. The choice seemed apposite. Barbara Ward (Lady Jackson, Dame of the British Empire) – as a press release of the Columbia University would later have it – was a 'noted British economist'. After graduating brilliantly from Oxford, she earned in her distinguished academic and educational career honorary degrees from the universities of Columbia, Harvard, Kenyon and Fordham. She had specialized in development economics and had written no less than fourteen books.

The constitution of Columbia University provided that a department of the university had to sponsor the offered chair and the administrators naturally turned to the Department of Economics. Its staff members were polled and by a majority voted to reject her. It was then decided by the administration that another department be approached and indeed the university's School of International Affairs and Graduate School of Business finally agreed to sponsor her. (I do not seek to disparage the important work done by this department, but the staff of the Department of Economics regard it as inferior within the orbit of the economic discipline.) When Columbia University announced the restructured appointment of Barbara Ward [20] in December 1967, it carefully avoided any mention of the previously frustrated appointment to a more eminent department. Nevertheless, one day after the news was published, the truth became known to the press both within and outside the United States. Why had Barbara Ward originally been rejected? Admittedly, she was a woman, middle-aged, and a foreigner. All these were attributes which, in varying degrees, might be regarded as misdemeanours. However, an anonymous 'senior official' of the Department of Economics disclosed that what was really wrong with her was that she 'lacked the particular scholarly qualifications of a modern-day economist, despite her eminence in other fields'. A cowardly 'high-ranking professor of economics at Columbia – who asked not to be identified – said that Miss Ward is a distinguished economic journalist but not really a scholar doing original work' [61]. That was the nub of the case against her: the Columbia professors did not actually catch her writing in salacious *Playboy*, nor was she proved to have earned her living by penning articles in plebeian tabloids. Implicitly, however, she was found guilty (and never denied the charge) of having been a contributor to journals like *The* (London) *Economist*, most readers of which do not have a Ph.D.*

At first glance it appears as if the pre-war world with its old-fashioned and intellectually meek economists, whom G.C. Allen has described, had survived in a university in Manhattan. Alas, the story only illuminates the dichotomous conduct of many

---

* Lady Jackson is a proud and stubborn woman. Though the embarrassing events at Columbia should have taught her that writing for *The Economist* (which she has done since 1939) blemishes one's standing as an acceptable economist, she has continued with this demeaning activity and was still at it twelve years later.

of today's university economists – and not only at Columbia! If
they restricted themselves to the teaching of abstract concepts of
economics and the construction of Indifference Curves, one could
perhaps appreciate their dislike of having somebody like Barbara
Ward enter their faculty lounge. Records, however, indicate that
few confine their activities to such constricted spheres. Many
indeed go slumming whilst wearing the uniform of a renowned
professor of economics: they write articles on economics for the
popular press, appear on television, and participate in mundane
political debates. The Columbia humbug epitomizes their split
personalities: they wish to be honoured as cloistered scientists
whilst simultaneously they solicit assignments from mass-
circulation journals and dream of lucrative lectures at the Lions
Clubs in Minnesota.

THEY WANT TO BE MEN-OF-ACTION

Post-war academic economists are eager to proclaim that their
discipline is not just concerned with theories and abstractions but
has many practical applications. This new spirit often begets the
conviction that the teaching of economics equips students with a
special capacity to plan the life of their fellow-citizens. It is perhaps
not surprising that many modern professors of economics have
convinced themselves that they can usefully perform also in
non-academic pastures: this gives them the added bonus of being
men-of-action.

A brilliant American economist was called upon to organize a
department of economics in the university of one of the countries
that had become independent after the war. He built up a faculty
which over the years has turned out many trained economists,
including a large number who are now pursuing successful
academic careers. The American professor himself added lustre to
his already distinguished scholastic name by original contributions
to economic theory which appeared in foreign learned journals.
His esoteric writings were of course incomprehensible to the
politicians of his adopted country. Nevertheless, they wondered
whether the acclaimed scholar in their midst could not be
harnessed to grapple with some of their daily problems. At first he
refused because he felt more at home with algebraic formulae and
complex curves than amongst the current concrete issues that

plagued the politicians. Finally, however, he relented and agreed to make a 'practical contribution'.

When the professor allowed himself to be recruited, the government was in a balance-of-payments crisis and had a growing domestic budget deficit. Applying his fertile mind, our public-spirited scholar devised a tax proposal that was intended to curb foreign currency expenditure and/or raise additional tax revenues. The professor's intricate, differential travel tax deserves to be enshrined in fiscal textbooks for its ingenuity and seeming fairness.

At the beginning the government was delighted, but soon this cleverly contrived tax proved largely unworkable: because of its cumbersome details it proved hard to administer; political pressures led to the abatement of the tax for more and more categories of travellers; the population was not averse to evading the tax – and did so. It became obvious that the learned economic expert had made a fool of himself and the scheme was quickly abandoned in the complicated form in which it had been introduced. The Minister of Finance was of course attacked for having introduced such an unsatisfactory fiscal instrument. He disclaimed publicly any intellectual responsibility for the fiasco by asserting that he, a non-economist, could hardly be blamed for the practical defects of a tax which had been fathered by a world-famous economist. There is more than one moral to this story.

Chapter II

THE LUCKY SEWAGE ENGINEERS

People like that should not be sewage commissioners, let alone hold office in the federal government.

*Walter Mondale**

FOUR UNSATISFACTORY ASSUMPTIONS

With some imagination one can conjure up situations in which economists are treated as being wholly redundant. This might be so in a besieged city where limited food supplies do not suffice to keep alive all the inhabitants till the relieving forces can be expected to raise the siege. Economists, philosophers and actors will surely be amongst the first to have their ration cards withdrawn to ensure the survival of sewage engineers, doctors and bakers. To escape such a fate, and for a variety of more prosaic reasons, economists are waging a public relations campaign to have economics acknowledged as a science, not just *a* science but one which is on a par with the natural sciences. Scientists, in our society, are said to enjoy a higher prestige rating than non-scientists. To help establish themselves as scientists, most economists manipulate adroitly four instruments from their tool-box.

(a) They work on the assumption that human beings ordinarily act rationally. I shall deal with this nonsense in Chapter VI.

* On the eve of the 1976 presidential election, General George S. Brown, chairman of the Joint Chiefs of Staff, made a political comment on US foreign policy which evoked a recommendation from the Democratic candidate, Jimmy Carter, that the General be reprimanded. His vice-presidential running mate drove home the point by making the cited, pejorative, remark on General Brown. The implicit disparagement of American public health engineers must surely have cost the Democratic candidate a number of votes.

(b) They work on the assumption that governments are generally able to enforce compliance with tax laws and economic edicts. Chapter IV will indicate that this is less true than economists would have us believe.

(c) They work on the assumption that individuals, companies and nations are propelled by the twin-gods of economic textbooks: 'optimization' and 'maximization'.

(d) They work on the assumption that only quantifiable things really matter. They do not actually say so explicitly but in most fields economists either ignore, or play down the importance of, factors that cannot be measured.

THE GLORY OF BEING A SCIENTIST

Some economists – amongst them I.M.D. Little – publicly sneer at their vain confrères who seek to be classified as scientists. Little mocks those of his colleagues who operate with unrealistic assumptions on the rationality of the average consumer and producer: 'If the man then fails to act in accordance with his preferences, how can one explain his behaviour? One must wash one's hands of him. Even if not mad, he is at least not an example of "economic man". So it would seem that the only people economists theorise about are satisfaction-maximisers.'[7] To Little, 'science' is an emotive word and he asks 'Why should it matter to anyone whether their study is called a science or not?' He expects people to reply that it does not matter, but actually it is of vital, bread-and-butter significance to many economists. Thousands of them would be unemployed if the buyers of their intellectual output did not believe that it has been produced with scientific accuracy. Without the cloak of scientific respectability they would not be able to sell their GNP calculations and forecasts.

We are supposed to learn from a series of annual GNP figures whether the people of a given country are now better off, and by how much, than in past years. The GNP is also intended to compare the national welfare level of different economies. No economist would maintain that the annual happiness and *total* welfare of a society – let us call it the whole social product – is identical with the annual quantifiable output of an economy, which is computed by aggregating the production of steel, hospital beds, nylon stockings, etc. The whole social product is a statistical imponderable. It is not within the competence of economists, or anybody else, to gauge the annual size of the national cake of happiness. Yet economists are surprisingly shy about revealing to the public that the GNP is an imperfect measuring rod of national welfare. Some economists have been so naughty as to imply that the non-material elements of the whole social product – which, being unquantifiable, are not incorporated within the GNP – are peripheral and relatively unimportant.

Non-material and non-quantifiable *ends* cause much distress to economists and this is enhanced by the existence of many non-quantifiable elements which encompass the *means* of producing the GNP. Few laymen are aware – how could they be! – that the human costs of the GNP are neglected by the architects of the national accounts. The uninitiated are led to believe that the citizens of country A are 10% better off than those of country B because it is reported in the tabloids that the *per capita* GNP of A is 10% bigger than that of B. What is usually not reported is that the working week in A is fifty hours whilst it is only forty hours in B. Nor do the economists, who merchandise the GNP data, disclose that A has a brutal dictatorship which tolerates no strikes and sends work-shirkers to concentration camps. (This non-disclosure is defended on the ground that it is irrelevant to the relative GNP dimensions of A and B.) It is probably safe to surmise that – by virtue of the higher output of washing machines, tanks and shoes – the material standard of living in A exceeds that of B. But does not common sense suggest that we should add to the material happiness of B the joy of living in a free society and deduct from the material happiness of A the unhappiness engendered by living in an oppressive society? There is no numerate answer to this and similar questions. That is why the size of the whole social product can never be ascertained and why the 'scientific' GNP is such a demonstrably inferior concept.

Economic forecasters, whose scientific virility is challenged, have been known to plead that as all scientists sometimes make forecasting errors it is unfair to pick on economists and challenge the scientific status of their discipline. When Robbins formulated his famous definition of 'economic science', he expressed resentment that non-economists paid so much uncharitable attention to the predictive failures of economists though practitioners in the natural sciences also experienced fiascos. Yet, Robbins complained, 'nobody in his senses would hold that the laws of mechanics were invalidated if an experiment designed to illustrate them were interrupted by an earthquake'. [2] The earthquake apologia highlights the two main differences, in the forecasting sphere, between the natural scientists and the economists. The prognostications of both groups are upset at times by adventitious factors – it happens very rarely to the former and very frequently to the latter. The predictions of natural scientists are frustrated by physical phenomena whilst those of economists are upset by the volatility, capriciousness and irrationality of human beings.

Some economic forecasters deserve to be treated with compassion. They do not regard themselves as competent to quantify the future, but are bullied to do so by non-economists who expect them to give a numerate performance. In the summer of 1975 I delivered a seven-hour presentation in London on the outlook of the UK economy to a group of mainly non-British executives who had paid for this dubious pleasure. As the evening approached the audience became restless. It was pointed out to me that I had not yet predicted the future exchange rate of sterling in terms of the US dollar. I replied that 'if the UK inflation in the next twelve months would rise by a given percentage, if the volume of marketed North Sea oil would reach a prescribed level, if ... then sterling in one year's time would be x dollars'. Some of my listeners could not conceal their disgust. Several stood up to say that they had come specifically to this meeting, and had waited patiently all day, in order to hear a 'scientific' currency forecast which would culminate in the unveiling of *one* future exchange rate. I was accused of not living up to their expectations by engaging in the barren exercise of outlining several options and predicting a number of future exchange rates. On that uncomfortable day I appreciated the lamentation of a financial editor: 'An economist without a forecast to his name is a sad thing to contemplate.' [9]

THE STERILIZATION OF WIGAN'S SLUDGE
Sewage engineers are a fortunate tribe and not only in a besieged city. They function in a climate which is professionally

more agreeable than that in which economists earn their living. Nevertheless, their status in society is in some respects inferior to that of economic experts on marginal utility. When James Lang gave his 1975 presidential address to the Institution of (UK) Public Health Engineers, and held forth on 'the present state of the country's economy', no national newspaper took any notice. No television channel was interested in his views on the recession. It is a fact that economists are frequently invited to television studios whilst sewage engineers are not called upon to air their views on the box concerning racial integration, the merits of Ireland joining the Common Market, and the likely price of Texan oil in 1992. It is even very rare for them to make a television appearance or be invited to write in the popular press to communicate on their own specialized, technical problems. But there are compensations, which is why I connote them as 'lucky' professionals.

Economists, as part of their training, learn how to construct Indifference Curves whilst sewage engineers are taught how to measure Suspended Solids Contents and gauge the Biochemical Oxygen Demand. These are non-controversial tools of the trade. There are, however, disputable matters – such as choosing for a given project either radial-flow settlement tanks or horizontal floor tanks – that do divide the profession and which can let tempers fly. From the paper of C.C. Parkman and G.N. Hindmarsh [75], we learn of certain happenings when the Lancashire municipality of Wigan commissioned new sewage-disposal facilities. The elected representatives of the town conceded that in this field they needed the services of an outside consultant. He advised that five methods of sludge treatment were practical propositions: heated digestion in anaerobic digesters, wet air oxidation, composting with refuse in windrows, chemical conditioning, and thermal conditioning. I confess that I have not followed up this matter to ascertain which technique was ultimately adopted, but we are surely on safe ground to surmise that the citizens of Wigan had no part in the decision-process. The councillors, who had to cast their vote, knew beforehand that whatever process they opted for, no one would boo from the public gallery and no pressure group would occupy the council chamber to express its disapproval. Amidst the agonizing selection of the most suitable method of sterilizing the local sludge, no partisan of one particular technique called the supporter of another a pig. As the options were debated, no capitalist or socialist banners were unfolded. I also doubt whether anyone in Wigan dragged the problem of multinational companies into the technical domain of the sewage specialists.

Only a fatuous layman expresses an opinion on the choice of rigid pipes and the selection of shallow manholes (that make access shafts unnecessary). However, sewage engineers' passions are aroused when they argue amongst themselves on such inanimate matters. From perusing reports of their annual conferences, I have been able to deduce that some technical experts are seen (with hindsight) to have made wrong recommendations. To an outsider it seems apparent that some public-health engineers propose certain structural changes because they have a bee in their bonnet. Without giving offence, it is not unfair to presume that a few may even occasionally take a bribe. However, sewage engineers are unlikely to face demonstrations of outraged citizens who threaten to change their party affiliation and voting intentions if the politicians decide that taxpayers' money shall finance the buying of vitrified clay pipes rather than concrete cylindrical ones. In any case, however wrong the technical recommendations of leading sewage engineers have been in the past, laymen will still not have any say in the future.

In the next chapter I am describing a contrivance – the *ceteris paribus* device – used by many economists to ensure that their forecasts turn out to be right but meaningless. When sewage engineers recommend, say, the use of pitch fibre pipes they also, explicitly or implicitly, do so with a number of reservations in mind. They may assume a given dry-weather flow of streams in the proximity, a local rainfall which does not exceed the maximum recorded in the preceding eighty years, and the absence of earthquakes. Their forecast that pitch fibre pipes will perform better than other pipes is therefore not a pure scientific prediction, because it contains some elements of conditional forecasting. Those matters, however, which might invalidate their technical recommendations have nothing or very little to do with the behaviour of human beings. On the other hand, when the economist introduces *ceteris paribus*, he does so almost entirely because of the imponderable foibles of his fellow-citizens and the unpredictable motivations that make politicians tick.

Political decision-makers who are given professional advice by economists are less concerned with its merits and factual accuracy than with the public's discernment of its merits and factual accuracy. This is a professional cross which sewage engineers and heart surgeons do not have to carry. Envied by economists, they can on the whole afford to ignore public opinion and the views of laymen.

Chapter III

SCIENTIFIC SOOTHSAYERS

*Beware of false prophets, which come to you in sheep's clothing,
but inwardly they are ravening wolves.*

St. Matthew

THE APTITUDE TO FORECAST

The Bolivian government agency, Comité de Obras Públicas, took
a full-page advertisement in a foreign financial daily in 1977 to
inform potential investors that the future of Santa Cruz had been
planned efficaciously. Things had all been worked out to ensure its
prosperous development. What better way to prove this than to tell
sceptical foreigners that 'we estimate reaching 835,306 (sic)
inhabitants by the year 2000!' Though others disagree,* I believe
that long-term forecasting does little harm. The players of the
game certainly do not find it hazardous: after ten-twenty years,
when the prophecies are supposed to have come true, who will then
remember them as the vain authors of quantified predictions?

Short-term forecasting has become a booming post-war industry which employs thousands throughout the world. It started with a bang in the US, when some government economists in
1945 – only a few months before the threatened doomsday – predicted erroneously a severe depression. (They miscalculated the
size of the GNP by 9%.) At a time when there were 1m unemployed,
they forecast (with a decimal point accuracy) that within nine
months their number would swell to 8.1m. (It turned out to be

---

* 'Long Range Planning is a most mischievously seductive pastime since,
provided it is sufficiently long range, those who by their erroneous
predictions have misled mankind cannot, because they will be dead and
forgotten, be duly charged with their misdemeanours.'[6]

2.7m.) Even the biggest British post-war forecasting failures cannot compete with such horrid errors. Occasionally some institution in the English-speaking world still publishes such an erroneous prediction as to expose itself to public ridicule but extreme failures* are now rare. The short-term UK and US post-war GNP forecasts by government agencies, international bodies (such as the Paris-based Organisation for Economic Co-operation and Development – OECD), famous research institutions, major business schools, and the (US) National Association of Business Economists, average annual errors of just under 2%.** (Their mistakes in predicting the balance of payments, unemployment, investment, consumer spending, etc. are larger.) Four kinds of alibis are produced by economists to vindicate their erroneous predictions:

(a) The errors are said not to be errors, because they appear in conditional forecasts. I shall have something rude to say about this cowardly approach at the end of the chapter.

(b) Regret is expressed that the predictions contained errors, but a plea of mitigation is entered: is it not, after all, a marvellous achievement to be wrong by only 1-3%? Many unthinking laymen accept this as a plausible defence. Let me try to debunk it. If it were true that a forecaster has to predict within such a wide statistical circumference as to allow for the GNP to either rise or fall in one year by, say, 50%, then indeed an error of only two percentage points would be a feather in the cap of a proud prophet. Whilst the wider public does not know it, economists are well aware that the post-war GNPs of most Western industrialized countries have been moving within narrow parameters. The numerate economic prophets can therefore – rightly – ignore the theoretical statistical possibility that the volume of the GNP may be transformed fundamen-

*The UK's premier forecasting body, the National Institute of Economic and Social Research (NIESR), in February 1975 predicted an annual 1.7% growth in the fourth-quarter 1975 national product – the actual outcome was a drop of 2.8%. The error of 4.5% is not however representative of the usual size of its errors. In any case the NIESR can explain away its faulty forecasts (see p. 40).

** Nowadays, national accounts forecasting is generally expressed in real, i.e. inflation-adjusted, terms.

tally (through a *large* fall or rise) in the succeeding twelve months.* Once one accepts the reasonable assumption that next year's GNP will not be so vastly different from this year's, seemingly small forecasting errors become big errors. Consequently, GNP predictions with errors of 1-2 percentage points are substantially wrong; those above 2 but below 4 percentage points are abysmally faulty; errors above 4 percentage points ought to land the forecasters in prison!

(c) This alibi concerns the bench-mark of forecasting. Predictions for year 2 are ordinarily published between the spring and winter of year 1. At that time, however, the forecaster does not yet know the size of the national product of year 1. In fact, even when the GNP of year 1 is published in year 2, its size is a provisional figure. Honest government statistical offices (as exist in the UK, US and a few other countries) regularly revise, over many years after the event, their estimates of the volume of the national output and its components – by year 4 they may have raised or lowered the provisional calculation of the GNP of year 1 by up to two percentage points. All forecasters have to labour under the tremendous handicap of not knowing the quantitative dimensions of the GNP which is to serve as their base-year. Yet, predictors rarely explain this to the public to which they sell their prophecies, because it would so obviously undermine confidence in their forecasts.

(d) We are told by an Anglo-American partnership that there is no factual 'support to the view that economic forecasting is a waste of time'.[49] The reason they adduce is that economists' predictions are more precise than 'naive predictions'. (The latter denote forecasts based on past trends or the assumption of no change.) It is true that most of the numerate prophecies by economists are slightly less erroneous than those which are computed purely by extrapolations. But this does not tell us whether predictions by non-economists, who forecast with intuition and after an intelligent reading of the newspapers, are

---

*In two out of the last twenty years (1959-78) the UK GNP fell slightly. In 14 years it rose by up to 4% and in only 4 years was the growth above 4%.

more or less accurate than those made by prophets with a Ph.D.

The accuracy of economic forecasting is alleged to depend on the skill of its devotees. During the last thirty years many 'experts' have been trained and the senior practitioners of this craft must by now have accumulated much experience. Have the forecasts of the current decade been superior to those of the preceding two decades? There is no evidence of it. It has been pleaded, ever since forecasting became a specialized vocation, that if only more money, bigger computers and refined electronic equipment were made available, things would surely improve. British government statisticians had always envied their wealthy American counterparts until in November 1972 the UK Treasury - I am sorry to say, somewhat boastfully - unveiled its new technical forecasting aids to the outside world. Until then the Treasury had relied on obsolete methods: it had used conventional batch-processing, suffered the proliferation of paper print-outs, and - they dolefully admitted - could never complete in one day more than three model simulations. All this was about to change because the Treasury was to have a direct link between its satellite computer and the main processor. It would now be possible to complete ten simulations in one day. A new dawn was rising for accurate predictions. An immodest, anonymous senior civil servant proclaimed that the Treasury computer for economic forecasting was the most advanced government application of its type in Western Europe. Has the computer made any difference? If we compare the Treasury spring forecasts of the five years before this proud acquisition with those of the subsequent five years, we can note no cognizable improvement. Taking a charitable view, one can only say that the impact of the new computer on the accuracy of the published forecasts has been nil.

According to one prosaic approach, economists actually perform worse than non-economists in the forecasting of economic trends. It is maintained that as the economic discipline does not demand vows of poverty from its members, and yet economists are generally not wealthy, it follows that economists are incompetent to anticipate correctly those events in the future, a foreknowledge of which would enable them to benefit personally. Economists dismiss impatiently and arrogantly this attack on their professional competence to forecast. The renowned Bernard Baruch once said that though he was aware of the economists' self-avowal in their own capacity to make shrewd predictions, it was nothing but vainglorious bragging. If they are so clever, why do they not make more money? [65] Keynes was thought to be an exception to this generalization but that myth too has lately been exploded.

Roy Harrod's story of Keynes's life was not confined to elucidating his original contributions as an economic thinker. As a biographer he set himself also the task of proving that *because* Keynes was a great economist he became a successful businessman. Harrod claimed that Keynes found it easy to enrich himself owing to his superior knowledge of commercial forces: 'His speculations were based on his judgment of economic trends ... he had the idea that it should be possible to turn an economist's understanding of the vagaries of the business cycle to profitable account.' [64] Harrod – out of ignorance or because he sought not to harm the sacred memory of his hero – did not dwell on the unfavourable details of Keynes's business affairs. But even those which he chose to relate make it abundantly clear that many of Keynes's deals in the City of London were unsuccessful, both when he speculated on his own account and when he did so on behalf of syndicates or as a manager of an investment trust. Keynes was rescued on several occasions by his family and adoring well-wishers. Harrod explains that 'it would indeed have been a disaster if the man, who has so recently set world opinion agog by claiming to know better than the mighty of the land, had himself become involved in bankruptcy'. Nicholas Davenport was a personal friend of Keynes and is now one of the last survivors of that circle of London businessmen who were involved in, or had first-hand knowledge of, Keynes's commercial activities. Davenport's memoirs [63] are imbued with affection for Keynes, the man and the economic theorist. Davenport, however, was not prepared to suppress unwholesome aspects of Keynes's speculative ventures in which he won and lost large fortunes. Thus, writing of the Independent Investment Trust (which Harrod merely mentions euphemistically to have been a non-success), Davenport recounts how the 'entire capital' – heavily subscribed by institutional investors who had been attracted, *inter alia*, by Keynes's magic name – was lost. Harrod, in his biography, is at pains to emphasize that when Keynes had successes in his speculations, this was not due to the receipt of inside information. Harrod says of Keynes that he traded only in the light of his personal, erudite understanding of the economic situation; not only did he not need inside information but he considered that such forbidden fruits mislead investors. Davenport, drawing on personal knowledge, asserts that Keynes, whilst never obtaining any in an improper way, did benefit greatly from inside information; he gives chapter and verse for one particular case.* It is only in fairy tales that brilliant economic theorists are deemed to command, by virtue of their professional training, those talents which are needed to make a killing on Wall Street or in the City of London.

An examination of the post-war performance of the Mutual Funds and Unit Trusts in the English-speaking world ought to provide a *coup de grâce* to the fable that economists can gauge the future more perspicaciously than their fellow-citizens who have never read a book by Ricardo or Milton Friedman. These professionally-managed investment vehicles yield profits which are no bigger than could be obtained from a random selection of stocks and shares. The (misguided) view that economists are good forecasters would be partly validated if only it could be shown that the institutional funds report relatively meagre returns on their investments because of widespread corruption on the part of their managing executives. It is a bewitching thought that the majority of the managers are really capable soothsayers who only fail to deliver high returns to their investors because – having made big gains through their putative expertise – they siphon off many of the profits to their private purses. Alas, most of these institutions are on the whole administered honestly, and it is not the wickedness of the managers which makes for the unexciting profits of the Mutual Funds and Unit Trusts. At their disposal are advanced computers and complex electronic gadgets; they spend much money on

---

* The veracity of Davenport's factual accounts of Keynes, the business-man, has not been challenged to my – or his – knowledge. I interviewed Davenport in May 1976, when he told me how much Keynes enjoyed speculating but how little his successes and failures were connected with his scholarly discernment of economic and political theories. Davenport remains convinced that these incursions into the financial world, whether successful or not, did ultimately make him a better economist than he would have been without these business experiences.

acquiring reference books and privately-commissioned research reports; above all, they can afford to hire and reward well-talented economists, statisticians and investment analysts. Yet, at the end of the day, they cannot surpass (and sometimes even lag behind) the showing of the *Financial Times* (London) and *Dow Jones* (New York) indexes. Despite the illustrious economists on their staff, the institutions cannot measure accurately the imponderables that make and mar economic progress, nor can they anticipate the vagaries of the capital market. The private investor in the UK is equally well served by using a pin. In North America – as one witness, in his testimony to the Senate Banking and Currency Committee, formulated it – administrators of Mutual Funds provide investors with a service which could also be procured by throwing darts and hitting random stocks.

THE BECKERMAN GAME

The British Economy in 1975 [59], which appeared in 1965, was marketed as a forecast. It is only fair to add that readers of the small print could have discovered the hedging provisions introduced by the authors to qualify their prophecies. Nevertheless, after all these years it still remains the most particularized futuristic tome of the British economy ever published.

With astonishing foresight, Beckerman and his associates predicted in the early sixties that in 1975 25.4 billion ton-miles of freight would be carried, the capital formation would then be 173.7% higher than in 1960, transport would account for 13.9% of personal expenditure, 121.6% more timber goods (at constant prices) would be needed to satisfy consumer demand as compared with fifteen years previously, etc.

Shortly after it was published I described it as a 'toy model' and held up this *magnum opus* as an example of the arrogance which inspires those who toil in the economic forecasting workshops. Not by accident, the book was brought out by a celebrated university publisher, thus imputing an even greater aura to the scientific foundations of its predictions. Although in 1965 concrete proof could not yet be offered, one was already on safe ground in conjecturing that all the tens of thousands of numerate projections, set out on 655 closely-printed pages, would ultimately be proved to have been wrong; if by chance any corresponded to the real happenings in 1975, it would be coincidental. Beckerman and his associates were the heroes of 1965 and probably still cherish today the academic reviews that praised their creation.

1975 is now behind us. Beckerman had forecast that the (current account) balance of payments in that year would yield a £550m *surplus* – in fact there was a *deficit* of £1,855m. Readers would be bored if I were to contrast other factual outcomes with the data in the forecasting exercise, which had been received with such fanfares. Suffice it to say that with very few exceptions 1975 did not live up to the predicted expectations.

One is struck not only by the numerate discrepancies but even more by the failure of the forecasting economists to emphasize those factors that proved to have had the most decisive influence on the state of the 1975 economy. Of course the authors were aware that there is such a thing as inflation but as, at the time of writing, it was of only puny dimensions, they failed to prophesy that the UK in 1975 would be dominated by a price explosion in excess of 24% per annum. Sterling devaluation? Between 1965 and 1975 the external exchange parity of the British currency fell by 28% against the US dollar. (It may be that Beckerman foresaw this but did not have enough space to include the item in his forecast, for room had to be found to state the more significant projection of the ton-miles of freight.) *The British Economy in 1975* does not mention petrodollars nor does it even hint at the quintupling of the oil prices, which surely was one of the outstanding features that moulded the economy of that year. This does not mean that the authors avoided prophesying the future of fuel prices for they fully recognized their importance. On page 304 we read: 'The expansion of the world's oil reserves and the improvement in methods of exploitation and production make a rise in oil prices unlikely in the foreseeable future.' Just as world-famous Norwegian econometricians failed to foresee the oil bonanza in their country, so Beckerman had no inkling of the (at the time still undiscovered) oil-gas resources in the British shelf of the North Sea. The insolvencies of British Leyland and Rolls Royce were not perceived in his crystal-gazing. There is not one word on the costs associated with the troubles in Northern Ireland.

The compassionate reader may feel by now that I have been knocking Beckerman too much and that it is unfair to reproach him for not having foreseen the economic consequences flowing from the Yom Kippur war. I value many of Beckerman's talents as a teacher of economic theory. Here, however, I am concerned exclusively with his predictive study on 1975. One is entitled to ask why he spent so much time on this fruitless exercise, why the National Institute of Economic and Social Research sponsored it, and why he led astray those of the public who might have taken his absurd projections seriously in 1965. Beckerman could and should have known that economic life does not run along a smooth path. It was *certain* when the book was being written that some yet unknown but important events would take place which would make nonsense of these numerate forecasts. As funds seem to be easy to recruit for such purposes, a group of economic 'experts' may at this moment be writing 'A quantitative analysis of the British economy in 1995'. We can be sure that imponderables will again make their predictions look ridiculous in the target year.

Beckerman may be a bad forecaster but he has a sense of humour. In Herman Kahn's preposterous book, *The Next 200 Years*, there are some uncomplimentary references to Beckerman, who retaliated by tearing Kahn to pieces in an article. It commenced: 'If there is one thing that convinces me that, after all, the end of the world is nigh, it is not the predictions of futurologists but the gullibility with which large, and often important, sections of the public swallow their pronouncements.' [93]

THE MORALITY OF FALSE FORECASTING

Economists, who believe in the validity of their own predictions, may be misleading others but in the process also deceive themselves. However, such honest-but-foolish forecasters do not belong to the tribe of practitioners who falsify statistical data and broadcast prognoses that they believe to be false. I have categorized below four situations in which they flourish: the first relates to the publication of false data on past events in order to lure people into wrong thinking about the future; the second is concerned with the suppression of forecasts; the third deals with the publication of wrong forecasts in order to save the face of the government; the fourth touches on deliberate cheating aimed at influencing the behaviour of people through the dissemination of mendacious predictions.

1) In many countries of the world the 'cooked' cost-of-living index provides the best example for this category, but in the Anglo-Saxon countries statisticians do not lend themselves to the concoction of deliberately falsified accounts of retail prices. In the UK, however, consciences are not pricked when the Bank of England's gold and foreign currency reserves are frequently presented in a peculiar manner. Ever since a former governor of Britain's central bank admitted it in a speech in the House of Lords, we have had authoritative confirmation that these monthly figures are not necessarily true and/or meaningful. The noble Lord naturally did not tell his peers that the Bank of England sometimes lied - such language is only used by the lower classes. Instead, he boasted about the strategy of responsible officials who decide what figures ought to be released in the national interest: he connoted this cheating as 'a tactical arrangement'. [56] In his memoirs, the former prime minister Harold Wilson implicitly endorsed this practice. Describing a fateful meeting at 10 Downing Street he said, 'The bankers proved to be constructive and friendly. One after another said how right the Treasury had been to publish the token figure of £25m for the July gold loss: everyone knew that the real loss was very many times greater, and to publish a patently derisory figure had had the right effect.' [73] Wilson was wrong in asserting that 'everyone knew' of the Bank of England's stratagem to publish misleading figures (Wilson euphemistically calls them 'token figures'). There were and are enough simpletons who place trust in the veracity of the statistics released by the central bank. If this credulity were non-existent, there would be no point in exploiting it by disseminating inaccurate reserve data.

2) The OECD's bi-annual reports regularly contain inflation forecasts. However, in December 1970 some predictions of price-rises were not published though they are known to have been prepared. The forecasts were suppressed because of successful pressure from the British government, which had learned of the OECD economists' intention to say in print that the UK in 1971 would be the only major industrial country in which the rate of inflation would rise. *The* (London) *Times* made the grave charge against Prime Minister Edward Heath that he had been so angered by this (as yet unprinted) prediction that 'his first thought seems to

have been in terms of cutting off British finance for the Organisation'. [142] The row was settled when the OECD gave in to Heath's displeasure. It did not publish the inflation prediction and also made other cuts in its UK forecast. If a member-country can bring about the suppression of routine predictions (of which it does not approve) by an international body, one can be certain that governments can do this in their national bailiwicks with less hindrance and without incurring the sort of odious publicity that was suffered by Heath for browbeating the OECD.*

3) The alternative to the suppression of honestly-prepared predictions may be the publication of false forecasts. The clamour to be told the official assessment of the economy's future has had perverse results. The campaign for the right-to-know has ostensibly succeeded in that governments now release forecasts on subjects which had previously been kept secret. But being under democratic duress, are governments not tempted to tell patriotic lies?

If anyone in the UK can give informed evidence on this, it is Alec Cairncross who used to be the British government's Economic Adviser. After his retirement, in a presidential address to the Royal Economic Society, he spelt out something which previously had only been suspected. In his experience, he said, governments 'hate issuing bad news at any time' and particularly 'if things are worse than is commonly believed'. Cairncross was surprisingly forthcoming to divulge that if bad news cannot be suppressed, 'there is also real risk that the government will insist on cooking the forecasts rather than reveal how awful the situation is'. [53] Galbraith, who has held important government appointments in the US, has testified in a similar vein about false, but not necessarily incompetent, official forecasting. In a sweeping generalization he maintained that 'the economist in high office is under a

---

* The fact that neither the UK government nor the OECD issued any denial provided *prima facie* evidence of the truth of *The Times's* dispatch. In the summer of 1976 I wrote to both Edward Heath and the OECD to inquire whether the substance of the accusation had ever been denied. I received courteous replies. The first stated that 'Mr Heath has asked me to let you know that he has no comment to make on the report'. [147] The second said that the press reports 'had caused as much interest here as anywhere else. I am afraid we are quite unable to give you any comment on them. Certainly, no statement of any sort was issued on the subject at the time, or subsequently.' [148]

strong personal and political compulsion to predict wrongly'. [77] According to Galbraith, this was particularly evident in 1967 and 1968 when the administration's economists based their intellectually honest, but unpublished, predictions on the assumption that the Vietnam war would drag on for many years and its financial burden would escalate. They could not, however, say so aloud, because it would have contradicted the official doctrine that the war would soon come to an end. Hence they made pronouncements in public on future trends (relating to the volume of defence expenditure and the rate of inflation) which privately they knew would not come true.

Let us assume that a government has proclaimed a rigorous 3% ceiling on all wage increases and has taken statutory powers to send to prison anyone breaching this rule. The government economists estimate in the privacy of their offices that substantial breaches will nevertheless occur and that accordingly the national wage bill will rise by 4.5%. Using this as their bench-mark, they then estimate its impact on budget policy, inflation, etc. It is obviously helpful to ministers to receive confidentially professional advice based on realistic working assumptions. If, however, the economists were compelled by public opinion to release their projections of the wage and price levels, they would thereby implicitly announce that the government's stated intention to stick absolutely to the 3% ceiling is either not genuine or not practicable. The publication of their estimates would be tantamount to sabotaging the credibility of their political masters. To escape from this dilemma some government economists are known to behave like tax-evading businessmen who keep two sets of books. Whilst publishing fallacious forecasts, they inform ministers of their genuine predictions. In a sense this can expose civil servants to unjustified ridicule. When the chickens have come home to roost and the published prophecies are proved to have been wrong they will be denounced as inept forecasters. With sang-froid they will then have to brook this unjust accusation, because they cannot reveal in public their true alibi, to wit that they had deliberately lied. Ash and Smyth, who have carefully scrutinized the British Treasury forecasts and found them to be frequently erroneous, nevertheless defend the competence of the seemingly incompetent government economists: 'It is possible that the forecasts published by the

Treasury are merely window-dressing and that they do not represent the predictions on which the government actually bases its economic policy.' [49]

4) The most degrading form of false forecasting is linked to what academic literature terms the 'reaction function', which depends on backlash, feedback and the announcement effect. Clearly, meteorological predictions have no feedback. The inches of rainfall that will pour down do not vary with the accuracy of the weather prophecies and are not affected by whether the predictions have been uttered in private or in public. Economic forecasts, however, differ in their impact as between those made privately and those disseminated in public. The outcome of the publicly-made prediction may be affected by its publication. Whilst clouds do not heed the prophecies of weather experts, human beings can and do change their intended behaviour if they hear the clarion-call of a persuasive economic prophet. When credence is given to a prediction that unemployment is set to rise to five million within twelve months, it may set into motion such an agitation as to induce the authorities to initiate a crash public-works programme which will limit the number of unemployed to four million.

Economic forecasts are made by journalists, economic institutes, academic luminaries, leading businessmen, non-government economists, economists in the service of the state, and politicians. Three elements determine how much attention is paid to any given prediction: the prevailing gullibility of the public, the track record of the prophet and – most importantly – the indirect* or direct prominence of the forecaster. Whilst one can safely assert that predictions made in public by a famous individual or organization will generally produce *a* reaction, the direction and extent of the backlash cannot be ascertained beforehand. In free societies the 'acceptance weight' of predictions is enhanced when several important and trusted forecasters prophesy the same trend. Thus, when the economic editors of the *Wall Street Journal, Washington Post* and *New York Times* all forecast a rise in the US GNP, this will influence strongly wholesalers to increase their inventory.

* The forecast of a young house economist of Pepsi-Cola (who can bask in the vicarious glory of his famous employers) is likely to be listened to with greater respect than the erudite prophetic utterances of an unknown economist (even when he has two Ph.Ds).

To summarize: forecasts made in private escape feedback; predictions by inconsequential forecasters are devoid of any feedback. All other forecasts, whether conceived by honest or mendacious forecasters, generate a backlash. Honest forecasters deplore this whilst to their crooked colleagues feedback brings grist to the mill.

In the *Three Sacred Cows of Economics*[5] I gave several concrete instances in which economists and politicians, who wanted to manipulate the future direction of the economy, circulated mendacious forecasts that were intended to throw dust in the eyes of a trusting public. By the dissemination of such false predictions, people were to be pushed into doing something which they would otherwise not have done. (Moralists will condemn hoodwinking as reprehensible *per se*; it is, however, also a dangerous feature because crooked forecasters cannot be certain that the desired backlash will be produced.) From several confessions we have an idea how such forecasting frauds are planned: a group of economists concludes that the economy is set on a course that would raise the national output in the coming year by 1%. They surmise that if this prognosis were published, the feedback might actually reduce the out-turn to 0.5%. What to do to help humanity benefit from a growth rate in excess of 1%? The Machiavellian economists use their elevated status, as government experts, to tell the public that scientific evidence at their disposal points to a 4% growth. Of course they do not expect the public to accept this prediction fully – in fact most businessmen are likely to treat the 4% figure as an exaggeration. Still, they are jolted by this 4% and whilst they do not alter their conduct to such an extent as to make the forecast come true in its entirety, they do adapt themselves to a higher growth rate than they had intuitively expected before the publication of the 4% forecast. As a result the GNP goes up by 2%. The 4% forecasters are of course then shown to have been very wrong. They do not mind. Chuckling privately amongst themselves, they recall that the 4% prediction was never the result of any 'scientific' prognosis. They had wanted to outstrip the 1% growth rate and can now exult in their 2% victory.

Academic literature, not meant to be read by laymen, unfolds before dishonest economists the vast terrain that awaits those who are prepared to divert their professional skills to manipulative exercises. Galatin is a newcomer to this game. He counsels economists, who are not bashful about abandoning 'accuracy of forecasts' as the criterion by which predictive endeavours are judged, that the feedback theory can be put to significant uses: 'It is possible that forecasts may become important tools of economic control when the forecaster wishes to *influence* the value of the outcome by his choice of forecast.'[78] No longer are economists enjoined to publish forecasts which correspond most closely to their glimpses of the future. Instead, they are advised to put forward such numerate prophecies as will have the biggest impact on the behaviour of the public. These knavish tricks can be balked if they are dragged out into the open from the crevices of learned journals.

COWARDLY OR MEANINGLESS?

We shall leave now the immoral economists and return to the honest forecasters. Whilst the former are sometimes happy when the outcome differs from their published predictions, the latter are downcast if events prove them wrong, because they must then seek excuses which can satisfactorily explain their forecasting mishaps. It may appear preposterous to the man-in-the-street but there are good and honest professors of economics who have expounded in detail why being wrong is not really a crime. They say that economists should not be judged by the degree of their forecasting success or failure but by the soundness of the theory on which they based their predictions. Accordingly, intellectual praise ought to be heaped on the sophisticated forecaster who works with refined techniques; from an academic standpoint it is not very relevant that he turns out wrong results. An English economist, who is engaged full-time on forecasting, wrote this: 'The first point to clarify is the difficulty of telling whether a particular forecast has been good or bad, which terms are emphatically not synonymous with correct or false.'[3] I like even better the fatuous lamentation attributed by Lesser[55] to a frustrated US econometrician: 'It is not the model which is at fault; it is the American economy which is wrong'

Half a century ago Irving Fisher was the world's most eminent living economist. In the days of 1929, when the US economy went from bad to worse, a few gloomy forecasters predicted that the lofty price plateau of the New York stock exchange would collapse.

But Fisher, with his prestigious authority, raised the morale of the despondent US investors who were happy to read his euphoric messages. There is no evidence that the great man produced his glad tidings without believing in his own rosy evaluation of the economic future. Even his adversaries have never suggested that he deliberately schemed to deceive the American public. He persuaded many that there was no cause for alarm: in his professional judgment the level of stock exchange prices was about right. Immediately after the débâcle in the second half of 1929 Fisher sat down to compose his apologia which was published in the subsequent year. Was it full of contrition? Fisher obviously could not shrug off the dramatic fall in prices on Wall Street, which had triggered off the crisis that was shaking the whole country. He could and did, however, dismiss suggestions that the events had cast a dark shadow over his intellectual capacity to forecast. In the book[79] Fisher says that his optimism in 1929 had been justified, because the American economy had then been in a sound condition – only 'peripheral factors' had led to the crash.

In our permissive age it is no longer obligatory to know Latin before being admitted to the economic faculty of a university. All students aspiring to become economists are nevertheless advised to familiarize themselves with a number of Latin phrases. The most important of these is *ceteris paribus*. (This is tagged on to the assertions, generalizations, prognoses and forecasts of economists to denote that they are only true 'on the assumption of other things being equal'.) The NIESR markets its quarterly journal[74] to businessmen and bankers who are not conversant with Latin; hence it uses an English-language equivalent to qualify its forecasts. To make sure that critics can make no valid accusations against the integrity of the NIESR, it has for twenty years hedged its UK forecasts by stipulating that they are intended to come true only 'in the absence of new government measures'. At first this *caveat* was hidden in the journal's text but later formed a separate signal in bold letters; the size of the warning sign has been increased over the years and so has the prominent blackness of the printed caution that beckons readers to beware.

The customers of the NIESR care mainly about its predictive exercises. They are even regarded by the BBC as such sensational pointers to the future that it gives them precedence over the Test

Match (cricket) scores. (Foreign readers will not be unduly excited about this but in the UK it is almost sacrilegious.) These quarterly prophecies on inflation and GNP growth are apparently so newsworthy that US, Japanese and Swiss correspondents cable them regularly to their newspapers. Whilst the NIESR can therefore proudly point out the fact that its forecasts are splashed around the world, it notes with regret that few reproduce them accompanied by the *ceteris paribus*. Even many of those people who actually peruse the *Review* take little notice of the explicit reservations that are displayed so conspicuously. The NIESR is not in the business of selling numerate, *unhedged*, predictions – yet a large number of its customers nevertheless treat them as such.

The NIESR arranges periodic post-mortems to determine the size and causes of its forecasting errors. When it does so it points to the useful proviso that guided its economists in the preparation of the forecast: 'we always assess what will happen if policy remains unchanged'. The Institute thus becomes morally entitled to argue that some or all of the discrepancies between the printed predictions and the outcomes are due to the government having changed its policy after the forecasts were published (by printing more money, imposing additional taxes, devaluing, etc). This 'conditional forecasting' provides a cowardly, built-in, alibi for errors and makes the forecasting exercise almost meaningless for most of its non-academic customers. If these were to understand properly what the NIESR and similar forecasting bodies in the world are selling – and there is reason to believe that many do not – they would realize that the forecasts do not foretell the likely development of the economy and are therefore not crutches upon which they can lean in their decision-making. To make meaningful predictions, forecasters must conjecture on the new policy-measures that the government may introduce in the years covered by the forecasting period. Were they to do so and incorporate them within their numerate prophecies, most of the – unhedged – forecasts would turn out to be very wrong. It is more cosy to practise 'conditional forecasting' with elusive *caveats* and thereby escape being denounced as false prophets.

Chapter IV

LIFE IS CLEAN AND HONEST

Testifying before a Senate committee, Exxon (the world's largest free enterprise corporation) confessed to falsifying its records to hide $51m secret donations to Italian political parties – from neo-fascists on the right to marxists on the left. Whilst Senator Church described such contributions by American oil companies as an 'epidemic of corruption', Exxon's spokesman explained that the motivation for giving this money was the company's desire 'to further the democratic process'.

DO ILLEGALITIES MATTER?

It is not only the lust for lucre which originates economic crime. Some choose to become criminals because they enjoy the excitement of the game. Others derive psychic – not material – pleasure from proving to themselves and their admiring friends that they are clever enough to evade the law with impunity. People are known to steal from their employers because of frustration at not having been promoted, and otherwise law-abiding citizens may deliberately evade taxes because they have some real or imagined grievance against the state. This chapter, however, is concerned exclusively with economic illegalities that confer riches upon the transgressor or the ethnic, religious, or political group on whose behalf he is acting.

Is there more illegal economic behaviour during the reign of Elizabeth II than when Victoria* ruled? The answer is in the

---

* The rich in Victorian Britain had to endure a peculiar corruption in their palatial homes. As the lady of the house did not do her own shopping in a supermarket, tradesmen importuned customers by offering lucrative 'kickbacks' to the senior servants.

affirmative but there is no proof that this is due to a decline in moral standards. The cause is to be sought in the structural changes that have transformed society: companies have become bigger; the state discharges many more functions; planning orders are both more important and numerous; politicians interfere increasingly with the environment, wages, profits, prices, international trade, currency movements; taxes are heavier and more complex. In short, the number of law-breakers today is greater than one hundred years ago because there are now more laws to break.

A Swiss banker once told me – presumably it was no more than an intelligent guess – that, per head of population, Swedes own more numbered bank accounts in his country than any other group of foreigners. The recurrent revelations by the Swedish press, ministry of finance and Rikspolisstyrelsen (police authority) about large-scale evasions of taxes and currency regulations describe graphically the widespread lawlessness in the economic sphere which prevails in the European country with the highest pre-tax *per capita* income. In July 1977 commenced the recruitment of a separate, financially well-endowed, police force to combat economic crime. Sweden delivers convincing proof that poverty is not the main drive behind economic illegalities: the West's most oppressive, personal income tax provides a more plausible explanation.

The simplest form of economic crime is to pilfer, steal or burgle. The quantitative dimensions of theft can be calculated with less inaccuracy than the magnitudes of other economic illegalities. In 1978 it was estimated that the amount of pilferage in the UK was equal to about 2% of the GNP. [52] Theft does not usually destroy wealth but redistributes it, albeit in a disorderly and (usually) unfair fashion. Stealing is thus different from other economic illegalities which sometimes generate economic distortions and may induce a waste of resources as exemplified by the felonious behaviour of the Russian street-cleaner which I shall soon relate. In another respect, too, stealing and allied operations are unrelated to the economic crimes which consist of transgressions of regulations and edicts decreed to direct the economy. If there were no exchange controls, import duties and income taxes, most of the illegal activities we shall be discussing would not take place. Theft, however, would continue to prevail on earth even if the functions of the state were heavily emasculated. Most illegal economic behaviour could be expunged by revoking the statutory rules which are being transgressed. This clearly does not apply to the sin of stealing unless one abrogates the laws governing private property.

R. L. Carter is amongst that small number of economists who are not afraid to talk about economic crimes; in his judgment 'theft is a matter of substantial economic importance'.[10] Without detracting from this, it can be convincingly argued that the other types of economic crimes are of considerably greater significance – both those already being perpetrated and those which the government fears would be perpetrated if some draconian tax or harsh edict were enacted.

Moralists will hardly relish the fact that illegalities, particularly but not necessarily only under a dictatorship, may help to redress absurdities devised by zealous state planners. The inability of the US government to control the concomitant illegalities associated with Prohibition engendered an atmosphere that led to its abolition. At the end, even people who originally thought that drinking should be forbidden by the state came to the reluctant conclusion that the ravages of corruption and the pervasive flouting of the law were socially more harmful. There has been less acknowledgement of the fact that many taxes and economic state regulations have been abolished, or amended, for precisely the same reason.

Not all illegalities are as crude as bribing an official or falsifying a tax-return – corporations sometimes offend the spirit of the law by 'bending the rules'. Governments can usually compel compliance with wage and price controls for only a short period; after the first bout of enthusiasm the planners become aware of the growth of illegal practices. A young Washington journalist went to the Soviet Union and discovered that its National Plan imposed production quotas, measured in square metres, on factories making plate glass. How did glass factories exceed the quotas and thus earn lucrative bonuses? They made the product as thin as possible. As thin glass is easily shattered, windows in Russian apartment houses suffer frequent breakages. Kaiser thought this was hilarious economic nonsense and implied that the Western system is superior to that of the Communists.[54] So indeed it is, but not when price-wage controllers are let loose in capitalist economies. The managers of the Russian glass factories must have learned their tricks from the Western corporations which try to evade mandatory price-ceilings by reducing surreptitiously the intrinsic quality of their products. Wage controls are similarly evaded. The now universally accepted term 'fringe benefits' was originally coined to describe the devious corporate responses in the US to the rulings of the National War Labor Board.[13] The law provided for the freezing of emoluments, but American managers and union leaders were adept in breaching the spirit of the controls by raising employee compensation through additional, unconventional payments. Until discovered and forced to retreat, the giant Mitsubishi Corporation employed such a stratagem in London during the 1977 wage controls. It declared sanctimoniously that 'as a foreign company we have no intention of defying British government policy. We have always strictly adhered to the pay code in terms of pay for staff.' Formally this was true, but in practice the Japanese company had given their British personnel an extra salary increase which was termed 'travel subsidy'. The experience of forty years of Western price-wage controls shows that they are abrogated, or not renewed, when politicians become convinced that there are not enough policemen to curb pervasive disobedience.

As a general rule a government only finds it worthwhile to legislate if it believes that it can carry its policy into effect; similarly, the imposition of a new tax is only justified when it has the potential of yielding (substantial) revenue.* This is where the *contingent* illegalities lurk in the background. Though couched in euphemistic language, we can cite supporting evidence from a retired, knowledgeable insider: he is a professional economist who for more than thirty years took an active part, as a leading administrator, in state-interventionalism and ended his career as the Head of the British Civil Service. D. Allen believes that the power of the central government may be declining for a number of reasons, one of which is the present 'radically different attitude to the law from that which existed a generation ago'. This experienced practitioner

---

* This is not always so. Some taxes are put on the statute book with non-fiscal objectives. No purpose was served by telling the Labour government that it would probably collect more revenue if the top 98% marginal income-tax rate, which was charged in the budget year 1978/9, were cut to 50%. The socialist politicians who insisted on the 98% rate were oblivious to its revenue effect – they wanted to prove to their supporters that they were soaking the rich.

in planning other people's lives has discovered that a great deal of existing legislation 'is not enforced because it is virtually unenforceable'. He concludes that awareness of these changed attitudes to compliance with the law may make politicians circumspect in the future when they contemplate widening the scope of their legislative powers. [66]

Wise politicians assess the prospective achievement of a new economic regulation on a *net* basis. They take into account that the greater the danger of large-scale evasion, the more urgent and costly it is to build an expensive enforcement apparatus. If the costs of implementing a new law and forcing a disobedient public to obey are seen to be unacceptably high, expedient politicians drop (otherwise desirable) legislative proposals.

The other shadow cast upon statutory economic edicts is the size of the illicit gains that can be obtained by infringements. Moralists assert that it is just as depraving to steal one dollar as to purloin one thousand dollars. It is possible that the Heavenly book-keeper records our pilfering sins without weighing them by the amounts pilfered. On earth, however, the volume of economic crime depends not only on the chances of escaping undetected but also on how attractive are the prizes awaiting the transgressor. Many an individual prefers to remain honest if violating the law will yield only a puny reward. This prosaic attitude has practical implications for the planners who formulate economic edicts or determine the rates of taxation. Few tourists, finding that the black market rate is only 10% above the official rate, will go out of their way to infringe the exchange controls of their host countries – if the premium is 100% they are certain to change their tune. Fraudulent under-invoicing of imports takes place more frequently when the import duty is 100% than when the tariff is a mere 20%. Unless, therefore, state interventionists can ensure by cheap and dreaded enforcement techniques that ordinances are obeyed, they are likely to frustrate the objectives of their regulations when they set the sights too high.

In 1975 the British government decided that to help the balance of payments it would forbid the import of South African gold coins (krugerrands). The Treasury officials who promulgated this prohibition were naive enough to believe that by just publishing such an order, all imports could be stopped automatically. It was therefore not considered necessary to ask for a budgetary allocation of £50m to recruit additional customs inspectors, provide lucrative rewards for informers, etc. The prohibition did not stop imports – it merely replaced legal imports with illegal consignments. At first UK residents were prepared to pay for the smuggled coins 30% above their intrinsic gold content but it gave smugglers such super-profits that many turned to this very lucrative economic crime, thereby driving down the premium to 5%. It appears that when people can make a profit in excess of the 5%, they are prepared to face the risk of going to prison but below 5% the reward is seen as being too small: they would rather remain poor but honest. Privately, and with hindsight, Treasury officials concede that the feasible objective of the absolute import prohibition would equally have been achieved by a 5% excise duty on legally imported South African gold coins.

TAX EVASION

In many parts of the world, the majority of individuals and businesses evade paying direct taxes on most of their earnings. In economies with relatively Satisfactory Tax Compliance – hereafter called the STC countries – evasion probably equals only 5-25% of the amount that would have been collected if all had made honest returns.* For the purpose of analysing the differential structural opportunities to evade taxes in the STC countries their economies can usefully be divided into the bureaucratic and non-bureaucratic sectors. To the former belong government departments, municipalities, non-profit organizations, nationalized corporations *and* the large companies of the private sector.

Notwithstanding popular opinion to the contrary, most large

---

* Obviously there are no reliable quantitative estimates. Occasionally, somebody hits the headlines by actually citing a percentage. Thus Erwin Kuester, the head of the Stuttgart tax fraud division, is quoted as saying that the German tax evasions equal 10% of the federal budget. [70] The British administrators of the Value Added Tax (the sales tax in the Common Market: VAT) surmise that less than 2% of the tax is evaded but the trade union of the VAT inspectors condemns this as a complacent figure; it claims to have evidence that the real dimension of evasion is 'several times the figure quoted'. Their plea, however, must be treated with some reserve because the Society of Civil Servants has a declared, vested interest in the recruitment of more tax-enforcement staff. [71]

corporations headquartered in STC countries do not practise tax fraud. In fact the corporate giants provide a textbook example of how taxes, in this case corporation taxes, can be imposed by the state and generally collected in full. Before elucidating why large companies are forced to adopt this angelic stance, it must be noted that if they choose to establish subsidiaries outside their home territory, they may face the additional impediment of finding it hard to adapt themselves to the fraudulent tax atmosphere of the host countries. An element of unfair commercial competition prevails when those multinationals, which are obliged to be tax-honest, operate in economies where all their indigenous (and some foreign) competitors do not pay the proper taxes. The following is taken from a frank report on the respective tax behaviour of foreign and indigenous corporations in Spain: 'the foreign investor ... is in a quite different position - particularly if standards of tax morality and discipline are high in his home country. While the Spanish entrepreneur can simply pocket his hidden profits, the foreign parent company cannot receive dividends or other remittances through legal channels without furnishing proof that all relevant obligations have been satisfied ....' [87]

The 1970s have thrown up a number of publicized instances, especially in the United States, where corporate tax fraud was organized by the salaried executives of some famous multinationals. By illegally reducing the corporation tax liabilities of the companies which employed them, they took *personal* risks which lent a strange, idealistic flavour to their conduct. Only a tiny proportion of the shares of the companies concerned was owned by the tax criminals. The cheating was not aimed at reducing their own personal tax payments, nor was it to obtain higher emoluments for themselves: the target was to increase the post-tax corporate profits which, overwhelmingly, accrue to the anonymous owners of the companies' equity.

These, however, were and are not typical examples of how managerial decision-makers in large companies behave. Most remember only too well that they are but salaried employees and have little personal material incentive to defraud the Revenue by cooking the accounts of their employers. This recognition dampens the eagerness of even the highest-paid US executives (with stock options) to take the risk of being indicted for crimes which, if undiscovered, largely benefit others. Few of the executives of the world's large corporations are angels. They are selfish humans whose enthusiasm to serve stockholders is muted when it involves corporate tax illegalities.

The hierarchical organization of businesses in the bureaucratic sector is also an antidote to tax evasion. Large corporations maintain internal discipline through rule books and prescribed guidelines. The keeping of two sets of books necessitates the active co-operation, and passive acquiescence, of dozens of employees. Middle-management executives, who may not have the courage to refuse to carry out criminal instructions, will nevertheless seek to cover themselves by asking for explicit, often written, orders from their superiors.

Those who talk glibly about tax evasion by large corporations usually know little of the practical difficulties in hiding black profits. Are they to be stacked away illicitly in some hidden safe? If so, who is to have the key? Alternatively, the undeclared profits may be paid into some dubious bank account in a tax haven. If so, who in the corporation has control over the illegal funds?

When the chief officers of corporate giants falsify the tax returns of their companies (or, more frequently, arrange for this to be done) they imperil themselves for years to come because some company executive with knowledge of the tax fraud may threaten to blackmail them. Many of the recent investigations in the US have been facilitated through information from disgruntled executives who were dismissed or not promoted. Revenue authorities all over the world have learned to depend heavily on discontented employees for hints on corporate tax evasion. This is therefore another reason why the managers of the top companies choose not to evade paying proper corporation tax. It is not because they are paragons of virtue but because they are egotistical realists.

Even critics, who find the above an ingenuous portrayal of the tax conduct of large corporations in the STC world, gladly concede that the propensity to evade direct and indirect taxes is very much greater in the non-bureaucratic sector. I hasten to add that this has nothing to do with morality but is explicable entirely by the concurrence of ownership and management. Not only self-employed craftsmen, professionals and small retailers but also

many (family-controlled) medium-sized manufacturing, servicing
and trading companies take advantage of the opportunity to evade
taxes. This helps to explain why many businesses, which lack the
muscle of the giants in the bureaucratic sector, nevertheless flourish
in the Western world. The small and medium-sized firms do not
enjoy the economies of scale of which their mighty rivals
boast – and yet they can compete successfully with them. Woolworth, with its concentrated buying power, sometimes obtains
supplies at prices which are 20% below those demanded from a
little store. But by the very nature of its organization, Woolworth
cannot evade VAT or corporation tax, whilst its pigmy rival can.
Tax-fraud is proving a lifeline for small firms and the self-
employed and is helping them to encroach upon the ostensibly
unassailable strength of the big battalions.

Only small groups of employees in the bureaucratic sector earn
emoluments which implicitly entail the partial evasion of personal
income tax. Municipalities assume that their refuse collectors have
some additional (unofficial) job-related earnings which they do not
declare on their tax returns. The nationalized corporation, British
Rail, is fully aware that the buffet-car stewards on their trains enjoy
an improperly derived, extra, non-taxed income. Large, respectable
food manufacturers know that some of their delivery personnel,
with the passive connivance of the retailers, regularly pilfer (and
then re-sell) supplies. There is an impressive list of occupations
with such illicit, untaxed, perquisites. Though many employees in
the bureaucratic sector thus can and do cheat on their income tax,
this does not demolish the broad generalization that the employers
in the bureaucratic sector generally cannot help their employees to
evade the full payment of direct taxes. This applies as much to the
office boy in the Dutch Ministry of Finance as to the chief
executive officer of a Swedish multinational. It follows that
dissatisfied employees in the bureaucratic sector cannot be induced
to stay at their jobs with the promise of having part of their wages
paid in black. Large companies can take money from the till for the
services of a temporary typist and window-cleaner (in the knowledge that the earnings will not be declared by the recipients), but
their financial rules do not allow this irregular method of payment
for the permanent staff.

The wages and salaries in the non-bureaucratic sector are usually lower than those paid in the bureaucratic sector, but this short-coming is more than offset by the ability of the small employers to pay part of the emoluments effectively tax-free. Firms in the non-bureaucratic sector often have a fund of black money out of which they can pay unrecorded wages, and this proves attractive to employees willing, nay eager, to evade taxes. In countries with penal income tax rates, employees are reluctant to do taxed overtime, yet bureaucratic employers have no choice but to report all overtime earnings to the tax inspectors. This is another field where the small firm scores over its big rival; the former can more easily induce its workers to do overtime whilst the latter, despite high premium rates for overtime, will frequently find no takers because of the unavoidable onerous tax deductions. Many employ-ees of bureaucratic employers prefer, as an alternative to doing taxed overtime for their main employers, to moonlight in the non-bureaucratic sector. This is why Chicago policemen become spare-time cab drivers and Whitehall clerks do night-work in Soho restaurants where they are rewarded with crisp bank notes. Germany's famous *Schwarzarbeiter* – who work in the lucrative black segment of the economy where there is no mention of VAT, social security contributions, trade union dues, income tax or corporation tax – are hardly ever full-time practitioners; most of them are moonlighters who have a respectable registered place of employment in the bureaucratic sector.

Few of the self-employed, small companies and medium-sized firms conduct *all* their transactions within the non-bureaucratic sector; most lead a dichotomous life in that they have dealings with suppliers and buyers of both sectors. Of course there are different rules for the two games. Prices for the same service or article may vary, depending on whether the buyer pays by cheque or in cash and whether he wants a receipt or not. A lawyer who is asked to defend a burglar may press the family for a cash payment, but when he prepares a brief for General Motors he will receive his fee by cheque and it will be recorded as a tax-deductible item by the corporate payer. A manufacturer of nails would never expect the naval dockyard to buy his goods without proper invoicing; on the other hand, the local ironmonger has good tax reasons of his own why he is happy to pay in cash for his purchase of nails, and does not ask for a receipt. Small hotels and restaurants are usually flush with money which they dare not bank; consequently, they tend to buy many supplies from non-bureaucratic bakers and grocers who are happy to sell for cash. Small US manufacturers of records are known to supply their distributors with three 'free', i.e. uninvoiced, records for every ten units bought officially.

The Geneva-based Investors Overseas Services (IOS) advised its salesmen that the most likely buyers of shares in the dubious Mutual Funds, which they were expected to hawk, would be the holders of black money. The IOS sales policy was highly successful; before the collapse it gathered one million customers who handed over more than $2 billion (a thousand million). In Latin America thousands of tax evaders arranged for their illicit earnings to be smuggled to Geneva. In Germany dentists formed the single largest professional group that fell victim to the blandishments of the IOS pedlars. It would be ungenerous and untrue to say that the reason why so many German dentists lost their money was because they were more foolish than other Germans. There is clearly another more plausible explanation. It probably tallies with the experience of the Swedish tax authorities who found that no less than 87% of five thousand medical doctors who were investigated had concealed a part of their income.

Ingenuity, risk-taking and immorality are the required ingredients to evade taxes in STC economies. Often it demands even more sophistication to store (or squander) the illicit gains from tax evasion. For humble beneficiaries of tax-frauds this of course is not a problem. No one will check the source of black overtime money which is spent on more beer or pocket money for the children. It only becomes a burning issue when the amounts are large. Worst off are the big crooks all of whose earnings may be entirely illegal. Many gangsters bemoan their fate of being unable to flaunt wealth by living in luxury apartments and owning race-horses: they must constantly be on guard lest they be asked to explain the sources of their money. The US Internal Revenue Service practically compels big-time crooks to have a genuine part-time employment so that some income can be declared as the spring whence cometh the wherewithal to pay for living expenses. Academic economists have not been helpful in advising harassed tax criminals on what to do with the proceeds from their crimes. To translate black cash into gold and jewellery is only a partial solution. Economists have little idea how dangerous it is in the English-speaking countries to bury valuables in bank vaults or hide them at home. All this is further complicated by the greed of most criminals who seek a return on their wealth which they cannot spend freely.

The majority of national tax authorities are literally forcing tax evaders to take their black money out of the countries in which it was acquired. Because of the hawkish eyes of the police the fruits of tax crimes cannot be squandered in conspicuous consumption at home. Nor can the criminals easily become patriotic investors. Too many questions are asked when black money is invested in the country in which it has been 'earned'. Tax criminals of a big enough stature are almost pushed to travel to Switzerland, which until now has provided lavishly for their needs.

Karl Marx never had cause to ponder over the miracle of Switzerland. When measured by the external exchange parity of its currency, Switzerland in the last few years has surpassed all other European economies. Why has the Swiss franc gone up and up in value? It certainly is not due to the frugality of the Swiss or because they work harder than other nationals. Once upon a time Switzerland relied for its foreign currency earnings on the tourist services of excellent hotels and the export of chocolates, medicaments, watches and machine tools, but these have played only a minor role in the recent ascent of the Swiss currency. The real strength of the Swiss economy is being constantly underpinned by the inflow of foreign funds. Only a small portion of this capital has been invested in Switzerland itself; indeed the yield on Swiss securities is amongst the lowest in the world. Most of those who transfer capital to Switzerland care little for the country's manufacturing and commercial activities: they are concerned almost exclusively with the favoured tax-treatment accorded to foreign capital and the bank secrecy which protects foreigners who crave to deposit the proceeds of illegal activities in a secure harbour. The Swiss – many of them are fervent churchgoers – are indignant when blamed for illicit trading operations, tax and exchange control transgressions, the corruption of state officials and purchasing officers, and the embezzlement of company funds, *outside* their borders. They plead passionately that as these crimes have been perpetrated neither in Switzerland nor by Swiss citizens, it ought to follow that the country of Switzerland is to be absolved from any associated blame. This is a formally correct apologia which, however, does not refute the reality that without the existence of numbered bank accounts (and all that goes with them) in Switzerland (and a handful of other *reliable* tax havens) it would often be senseless for foreigners to commit certain economic crimes. The Swiss are aware what a bad name they have earned for themselves by attracting dirty money. To prove their good faith they have in a few cases actually lifted the anonymity of Swiss bank accounts when foreign governments could point to particularly heinous – *but not economic* – crimes. The public relations officers of the Swiss banks have also been busy telling the Western world that in future they would be more selective in accepting faceless customers with funds of dubious origin.

There are many people within Switzerland who are hostile to the present system. They feel that their national honour is being impugned by allowing the profits of foreign economic crimes to be hidden with impunity in Swiss banks — to the shameful advantage of the standard of living of the Swiss people as a whole. In March 1977 senior officials of the Swiss central bank chose to go on public record to denounce the numbered accounts as a 'national embarrassment'. In May 1978 the Social Democratic party wanted to loosen Swiss banking secrecy – not, heaven forbid, abolish it! – in a number of instances including foreign tax evasion. Some Swiss politicians joined foreign critics in publicly deploring that Switzerland has become a centre which absorbs fugitive capital to the detriment of other countries. The Bankers Association countered this subversive demand by arguing that if the banking laws were radically reformed, this would constitute a danger for the Swiss economy – proving thereby, by implication, that the numbered accounts have made a decisive contribution to recent Swiss prosperity. Until a fundamental change has occurred, Switzerland's bank secrecy will continue to prop indirectly economic law-breaking in the rest of the world – and the Swiss franc will retain its extraordinary vigour.

BRIBES*
Between 1974 and 1977 innocents in the STC countries suddenly

* When A.C. Kotchian, the former president of Lockheed, gave evidence under oath before the Church Committee, he was displeased with the word 'bribery' to denote his company's admitted corrupt practices. He

became aware that corruption was one of the components in the murky life of some celebrated companies in the bureaucratic sector. There are teachers of economics who learned for the first time what knowledgeable corporate investors, and most large exporters, have had to digest gradually: in many parts of the world commercial success will elude those corporations which are not willing to bribe on a massive scale. Chaired by Frank Church, the open hearings of the US Senate subcommittee on multinationals opened the eyes of many simple professors of economics. Equally revealing have proved the demands of the Securities and Exchange Commission in Washington (SEC) for voluntary disclosures by guilty corporations; when met with refusal it applied to the courts to force them to tell. Not only practices by US corporations were publicized. The scandal involving the Royal Dutch family and the exposure of corruption in the Japanese cabinet made headlines – and nonsense – of much of the teaching of economics at school. In the United States guilty executives were not sent to prison; they were only required to confess in public and beat their breasts for having misled the SEC, auditors and stockholders. It was different in the Comecon world where, in this same four-year period, governments found it expedient to tell the Communist masses of the savage prison – and even death – sentences on officials in charge of buying foreign equipment, who had been found failing in their socialist duties. These were also the years when British public opinion had to shed the belief that bribery was alien to domestic business practices. (Hitherto it had been thought that corruption was only wide-spread when trading amongst foreign savages.) The idealistic British concept, which affirmed the unshaken honesty of public servants, was corroded when a number of politicians, municipal councillors, high civil servants and purchasing officers of nationalized corporations were indicted and some sent to jail. The worst blow was delivered in the summer of 1976 when the Report of the

---

said that he much preferred 'gift', because the money had been earmarked 'to establish a general climate of goodwill to foster our sales'. The mighty US corporations, which have been forced to publicize their misdeeds, generally shy away from such vulgar words as 'bribery' or 'corruption'. Amongst the euphemisms employed are Chrysler's 'unusual payments', Pullman's 'facilitating payments' and Coca-Cola's 'improper payments'.

Royal Commission, under Lord Salmon, confirmed publicly what
had been whispered in the dark for years. It shattered the carefully
nurtured illusion that there were only a handful of black sheep
amongst the commercial decision-makers of the UK public sector.
The Commission noted in euphemistic, muted, language that
there was a 'significant minority' which 'did not measure up to
acceptable standards'. [67]

In times of shortages bribes are given to jump the queue for the
procurement of goods, while during a buyers' market it is the
purchasing officials of the customers who are rewarded illicitly. A
few remarks on three broad legal aspects of bribery: (a) most
countries have laws which forbid the corrupting of their own
public officials but these laws do not necessarily apply to the
corrupting of officials abroad. Only a few states – Sweden enacted
such a law in 1977 – also make it unlawful to corrupt the
purchasing officers of domestic business firms in the private sector.
(b) Some countries do not permit the expenditure on bribes as a
tax-deduction. (This, however, is often a theoretical dictum only,
because it depends on how bribes are paid and how they are
recorded in the company accounts; the tax inspectors can do little
when the 'gift' is described as entertainment expenses or as a
commission.) In many other states, bribes are an explicitly
recognized tax-deductible business expenditure though domestic
and foreign bribes are sometimes treated differently. A recent
Dutch ruling had it that bribes may be deducted from corporation
tax liability and the payer need not disclose whom the money is
paid to. The Finance Court of Lower Saxony has adjudged that
when employees of German companies are arrested in Eastern
Europe for handing over bribes on behalf of their employers, the
companies can charge to German corporation tax the fines and
penalties which are imposed by the Communist governments as a
condition for freeing the salesmen from incarceration. (In one case
the Romanian authorities demanded, and received, $290,000 from
a German chemical concern as an indemnity for the release of its
employees who had been indicted for bribing Romanian officials.)
The UK tax laws are the world's most liberal in that the Inland
Revenue recognize bribes as a valid tax-deduction and will not
disclose them even when the recipients are British government
officials. As for UK corporations paying bribes abroad, these are

managed on a gentlemanly basis with the authorities. When, for example, some British exporters found that their foreign customers did not wish to be bribed in sterling, it was easily arranged with the Inland Revenue and the Bank of England's exchange controllers – unofficially of course – that the corruption gratifications could be remitted in dollars to Swiss bank accounts. (c) The reason why many US companies have had their bribery escapades made public had nothing to do with US laws against corruption or tax offences. The SEC accused them of having run foul of the rules governing the *fullest* possible disclosure of corporate information to the *investors* in publicly-traded securities. (Only in 1978 was legislation enacted outlawing the payment of bribes by US companies to foreign government officials.)

Those who object to corruption on principle do not care about the techniques of bribery; these, however, are of burning interest to less morally-inclined executives of many businesses. There are few problems for non-bureaucratic companies which have black cash, particularly when the owner-managers in person transmit the filthy lucre (as moralists would describe it). Firms in the bureaucratic sector also pay in bank notes, taken from the till for petty cash, but it is mainly to sweeten minor officials – with 'tips', 'grease' and 'baksheesh' – to expedite customs clearance, the installation of telephones, etc. The difficulty in the bureaucratic sector starts when the amounts are large and the corporate payers are intent on recording the illicit payments, with receipts, in the company accounts*. Most corrupt officials want to be paid in cash but giant companies usually have no big slush funds of hoarded black cash notes. People who accept bribes are not in the habit of handing the donors a signed receipt. Lockheed somehow solved both these problems for it was able to reward the corrupt Japanese politicians

---

* A sound bribing technique was admitted to by the Pullman Corporation. [8] 'In accordance with a not-uncommon practice in such country', a foreign Pullman subsidiary paid by cheque $5,000 to an overseas office of its *own* independent auditors (a world-famous accountancy partnership), which then turned over this amount to 'a taxpayers' association in such foreign country and, presumably, passed on to an official of such foreign country who could influence the outcome of the subsidiary's tax situation'. The furore caused by this revelation, and other disclosures, make it unlikely that US accountancy firms will render such client services in future.

with suitcases of cash. Furthermore, Lockheed's agents in Japan, who bribed government officials on its behalf, were helpful to the company's accountancy system by sending to the US parent company signed receipts for '100 peanuts' whenever 100 million yen were transferred. Many multinationals do not have to go to the lengths of Lockheed and are able to persuade corrupt officials to accept their bribes in the form of cheques, drawn on bank accounts housing 'off-the-book' funds, which usually end up in the recipient's numbered account in a tax haven.

The Church Committee and investigating bodies outside the US have established that large corporations do not always need Swiss cheque books or cloak-and-dagger couriers with money-suitcases. Corrupt payments can be made to look innocuous when entered in the books as commission, research costs, advertising expenses, etc. Bribery at home can also be effected through goods-in-kind, entertainment, jobs for relatives and the promise of a sinecure for the corrupt official when he leaves his position of power.

Earlier in this chapter we mentioned that the contingent disloyalty of employees acts as a brake on corporate tax-frauds because chief executives are frightened of being blackmailed. Potentially dishonest salesmen also limit the scope of corporate bribery: how does a board of directors *know* that a sale in country A can only be effected by bribing B with C number of dollars? When bribes are handed over in cash, there is a distinct risk that the employee, who carries the suitcase to the foreign procurement official, will grab some of it on the way.* Several corporations believe that this has actually happened to them though they obviously cannot prosecute. Giving a cheque is somewhat safer but not wholly so. Whilst no company has yet said so in public, there

---

* In September 1977 one of the top officers of an American trade union was charged with extorting money from United Brands; he was alleged to have taken $124,000 from the company in return for ensuring that its perishables were unloaded without any disturbances even during a strike of the longshoremen. An executive of United Brands gave evidence that after approval by his superiors he had made various black cash payments over lunch to the accused. The union official's attorney told the jury that no bribes had been given. He charged that 'certain United Brands officials, fearful of their jobs during a period of management turnover, took the money themselves from an alleged company slush fund'[12]. Whether United Brands paid bribes or not is irrelevant in this context. The fact that the accused's attorney could counter an open admission by a

are grounds to suspect that some corrupt foreign officials have split their bribes with executives of the company which paid them. There is overwhelming evidence that firms, that are unwilling to sully their corporate hands by negotiating directly with corrupt ministers and officials but use local agents instead, often pay extra commission – intended for corrupt objectives – which remains in the pockets of the agents. Bribing is a messy business, particularly if a company has to guard against treachery in its own ranks.

No corruption is more startling than that associated with multi-nationals selling in the Comecon markets. The specialist Vienna weekly, *Eastern Europe Report,* has been monitoring the trials – in Bulgaria, Poland, USSR, Romania and Czechoslovakia – of both foreign sales executives and their accomplices, the native managers of state importing agencies. Considering the risks involved for both parties, one can only marvel – with admiration or disgust – at how obsessed certain companies are to effect sales and how avid is the urge of some Communist bureaucrats to enrich themselves. In October 1973 a government official, Ion Tudora, was executed for an involvement with foreign farm equipment manufacturers that was considered detrimental to the Romanian economy. In April 1975 another Romanian, an expert on wood lacquers who was influential in steering business to a foreign supplier, was also sentenced to death though there is no confirmation that the sentence was actually carried out. Apparently, the usual form of bribery is to offer the corrupt Communist purchasing official an illicit commission which is deposited in a Swiss banking account. Sometimes, however, the payment is made by the foreign firm in black Communist money and goods-in-kind. [72] According to Bulgarian newspapers, several of their foreign trade officials were prepared to receive shirts, spare parts for cars, shoes and watches in return for revealing sensitive price information to foreign buyers of Bulgarian agricultural exports. Whilst several Czech bureaucrats insisted on having their bribes paid into bank accounts abroad, other colleagues were satisfied with gold coins, watches and jewellery. In March 1975 a Moscow court sentenced Y.S.

---

bureaucratic corporation, to have corrupted a union official, by asserting that the money had in fact been embezzled is symptomatic of the dangers to which executives expose themselves when they enter the dangerous minefield of bribery.

Sosnovsky, general manager of the Soviet furniture manufacturing concern Soyuskomplektmejbel, to death by a firing squad and a Swiss businessman to ten years' imprisonment. (Communist morality would have it that it is more dastardly to receive than to give a bribe.) The Swiss transgressor was arrested at the Moscow airport trying to smuggle 45,000 rubles into the country. It was alleged that they were intended for poor comrade Sosnovsky who is said to have already received on a previous occasion 107,000 rubles in bribes as well as a radio, tape recorder, watches and overcoats. All these 'gifts' – to use the Lockheed terminology – were in exchange for granting several substantial orders to a Swiss woodworking machinery company. The Russians were apparently incensed that the Swiss had taken the corrupt payments into account when submitting their adjusted prices.

The danger of blackmail by discontented personnel is particularly rampant with corrupt practices in Eastern Europe. *Eastern Europe Report* claims to know of cases where disgruntled employees informed the Comecon authorities of bribes that their employers (sometimes their ex-employers) had given to Communist trade officials. In one case an employee with a grievance against his company – an Austrian firm – copied a bank statement showing a money transfer to a Swiss bank account for the credit of a Romanian procurement official. When the sales manager of the Austrian company was next in Romania, he was confronted with a photocopy and arrested.

After his appointment as Secretary of the Treasury in the Carter administration, Michael Blumenthal told Congress that 'paying bribes is simply not necessary for the successful conduct of business here or overseas'. Had Blumenthal disavowed corruption on moral grounds, he would have deserved applause. To assert, however, that it is 'not necessary' justifiably evokes hollow laughter. An association of the world's multinationals – *with powers of enforcement* – could eliminate many forms of bribery, but Blumenthal (the businessman-turned-politician) knows that this is an utopian proposition. Whatever one may think of the wisdom and morality of Lockheed's executives who sought to keep alive their troubled company, they were certainly more accurate than Blumenthal in describing corporate handouts as 'necessary in consummating certain foreign sales'; they could well have added that but for bribery the Lockheed company might have faltered.

A very small number of firms, whose products or technology are unique, can haughtily adopt the attitude of 'take it or leave it' when approached by buyers. They do not find it necessary to do more than wine and dine prospective buyers. Such corporations readily agree with Blumenthal that corruption is not a necessary adjunct to their foreign sales campaign. Clearly, when there is a sellers' market, buyers do not have to be given illicit gratifications by the vendors.

The overwhelming majority of Western firms, however, are not in such a fortunate position. They have been forced to recognize that the (unofficial) commercial rules in most parts of Africa, Asia, Latin America, and in some countries in Europe, differ fundamentally from those in the STC economies. Partly or wholly, imports may be at the discretion of (corrupt) government officials who alone can grant licences and/or allocate foreign currency to finance them. When the government (or a nationalized corporation) is the only potential buyer – that, according to experienced exporters, is frequently the biggest impediment to honest marketing in many parts of the world. Where there is a private sector to sell to, the importer or agent may demand – this means breaking the law but is not bribery – that the foreign supplier help him evade paying taxes; the provision of a false invoice, together with the payment of an agreed amount into a Swiss bank account, is often a condition of purchase.

No divine injunction impels companies to market aeroplanes in Japan, oil in Italy and trucks in Bolivia. In this sense Blumenthal is correct when he pontificates that even in areas which are derided for their corruption it still is 'not necessary' to pay bribes; multinational A can determine not to do any business there though it knows that multinational B will gladly replace it as a supplier. I know of two Californian firms which, as a matter of principle, decided (long before the 1974-77 revelations) that they would cease trying to sell in markets where success could be attained only with bribery. Lest they be admired as being more honourable than other US companies, one must bear in mind that the trade which they voluntarily abandoned was an insignificantly small segment of their global sales – they could *afford* to bask in the moral glory of being untainted by corruption. Many corporations, of which aircraft manufacturers are an outstanding example, cannot give up so easily vast overseas markets when this would make such dents in the global profits as to imperil their very existence.

In the wake of Blumenthal's exhortations, many business leaders have joined in to preach on the ethical aspects of bribery though few have considered the economic significance of corruption. Are bribes akin to theft and embezzlement in that they primarily redistribute wealth without causing any major material damage to society? I hope to show later that many forms of bribery lead to a severe misallocation of resources and are therefore harmful both for moral and economic reasons. First, however, I want to deal with some corrupt practices which – though obviously obnoxious by moral standards – have only trivial detrimental economic consequences. My model is a self-contained community in which an organized group of gangsters plans to extort protection money from *all* retail outlets. If the gangsters are only partly successful, then some market distortions would ensue because of the resultant unfair competition between shops that do and those that do not have to bear the illicit protection costs. Should they succeed in blackmailing all shopkeepers but collect the ransom in the form of a flat-rate tax, some (differential) economic damage would still be caused. As nowadays even the worst hoodlums can afford to take professional advice, they might well call in an economic consultant. He would surely counsel them to vary the amount of the protection money in accordance with the turnover or net profit of each retail outlet. Such an illicit tax would be 'just' and cause few economic distortions.

Under the Nkrumah regime, foreign firms which wanted to do business in Ghana were compelled to make unofficial payments to the dictator's political party. Foreigners knew that if they did not comply, they would not be given any contracts or import licences. If one is to believe certain unconfirmed reports, the Ghana authorities extorted *identical, pro rata,* political bribes from all major foreign suppliers and contractors.

A similar equitable system was inaugurated when the oil companies were compelled to pay massive bribes to the Italian political parties (which formed the coalitions or played a key role in parliamentary committees). The salient point is that all oil companies were in the same boat. The Unione Petrolifera negotiated on behalf of all indigenous and foreign oil companies with the political decision-makers on the aggregate amount of the industry's bribes and the proportional allocation to the coffers of the various parties. This trade association in turn saw to it that each individual oil company chipped in 'fairly' by contributing a quota that was commensurate with its share of the national oil sales. In the Italian and Ghana examples, as in the model of our gangster-infested community, it was impossible to conduct any business except on the terms imposed by the men who held the reins of power. The outstanding feature of these bribery arrangements is that they were economically less injurious than many other forms of corruption in that they did not discriminate between different suppliers provided these were willing to play by the rules of the game.

The Church Committee, the Salmon Commission and the Japanese disclosures prove conclusively that the above examples are not typical: bribes are ordinarily not a *uniform* business expense that each acquiescing company must bear when selling in a country where corrupt ministers and officials make the purchasing decisions. Bribes are rarely a neutral tax. Two kinds of corruption are common in this field. The purport of the first is to induce the tainted procurement functionary not to buy the superior goods of company A but, in exchange for a personal reward, to acquire the goods of company B that are of inferior quality. Suppliers hand out kickbacks to dishonest decision-makers (or technical experts) to ensure that they deliberately fail in their designated duties as trustees who are charged with making a best-buy on behalf of the public or their employers. This kind of corruption has the economic effect of encouraging the sale of inferior goods and discouraging the use of goods which are technically excellent but supplied by companies unwilling to bribe. The lower the quality of the goods of B, the bigger the bribe which the salesman of B will offer.

The other kind of corruption relates to situations where the decision-makers exercise their technical expertise to choose the superior product provided they are given an illicit commission. In this case the economic damage consists of paying more than necessary for the goods because the vendor has incorporated the bribe in the selling price. It is a fatuous and hypocritical defence, often put forward by corrupt officials, that the bribes they have received reduce the profit of the supplier. Most firms have two prices: one for markets where no bribes are paid and one where an 'extra commission' is calculated in the invoiced price. There is an unauthenticated story that a European company regularly raised its standard prices by 4% when invoicing the Cuban government in the days of the Batista regime, because 4% was the agreed kickback. When the Communists came to power the firm was told that they knew of this arrangement. They wanted to continue buying from the same company but, as no more bribes were payable, asked for the removal of the 4% surcharge. The supplier was happy to oblige.

Youngsters, listening attentively to their professors of economics, are taught that in a free-market economy firms compete with one another primarily in terms of quality and price. They are also told that cartels and monopolies mar this idealized picture but corruption is not deemed important enough to be stressed. In textbook theory a procurement official in the bureaucratic sector takes no cognizance of how salesmen behave to him. According to the rules of free enterprise, he does not care whether the vendor's representative is obsequious or not – all that interests him, as a buyer, is the quality and the price of the offered goods. Were this true then airlines and airforces would select new aircraft exclusively by their potential technical performance. The buyers would rely entirely on hired economists and engineers who have prepared cost-benefit options for different aircraft. Suppliers would find it unnecessary even to dine and wine the decision-makers. Alas, we know from the Church committee that massive bribes have often been the decisive factor in choosing one aircraft rather than another. I recently perused a thick book used widely in English-language university seminars for students who take marketing degrees. The sophistication of the models was intellectually overpowering. Yet in over 800 pages there was not one single line which elucidated to the budding marketing executives how to recruit prostitutes for their customers and how to ensure that buying agents, who have had bribes credited to their Swiss banking accounts, can be made to keep their word and actually purchase inferior products at high prices.

SMUGGLING

This section deals with the unlawful import and export of merchandise. Leaving aside special cases (contraceptives, hard drugs, weapons), smuggling is only lucrative when import or export licences are needed but not freely available and/or the government imposes heavy import or export duties and indirect taxes. The rationale of the smuggling of banknotes, gold and diamonds is ordinarily a function of arbitrary currency rates and capricious exchange controls which are the subject matters of the next section.

The chairman of an important British watch company once complained that its legitimate trade was adversely affected by an estimated annual smuggling of two million watches into the UK. [76] In the sixties 90% of all cigarette exports from Switzerland are said to have been 'unofficial', a euphemism for being smuggled into neighbouring countries. [80] The border between North and South Ireland has provided profitable business for generations of adventurous smugglers of cattle and butter. But despite these few irregularities, smuggling in Western Europe is an unimportant element which does not distort the external trade patterns. One can consequently trust the official import-export statistics which (with a number of exceptions) are reliable indicators of the national movements of merchandise.

The same cannot be said of most states in Africa, Asia and Latin America. The external trade statistics which they publish solemnly, and the so-called 'certificates of origin' issued by government offices and local chambers of commerce, are often a travesty of the truth. Smuggling can and does falsify substantially the official statistics of many countries. In some respects Jagdish Bhagwati is a black sheep amongst academic economists, for he has devoted much of his research to the forbidden theme of measuring, and theorising on, illegal transactions in international trade. Many of his university colleagues tend to belittle the momentousness of his numerate analyses of the under-invoicing of Turkish imports and the propensity to smuggle in Afghanistan. He, however, is unrepentant on the 'urgent need ... to integrate the analysis of illegal trade phenomena into the pure theory of international trade .... These illicit phenomena vitiate not merely the accuracy and use of foreign trade statistics. They must also affect the policy prescriptions from the theory of trade and welfare that economists would bring to the policymaker.' [11]

Ecuador provides a small but interesting case-study of an economy in which the volume of a large number of smuggled items can at times match the legitimate imports. Across its northern border from Colombia come vast quantities of textiles, coffee, shoes, cosmetics and chocolates. Not all illegally imported goods are smuggled physically into Ecuador. For example, contraband electrical appliances, said to supply half of the domestic market, come in unlawfully by avenues which include the bribing of customs officials – especially 'around Christmas and Easter when they need extra cash'. [82] At one time Indonesia was the classical economy in which widespread smuggling thrived. In Simkin's study on 'Indonesia's Unrecorded Trade', [11] emphasis is laid on her illicit exports. He found that in one particular year official coffee exports of $16 million were surpassed by smuggled exports totalling $37 million.

'Unofficial trade, in most cases more properly dubbed smuggling, plays an important part in inter-African trade – in fact so important is it that it is thought in some cases to account for more than half the goods crossing the borders of a given state.' [81] This is taken from a dispatch published in *The Financial Times*. Standing by itself such a journalistic generalization is not likely to persuade academic sceptics because no *quantitative* proof is given. In this case, however, the correspondent was able to provide a numerate illustration from official sources. According to the Ministry of Animal Production in the Republic of Niger 64,267 calves were exported in 1969 to neighbouring Nigeria. The official trade statistics of Nigeria in that year registered an import of 195,000 calves from the Republic of Niger.

International companies, headquartered in STC countries, may face moral and commercial dilemmas when they seek to do business in regions where smuggling (in both directions) is a pervasive fact of life. Manufacturing companies with world-renowned brands, which have set up their own retail outlets or assembly plants in host countries where illegalities are rife, are sometimes hit hard by severe competition from smuggled imports. The same fate is suffered by multinationals which market through native agents and distributors who are expected to obtain supplies only lawfully and directly from their principals. A big-volume producer in an industrialized country can do little to prevent middlemen buying his branded goods for re-sale to smugglers who then successfully undersell the appointed foreign distributors. Except with heavy capital goods, such practices are difficult to control. (Some firms instruct their official outlets abroad not to service appliances that cannot be proved to have been imported lawfully.) There are instances of powerful companies which have given up attempting to play it straight. Shamelessly – but of course unofficially – they leave their appointed native agents in the lurch and concentrate on selling to disreputable intermediaries who are prepared to buy considerable quantities of goods for the smuggling organizations. The smuggling is in the reverse direction but the moral-cum-economic issue is the same when, through traders in New York, major US food firms regularly buy large amounts of coffee beans which they implicitly know to have been shipped illegally out of Latin America.

Countries with extensive illegal cross-border trade periodically launch anti-smuggling campaigns which end by sending some lowly customs officials to prison. When corruption is not regarded with disdain by the ethos of a society, and the government lacks effective coercive powers to stamp out economic illegalities, smuggling is only curtailed by abating the gains that can be earned from it. In 1971 Indonesia publicized itself as an attractive location for new foreign investors. The government was therefore perturbed when Unilever, one of the few multinationals already established in the country, ordered the temporary closure of its Djakarta factory because of a disastrous drop in sales. This was not due to falling consumer demand. The Anglo-Dutch giant had always faithfully obeyed the laws of its host country and consequently the goods which it marketed bore the full brunt of the hefty turnover tax. [83] Unilever met with unfair competition from native traders who sold soap, margarine and toothpaste which had been smuggled in from Malaysia and Singapore and were of course 'exempt' from import duties and the turnover tax; in addition, they carried the prestige of a 'foreign-made' tag. The Indonesian authorities had built their fiscal policy on two erroneous assumptions: heavy import duties – some were as high as 280%! – protect domestic industry and, if imports nevertheless come in, the Treasury benefits accordingly. In reality the exact opposite was true. The higher the import duties, the greater were the fortunes which tempted the smugglers. The Unilever shock, and the decreasing revenues from import duties, induced the Indonesian government to fundamentally alter its position. In June 1971 it slashed the import duties on the favourite items of the smugglers with immediate beneficial results for the economy. The reduction in the level of import duties led to a drastic curtailment of illegal

imports and a considerable increase in the revenues collected from
legal imports.

BREACHES OF EXCHANGE REGULATIONS

The external exchange parity of a currency, when there are no
exchange controls, is determined largely by the country's international trade and capital movements. The *raison d'être* of exchange
controls is the intent of rulers to fix an arbitrary rate that is
unaffected by the free interplay of market factors. To defend an
artificial currency rate, exchange controls are imposed to restrict
the cross-border movement of capital, to regulate foreign trade and
to prohibit the unauthorized import or export of local paper-
money. The ideology behind arbitrary exchange rates is that the
planners know best. They are admittedly aware that they can
control only one side of the equation because foreigners cannot be
bullied to exchange their currencies at an arbitrary rate. Exchange
controllers, however, imagine that they have the capacity so to
regiment the citizens of their own country as to ensure that the
rate, or rates, which they fix can survive any onslaught from
conventional supply-and-demand forces.

Many governments, which start by laying down *one* fixed
exchange rate, after some time become intoxicated with their own
putative wisdom in regulating the external relations of the
economy. They then refine the system by promulgating multiple
exchange rates. When importers are allocated foreign currency, say
dollars, to pay for the import of essential goods – essential being
defined by the bureaucrats or politicians – they are offered a
favourable rate in terms of the local currency: they become
privileged to buy cheap dollars. On the other hand the import of
non-essential goods is prohibited altogether or made subject to
quotas and/or can only be financed with dear dollars. Multiple
exchange rates offer ample scope for a dishonest trader to 'switch'
from one category to a more propitious one by making false
declarations or forging bills of lading. He applies to the authorities
for the allocation of cheap dollars to bring in essential goods whilst
actually importing inessentials that ought to have been paid for
with dear dollars: for example, luxurious air-conditioners may be
imported under the cloak of industrial machinery; silk dresses may
be fraudulently labelled as industrial overalls.

Arbitrary exchange rates inevitably produce breaches of the regulations and thereby generate a currency black market. The economic impact of the resultant illegalities varies in accordance with the premium of the official exchange rate over the black rate. When it is less than 15% the effect is minute but obviously becomes very weighty when the premium is several hundred per cent as was once the case in Pakistan. The first chinks in the wall, protecting the exchange controls, usually appear when people request currency allocations for foreign travel. If these are refused or only a derisory sum of, say, $100 is made available, the travellers may be tempted to smuggle out physically local paper-money and bank notes in order to exchange them abroad for dollars (albeit at a discount on the official rate). Alternatively, dollars may be acquired unlawfully from tourists by offering terms of exchange which are superior to the official rate.

What happens when Beatles' records are condemned as decadent and classified as inessential imports for which no dollars are made available? John in San Francisco used to send every quarter a cheque for $100 to his aged mother who remained in the old country – now, instead, he buys records for $100 and dispatches them as his filial support. Thanks to this stratagem his mother is better off. The amount of local currency obtainable from selling $100 of goods which cannot be imported officially is bigger than the sum which she would receive were she to exchange a $100 cheque at the (low) official rate.

Yugoslavia was not prepared to allocate foreign currency for the import of cosmetics from the West. Consequently, Yugoslav workers in Germany, who returned home periodically for visits to their families, found it more profitable to bring with them branded lipsticks and perfumes rather than marks. It certainly was not helpful to the Yugoslav economy but for the Yugoslav *Gastarbeiter* it was a very much better proposition to sell the luxury goods (they had acquired for marks) within Yugoslavia instead of exchanging their German savings for dinars at the official rate.

When the exchange controllers make available cheap dollars, the door is opened for unscrupulous importers to abuse the system provided they are aided by foreign suppliers who provide fake invoices. Though the consignment of soya beans costs $4,000, the *pro forma* invoice reads $5,000 which enables the dishonest importer to acquire the $5,000 cheaply. What happens to the $1,000 that has been remitted to the supplier who holds them in trust for the importer? The dollars can either be exchanged on the black currency market at a favourable rate and the proceeds repatriated unofficially or the importer can retain the $1,000, unlawfully, outside his country. (Brazil and India have long suffered from such 'unofficial' capital movements.)

Over-invoicing makes sense when cheap dollars can be acquired whilst under-invoicing is profitable when imports of inessentials are restricted by quotas and/or have to be financed by officially allocated dear dollars. A journal, specializing in Latin-American economics, reports that the imports of Japanese electric durables are often invoiced with 'errors in weight' or are undervalued in collusion with corrupt government officials. [82] The game can only be played when the crooked importer receives collusive help from his supplier. The latter sends a *pro forma* invoice for $100 and the importer pays a great deal of local currency for the dear dollars that are officially assigned to him to finance a $100 import. He arranges, however, for the supplier to send goods with a value of $150. This means that to complete the circle he must acquire $50 on the black currency market in order to pay his supplier in full. The profit on the sale of import-restricted goods is likely to be so considerable that the importer can afford to buy the $50 on the black market, disburse some bribes and yet remain with a handsome gain.

Exchange controllers in many countries exhibit an ambivalent attitude towards exporters. When multiple exchange rates prevail, the treatment of companies varies in accordance with the type of goods they export. Some groups may be smothered with kindness, i.e. receive very favourable rates for their export earnings, whilst others – believed to be in a weak bargaining position *vis-à-vis* the state – are allotted unfavourable rates.

Not all exports are patriotic ventures; this iconoclastic view is set out in Chapter V. Most planners, however, swoon for joy when they hear of propositions which would swell the volume of their country's exports. Exchange controllers therefore frequently offer lucrative exchange rates to prod selected producers into becoming exporters. To be granted such a favour the applicants must convince the bureaucrats that without the help of an advantageous exchange rate it would not be commercially feasible for them to export. There is evidence from several countries that the exchange rates fixed for favoured exports often prove so attractive as to make it worthwhile for dishonest companies to sell abroad goods for $50 but remit home $90, the latter amount being reported to the authorities as the sum for which the exports were (allegedly) sold. The government, in its folly to encourage certain exports at any price, exchanges (what it imagines are all genuine) export-dollars into local currency on such favourable terms as to leave our crooked exporter with enough funds to buy on the black market the incremental $40 and still make a profit on the transaction. To readers in STC economies this may appear incredible and ridiculous devilry but it is viewed in a different light by those businessmen in developing countries, with arbitrary exchange rates and complex trading controls, who have become proficient players of this lucrative game.

The exchange controllers are tough with exporters, who are at their mercy. Producers of goods that cannot be marketed domestically in large quantities – cocoa in Ghana, bananas in Jamaica, coffee in Brazil – are punished for being captive exporters and offered unfavourable exchange rates or are subjected to an export tax. Sometimes a too inflexible stance by the government manipulators of multiple exchange rates boomerangs. As most Argentinian farmers could not resort to smuggling, the administrators (during the second Perónist regime) fixed a derisory exchange rate for exported meat. Told to take-it-or-leave-it, many farmers responded by curtailing their production of cattle. Colombia provides another example of an economy in which one branch – the coffee producers – which had no domestic outlet for its output was bullied by the government into selling abroad on unsatisfactory terms. Whilst Colombian exporters of other products received many valuable incentives, coffee producers were discriminated against by a combination of factors: an unreasonably low official selling price, a high export tax and an adverse exchange rate. It has been said that Colombia and the world benefited when, in the sixties, the coffee growers rebelled against the oppressive operation of the multiple exchange rates; they smuggled out of the country (mainly through the island of Aruba) coffee for tens of millions of dollars. Though the authorities in Bogota promised informers and captors of illegal consignments rewards equal to 85% of the

confiscated contraband, the illegal trade did not dry up immediately. By 1976, however, most of the coffee growers were finally
beaten into commercial submission: only about 35% of the
country's crop was then still exported illegally and this came
mainly from the border areas. The coffee growers, who could no
longer smuggle out their products, complained that the government's official export terms would yield, in pesos, one third of what
they would have received if they could have exported freely to
New York and sold the dollar proceeds on the open market. As a
result, many growers reacted to the – now largely effective – arbitrarily low exchange rate for exported coffee by burning existing
reserves and vowing in future to grow other crops destined
primarily for the home market.

IN THE FATHERLAND OF SOCIALISM

Critics of capitalism enjoy pointing out the illegalities which play
such an important role in the non-Communist world, but they find
it harder to explain why the death penalty has been introduced for
economic crimes in various countries of the Comecon. Stalin, in
1947, had abolished capital punishment as a penalty for serious
economic crimes against the state – the 'liberal' Khrushchev was
pressured by events to revive it. When viewed in the perspective of
the heavy punishments meted out to transgressors who infringe
Communist state planning regulations, it is surprising that many
citizens of the communist states are not only contemptuous of the
orders of the central planners but successfully frustrate them.
According to Kaiser there has grown up a huge unofficial economy
which thrives beyond the reach of the planning mechanism. [54]

Local managers do not always find it expedient to tell the chief
planners in Moscow that their local plan cannot be executed because
spare parts are unavailable – instead they procure these by unorthodox (i.e. illegal) means. It does not matter greatly whether the
laid-down targets have actually been achieved. However, it is of
vital importance that a production report be sent to the planning
authorities which contains completion-data that correspond to the
projections in the National Plan. My favourite illustration concerns
comrade Isaev, a minister of the Kirgiz republic, who was caught
buying butter from state shops in order that he could deliver larger

quantities of butter to state depots and thus make his output statistics appear more impressive. [85]

In 1975 the Russian grain harvest failed badly but not enough foreign currency was allocated for the import of cereals. Orders went out from Moscow to cut drastically the amount of grain which was to be apportioned for the feeding of livestock. The price of bread was kept at an arbitrarily low level through the supply of flour to the bakeries at below accountancy-cost prices, i.e. with subsidies as we would say in the West. The policy entailed the premature slaughtering of animals and a concomitant rise in the price of meat. Even in the fatherland of socialism, market forces sometimes break through the maze of a distorted price structure. A Russian woman street cleaner, 250 miles out of Moscow, schemingly calculated that since her betters were curtailing official grain supplies for livestock, the resultant high price of meat would make it profitable to feed animals with the cheap bread which was freely available. Conscious that the law forbade it, she nevertheless fed forty-five pigs on her private farming lot with subsidized bread. We know that her pigs were confiscated and she was sent to a labour camp for one year. We do not know why *Pravda* found it right to tell Russia and the world about this wicked woman. [86] Ought the name of this criminal not be immortalized in the Communist and non-Communist textbooks on economic planning?

WHY ILLEGALITIES ARE SWEPT UNDER THE CARPET

Some economists are very good at describing the impact of a new tax on income distribution. Articles in learned journals explain why wage controls narrow the differentials between the emoluments of skilled and unskilled operatives. Proposals for import restrictions invariably provoke some professor to hold forth on television on the distortive influence this would have on the trade pattern. Economists, however, rarely discuss whether the reaction of the public to new taxes and controls might take the form of transgressing the law. It is not difficult to illustrate this disdain of economists for the importance of economic illegalities. One only has to examine the ten most popular textbooks currently used in the teaching of economics. The majority of these books leave out altogether economic crimes as if they played no role in the real world. The few academics, who do lower themselves to mention illegalities, perform this ignoble task in footnotes, thereby hinting to their pupils that transgressions of the law have nothing, or only very little, to do with economics. Some Anglo-Saxon teachers regard this as a dirty subject which has no relevance for a study of STC economies and need consequently be taught only in relation to under-developed countries. I have discerned three reasons why actual and potential economic crimes are treated as bagatelles by the majority of professional economists.

1) Many economists are still ignorant of the amplitude of economic crime. This ingenuousness used to be very pronounced in the past but is now receding in view of convincing evidence that is converting even pious academics. Nevertheless, though now fewer in number, there are still economists who are genuinely unaware how human villainy can deform a polished economic theory.

2) Even economists who concede that sinful behaviour is widespread are not prepared to amend the textbooks and give illegalities the place of dishonour which they so rightfully deserve. In their craze to be regarded as scientists, economists tend to lean heavily on quantifiable factors and of course there is little documentary evidence enabling economic 'scientists' to measure the dimensions of sin within their sphere of work. Economists worship official data as respectable sources of knowledge. Most statistics are collected by the government and semi-official bodies; with few exceptions, these omit to record illegal earnings and such unmentionable activities as smuggling and black market trading. It is very rare for tax authorities to produce annual revenue statements which say: '$x collected and estimated $y not collected because of evasion'. In other social sciences the practitioners are not ashamed to avail themselves of non-quantifiable evidence which may be gathered from fieldwork, newspaper reports, court proceedings, etc. Economists fear that if they were to emulate the sociologists, their findings would not pass the test of scientific reliability.

3) Ambitious planners have an additional reason for seeking to minimize the volume of economic law-breaking. Galbraith, as an elder statesman, is now preaching from many pulpits how virtuous wage-price controls are and how blessed the US

would be if only it had more state-interventionism. In his youth Galbraith had an opportunity to practise actively the craft of regimenting other people's economic behaviour. He rose to prominence during the war as America's celebrated controller of prices. It had little to do with his personal competence that historically the US price controls are considered to have been a relative failure. Nevertheless, more than thirty years after leaving the job, Galbraith still feels the urge to proclaim publicly that his controls had been successful and had not been frustrated by large-scale evasions.* Many contemporary observers deny this boastful claim. But, be this as it may, why does Galbraith find it necessary *now* to rake up the glory of his past 'success' as a price controller? One explanation seems to be that unless he can establish his credentials as a proven planner, who once successfully regulated the US public, less credence will attach to his current passionate television appearances in which he pleads the case for economic controls in the future.

Galbraith's dilemma is shared by many economists who seek to sell planning prescriptions to politicians. Economic illegalities on a modest scale should not seriously interfere with the ambitions of state-interventionists. But what if economic crimes on a large scale threaten to make the planners look foolish? As Galbraith has done, there is always the temptation to say that illegalities are too peripheral to matter. Planners have a vested interest to play down the significance of economic crimes.

---

* In mounting his defence that there was no serious black market in the US when he was in charge of price controls, Galbraith points to the slow rise in the consumer price index during this period. Yet he has to admit that in the US in those days, as in many other countries, the official cost-of-living index did not incorporate black market prices.

Chapter V

THE EXPORT MYTHOLOGY

What kind of policy is it that leads to a Scottish client, who has never built except on the Clyde, building in Norway with a special Norwegian low-interest loan, whilst we are building for a Norwegian friend an almost identical ship on a special British low-interest export loan? The current craze, exportmania, is - in fields like my own - nothing less than economic sodomy.

William Lithgow
Kingston Shipbuilding Yard, Glasgow

THE WICKEDNESS OF MARKS & SPENCER

Eminent economists plead in vain that 'there is no special virtue in exports as such'. [18] They also have little success when trying to educate legislators that the production of import-substitutes 'for sale in the home market' can be more salubrious than manufacturing for export. [19] There are few themes on which economists display such intellectual agreement as in their united opposition to the populist 'thinking' on exports. No professional economist would subscribe to the formula that exports are automatically virtuous and imports inherently wicked. Yet the economic discipline has failed to mar the images which depict exporters as lovable heroes and importers as parasitic villains. In communist and capitalist societies, in developed and under-developed countries, economic analysts have been unable to shake the dogmatic beliefs of the faithful that it is meritorious to sell to foreigners. In the United Kingdom, Conservative and Labour governments have dragged Her Majesty into upholding this fetish by instituting the Queen's Award for Export Achievement. Republican countries are obviously at a disadvantage because no royal accolade can be bestowed on exporters but, as an inferior alternative, their presidents are wont to invite saintly exporters to special cocktail parties. Whilst the British Queen makes the Award by handing out a trophy, republican governments present their national heroes with medals.

The US Immigration Service is charged with keeping out certain categories of undesirable aliens with dubious background but they are sometimes allowed to bend the rules if the foreign individual can persuade them that his journey to the US is for the purpose of aiding US companies to export. Citizens of countries, where exit visas are difficult to obtain, find it useful to state on the application form that the purpose of their intended journey is to further the export drive.

Since the end of the war, British prime ministers have made many recommendations to the Monarch concerning the elevation of successful exporters to a peerage, but no announcement has ever been made, on the eve of the Monarch's birthday or at any other time, to say that a businessman was honoured for increasing imports. Has a citizen of the United States ever been praised by the President for his skill in buying goods from foreigners, on advantageous terms, to market them in the domestic US market?

All governments employ special civil servants to help with export promotion. (Some states actually have a separate ministry of exports.) When there are calls for an across-the-board cut in government expenditure, export aid is usually exempt. No Western society disburses taxpayers' money to reward firms which buy in the cheapest foreign market. The very thought that an industrialized country might wish to devote national resources to subsidize imports and reduce exports is as abhorrent to politicians as a recommendation that the state should organize a chain of hygienic brothels.

Apart from aberrant exceptions*, the maxim of exporting-is-patriotic has become enshrined in modern economic legislation.

---

* In recent years the Japanese government has roused its multinationals to proclaim publicly their eagerness to help foreigners export to Japan. These corporate giants beat their breasts (in English, French and German) to declaim that no overt or covert import restrictions exist in their country. I know of a case where one of Japan's biggest exporters ostentatiously aided a foreign company to market its goods in Tokyo. The former had no pecuniary reason for doing so; its sole interest was that this charitable act should become widely known in the outside world. Despite

Anti-trust laws are directed against rapacious cartels and exploiting monopolists. These condemned practices are lauded and abetted when employed by manufacturers to penetrate foreign markets. A number of countries, none as generously as the Republic of Ireland, have statutorily reduced, or abrogated altogether, corporation tax on export profits.

The export craze has also affected London's Ritz and Savoy where British company chairmen have always enjoyed lunching. Until a few years ago the cost of the meals could be deducted from corporation tax, provided actual or potential customers were feasted. Now that Parliament has outlawed entertainment allowances, tax-free lunches have become a thing of the past. One exception, however, was written into the Finance Act: foreigners who might be considered potential buyers of British goods can be wooed at the expense of the taxpayers (and the shareholders). The social spirit of present-day British society regards it as obscene when corporate executives eat at the Ritz and the Savoy without paying for it from their own pockets. The tax law, however, consecrates their caviar and champagne when the accountant is satisfied that there was also present at the table a righteous foreigner who passed muster as a prospective customer of UK-made goods.

In 1967 the British government of the day amended the Company Act, making it a mandatory duty for each company to disclose in the Annual Report the value of its exports. The then Labour administration wanted to put to shame all those unpatriotic UK corporations which did not export enough. The message, which this legislation was meant to convey to the wider public, was that some lazy British firms concentrated on the home market whilst others were commendably diligent and sold a large proportion of their output abroad. The foreign sales figures, which the law now forces each company to disclose, are not indicative of the *net*

---

such (sometimes genuine, sometimes cosmetic – but always well-publicized) operations, Japanese society continues to believe fervently that it is exporting, and not importing, which ought to be their industrialists' holy vocation. Occasionally, the government finds it expedient to support imports into Japan but this is part of a strategy to *increase* Japanese exports by countering protectionist threats in foreign markets.

gains accruing to the balance of payments by virtue of the (reported) exports. They also do not tell whether the export glory ought to be attributed wholly to the company which is the nominal exporter or whether it deserves to be shared with its British suppliers whose export contributions are condemned by the legislators to remain unacknowledged. I have in front of me the 1975 Annual Reports of three large UK corporations: P & O Steam Navigation, Marks & Spencer, British Leyland. The directors of the first company clearly do not love their country – the law makes them admit that out of a turnover of £635m not a single penny could be designated as export earnings. (In reality, of course, P & O aided tremendously the balance of payments by carrying the freight of foreign companies; also, if the company had not existed, British traders would have had to pay in foreign currency for the services of non-British shipping companies.) Wicked Marks & Spencer is seen by the new legislation to be slightly more praiseworthy than P & O but the gruesome figures in the 1975 accounts still make it look like a corporate parasite: a mere 4% of their total sales of £901m was sold abroad! (Apart from its policy of selling domestically a larger proportion of British-made goods than most of its competitors, the company is a large 'invisible' earner of foreign currency, because a substantial part of its domestic sales, particularly in Central London, is accounted for by the purchases of foreign visitors. Its major positive contribution to the welfare of the British people is its universally praised, honest and efficient merchandising.) The hero of this trio is British Leyland which exported 30% of its £1,868m. The only thing wrong with this lofty export record was the announcement, in the same report, that the corporation had made an operating loss. (Its miserable performance, which included uneconomic exports, soon became so startling that no private investor was prepared to lend it money and this remarkable exporter has since had to be rescued from insolvency with taxpayers' money.)

When the socialists buttressed their export-worship with this novel statutory disclosure rule, the Conservatives, as a party, did not dare to expose it as puerile nonsense. They were afraid that if they did so, the Labour government would wield a heavy stick to denounce them for playing down the importance of exports.

There was however an *enfant terrible*, a Conservative Member of Parliament, J. Vaughan-Morgan, who did not moderate his language to lampoon this amendment to the Company Act. He reserved his most caustic scorn for that part of the legislation which implicitly denigrates British manufacturers who 'only' export indirectly and consequently need not quantify foreign sales in their Annual Report: 'I am never certain why it is virtuous to ship carbon-brushes abroad to be included in Volvos or Volkswagens which are brought back to this country, but wrong to send them to Coventry to be included in motor cars which are then sent to the American market.'[21] All economists would treat this as sound logic. Not so, however, some of the supporters of the new legislation. Up stood a Labour Member of Parliament, Robert Sheldon, to aver that no virtue deserves to be ascribed to a British manufacturer when he sells his output to another British manufacturer who in turn incorporates it in his export merchandise. Sheldon explained: 'To me, an exporter is a person who goes overseas to find markets for himself. The person who supplies goods to another company which exports them is not an exporter.' Nobody laughed and no editorial described his argument as economic illiteracy. When the House of Commons can lay down such dubious standards by which British manufacturers are to be adjudged worthy or unworthy of public approbation, what hope is there for economists to enlighten the man-in-the-street on the economic significance of exporting?

SOME IMPORTS ARE MARVELLOUS
It is a popular belief that a community's material welfare, somehow measured by the size of the nation's output, can be enhanced by an increase in exports. At best, this is a half-truth. The material living standard is determined by the size of the GNP plus imports: *it is lowered by exports*. An economy that manages to import more than it needs to export, thereby becomes better off (at least in the short run). In this sense Ireland, Israel and Italy enjoy a higher living standard than is justified by their GNP. They successfully import more than they export, thanks to charitable, religious, political, investment and military funds which are supplied by friendly governments, foreign sympathizers and expatriates. Notwithstanding what television commentators may instil into the minds of

trusting viewers, imports are not necessarily a curse and in fact can be a blessing when there is no immediate need to match them with exports.*

In many situations exports aggravate inflation whilst imports have the opposite effect: the more goods flood the domestic market, the greater the downward pressure on prices. (The cheaper the imports the bigger the anti-inflationary impact but, as already noted, traders who bring in low-priced imports certainly receive no lollipops from ungrateful politicians.) Though governments ordinarily treat exports as a sacred cow, they are nevertheless compelled to recognize that exports sometimes worsen a domestic inflation. This is why the British authorities have been known to forbid the sale abroad of UK scrap metal. In April 1977 the Indian government put a hefty export duty on tea; this made it more profitable to sell domestically than to export. The avowed purpose of the levy – which was of course condemned by the tea industry – was to make more supplies available for the home market and thus reduce the price for the Indian consumer. In 1974 the US government was so concerned with the rise of food items in its cost-of-living index that it banned unilaterally the export of soya beans, hoping that this would have an immediate anti-inflationary effect. In March 1973 two of Warsaw's main foodshops were wrecked by shoppers who complained of shortages and high prices; they blamed this on excessive Polish exports of meat and dairy products. The Politburo of the Communist Party publicly promised to slow down such exports and provide foreign currency for more imports of some foodstuffs.

Indirectly, imports are a force for good in that they furnish wholesome competition to indigenous manufacturers who are thus

* This economic truism is difficult to sell to the uninitiated. The quintupling of the oil prices at once had a disastrous effect in those oil-importing economies where no petrodollars were deposited or invested. It did not, however, directly cause an immediate, substantial, drop in the living standards of a few privileged countries (amongst them the US, Switzerland, France, Germany, Canada and, until 1975, the UK) because the oil exporters were prepared to accept payment in the form of pieces of paper. Only now, as the OPEC suppliers increasingly insist on being paid with exported merchandise, is the higher price of oil imports causing the maximum of material pain.

often spurred on to improve the efficiency of their operations. The relatively inefficient modes of production, and the preponderance of shoddy goods, in the Communist countries is to be explained partly by the absence of the competitive challenge which imports provide in many capitalist economies.

Not all imports, however, are beneficial. They are sometimes damaging when they are a reaction to economically extravagant, and/or subsidized, exports. Post-war British trade ministers have mollycoddled exporters for thirty years and Peter Shore was no exception. He differed from his predecessors in that as a professional economist his conscience pricked him when he had to announce a further bout of export subsidies. He heretically expressed the fear that the measures might lead 'to an increase in exports which was simply offset by greater imports of engineering goods'.[96] Only in a fully regimented economy can the government forcibly maximize the export of certain goods and simultaneously prevent the void being filled by imports. Castro's Cuba, in order to boost sugar exports, successfully deprived its citizens of sugar they would otherwise have consumed. Yet, thanks to an authoritarian grip over imports, Cuba also prevented any (foreign currency) backlash. The following examples indicate what happens when export-crazy governments lack Castro's dictatorial whip.

(a) In normal circumstances unrestricted imports are to be welcomed because they provide consumers with the freedom to choose between a local and foreign make. The 1975-77 flood of car imports into the UK can hardly be justified on this count. The rise in the sale of foreign cars was due in part to government pressure on domestic manufacturers to behave patriotically by selling abroad a large segment of their output. This forced many British car-buyers to purchase imported cars, because the locally-made cars they originally wanted to acquire had been sent abroad to serve in the holy war for exports.

(b) Israel, at the beginning of its statehood, bullied citrus growers to send abroad the maximum quantity of fruit. Through rationing, the government successfully prevented its people from eating all the Jaffas they would have liked to eat. This strategy of maximizing citrus exports was abandoned when it was discovered that, indirectly, it had led to a net loss of foreign currency earnings: Israelis, whose demand for indigenous citrus fruit had remained unsatisfied, ate instead (legally and illegally) imported fresh and canned fruit.

(c) Before the Republic of (Southern) Ireland joined the Common Market, it taxed its people to find money for heavy subsidies on its dairy exports: the same packet of butter, which was high-priced in the Republic, could be bought cheaply by foreigners. Northern Ireland, as part of the United Kingdom, was the nearest export market which benefited from the subsidized butter of the Irish Republic. The export sales of (Southern) Irish butter in Northern Ireland rocketed thanks to the naughty merchants in the Republic who imported from Northern Ireland (illicitly of course) the cheap butter that had originated in the South.

(d) The land border between Northern and Southern Ireland also made nonsense of the policy of the (British) National Coal Board to export subsidized coal. In their London head office they decided that coal sent to Northern Ireland must obviously be merchandised at the price applicable to all domestic UK consumers, whilst Southern Ireland was to be blessed with cheap coal for it was treated as a foreign market. Londonderry, the second largest town in Northern Ireland, loves British coal. Being situated near the border, it prefers, however, to import its coal from Southern Irish suppliers, who can procure cheap (subsidized) British export coal, rather than buy dear coal direct from the National Coal Board.

(e) The foreign currency receipts of Spain depend considerably on tourism and citrus exports. These two branches rightly boast that they are big dollar-earners. However, they somewhat overstate their importance to the Spanish balance of payments by omitting to spell out the foreign currency cost of their imported inputs; this is particularly significant in the hotel trade, which imports special foodstuffs for the foreign visitors. Economic common sense made the authorities realize, belatedly in 1975, that Spain's net foreign currency earnings would be increased if citrus exports were decreased. The government recognized that instead of encouraging citrus growers to export all the available oranges, it would be more propitious to put part of the crop into cold storage and sell the fruit in the summer to the tourists, which in turn would lead to a smaller import bill for other foodstuffs.

Between 1973 and 1977, under both Labour and Conservative governments, a combination of administrative follies helped to suck in certain, economically unhealthy, imports. The price controllers had no jurisdiction over exports and only vetted tabled price increases by local manufacturers. To have these approved the bureaucrats had to be satisfied that the proposed price increases were unavoidable because of the rise of 'allowable costs'. Increases in domestic production costs were not always allowed to be fully reflected in price rises but imports, at whatever their acquisition price, were automatically treated as 'allowable costs'. This produced tragi-comic results. UK companies greedily scooped up the cheap, subsidized, products of the (nationalized) British Steel Corporation and exported them to foreign markets where in those days high, unsubsidized, prices prevailed. Sometimes the same UK firms then bought foreign steel products for import into the UK.

As the price controllers allowed only a meagre profit on domestic sales but did not mind companies earning exorbitant profits on exports, it was not surprising that some UK manufacturers, for example in the chemical industry, did not supply their traditional British customers but instead exported to foreign markets where (uncontrolled) prices were sometimes up to 70% higher than the (controlled) prices they were permitted to charge in the UK. The jilted British customers were then forced to import their requirements. In 1974 Shell Chemicals brought the matter to public attention by informing British buyers that in view of the government's unrealistically low prices for its polystyrene, it would no longer supply the home market but would divert its output to the Continent. (The government became so concerned with this export threat – which would have meant increased imports – that the Price Commission was instructed to raise by 50% the price ceiling on goods of Shell Chemicals.)

Not only in Britain have price controls given birth to contrived exports and imports. When the US played around with ceilings on prices and profits, similar anomalies were created. It is reported that US cattle ranchers, during the Nixon price controls, would export their animals to be slaughtered in Canada and then bring back the imported meat.[158]

NOT ALL EXPORTS ARE WONDERFUL

Under a system of multiple exchange rates, a country can actually lose foreign currency through exports. When $100 of imported materials are incorporated within an article that is sold abroad for $90, the national balance of payments suffers though it may prove to be a profitable venture for the exporter. This depends on the differential rates of exchange at which the government buys and sells foreign currencies in the dealings with its citizens (see pp. 69-71). The exchange controllers in their wisdom may sell, at a low unit price, the $100 allocated to acquire the imported materials and buy, at a high unit price, the $90 export proceeds.

The above is a lawful lunacy, whilst phantom exports are clearly unlawful. In the preceding chapter we referred to exporters who abuse the multiple exchange rate system by selling goods abroad for $50 but remit home $90. This crooked transaction entails reporting to the authorities that $90 are true export proceeds which are entitled to be exchanged at a favourable rate – so favourable indeed that the exporter can afford to buy the incremental $40 on the black market and yet remain with a profit. In some economies criminally-inclined entrepreneurs have gone a step further: why, they ask, do we have to carry out any genuine exports at all? Surely, they reply, it is enough to go through the formalities of exporting and then buy all the dollars (said to be the foreign currency export proceeds) on the black market. To implement such nefarious schemes, documents have to be faked; the crates, which are to pass through the customs as allegedly containing valuable export merchandise, must be filled with sand, stones or bricks; it is necessary to recruit co-operating dockers or longshoremen who will drop the crates into the sea. During the last thirty years, exchange controllers in several countries have caught out exporting tricksters playing this profitable game but, if a press report can be believed, [91] it is still in full swing in Brazil. The Brazilian authorities subsidize generously manufacturers of leather goods who are out to capture new foreign markets. This is why crates, filled with bricks, are so frequently marked as containing export consignments of leather shoes. No fewer than 230 such conjuring exporters are said to have been caught, in the Sao Paulo area alone, in 1978.

Such exotic examples can nowadays be reported only from

developing countries because the industrialized economies of the West abolished multiple rates within fifteen years of the end of the war. The latter, however, tolerate other kinds of nonsensical exports which are often induced by the lavish application of open or surreptitious subsidies. At one time British eggs were sold abroad at below-cost prices; the farmers did not lose by this dumping because the UK taxpayers provided the subsidies. The foreign currency receipts from some of the egg exports were estimated to have been smaller than the foreign currency costs incurred for the imports to feed the chickens. This is an extreme example of a type of loss-making export which nowadays is probably non-existent in the West. But there are still many instances where the economic viability of certain exports is very doubtful if they are properly evaluated by their *net* contribution to the balance of payments.

Multinational corporations, with subsidiaries in economies where exporting is attired in virtue, have found it expedient to publicize their exports as a numerate proof of the blessings which they are bestowing upon the balance of payments of their hosts. Public relations agencies are hired to advise on the contents of the expensive advertisements which are placed in the popular newspapers to disseminate their, seemingly impressive, export boasts. When a famous US corporation announced in the UK media that the exports of its British subsidiary had earned the UK balance of payments £170m, we were not told simultaneously that in this same period the company had spent *more* than £170m on imports into the UK and (profit and royalty) remittances to its parent.

The foreign currency *value-added* of exports determines the benefit which accrues to the balance of payments from exports. It is calculated by deducting from the export sales proceeds all the foreign currency expenditure on the direct and indirect imports which were utilized in the production of the exports. When £100 of exports are manufactured with directly imported inputs of £30, the apparent value-added (for balance of payments computations) is £70. When the export merchandise also embodies £30 of components bought from local suppliers, again assumed to have an import content of 30%, the foreign currency expenditure on indirect imports is £9. In this example, therefore, the manufacturer's patriotic export accomplishment is not £100, as he is likely to publicize, but £61. It is to the credit of ICI that when it proudly advertised record exports of £586m, it added modestly that it had imported goods for £236m in the same year and therefore asked to be praised, as a benefactor to the UK balance of payments, for a contribution of only £350m. Even this might still be slightly too high because it leaves out the foreign currency expend-iture on ICI's indirect imports but nevertheless evinces an intellectual honesty that the vast majority of bragging exporters lack.

There is no virtue *per se* in manufacturing a product with a high or a low value-added. The exporter of Welsh sand (90% foreign currency value-added) is neither a better nor a worse performer than the exporter of polished diamonds (10% value-added). The only time when the value-added concept assumes commercial significance is when the state hands out subsidies, as it frequently does, in relation to *gross* export proceeds. Let us assume that every exporter is handed a $20 bonus when he sells $100 of goods in foreign lands. This means that an exporter with 90% value-added receives from the taxpayers $20 for a $90 net gain to the balance of payments which is equivalent to an effective subsidy of 22% per net export dollar earned. An exporter with 10% value-added, who receives $20 for a $10 net gain to the balance of payments, is granted an effective subsidy of 200%. Most exporting manu-facturers are somewhere between these two extremes. Neither exporters nor the government are charmed with such an evaluation of export subsidies. It can prove highly embarrassing to compare the subsidy with the net gain to the balance of payments.

The most weighty of the UK's many open and hidden export incentives was and is the subsidization of export credits: the commercial banks extend practically unlimited export credit, the low-interest level of which is not fixed by them but by export-friendly politicians. As the banks are not philanthropists, their export loans are state-guaranteed and they are reimbursed for the difference between the subsidized interest they are told to charge and the interest they could otherwise have earned on conventional domestic loans. Is this an effective subsidy per net export dollar of 10%, 20%, 30% or more? There are only obscure answers to this sensitive question. The consequences flowing from Britain offering its main export incentive in the form of cheap credit can be stated but not quantified.

The imports, which are specially brought into the country as inputs for export merchandise, are usually not bought on credit; this necessitates a foreign currency expenditure before the export goods are manufactured. As the UK allows its exporters to sell on credit, it follows that even after the dispatch of the exports, the UK's balance of payments is not immediately credited with export earnings. If we assume that UK capital goods, sold on twelve-year credit, have a 30-40% import content, this means that the UK's foreign currency position actually deteriorates in the first three or four years of the credit span.

British post-war governments have encouraged exports by giving preferential favours to credit-buyers. Whilst there is no definitive estimate of the average subsidy paid per net export dollar, there is no doubt about the paradox that the longer the credit the bigger is the export subsidy. Worst off is the foreigner who is prepared to pay cash for UK goods. He is given no alternative bonus when he does not partake of the hidden bounty incorporated within export credits.

Too many companies have been bruised heavily for this to happen now. Until a few years ago, however, Machiavellian foreign companies were received with open arms when they proposed to buy British goods, on long-term delivery contracts, at fixed sterling prices and of course on credit with subsidized interest.* Many of the clever foreigners had in mind that windfall gains awaited them if most of the instalments of the sterling-denominated credit contracts were payable after the currency depreciation of sterling which they confidently predicted. Hard-headed British executives were so enamoured of the privileged opportunity to export that they played down the dual risk of a currency devaluation and of rising production costs. Some were later to claim that the

* In February 1977 the government put a stop to this racket and insisted that henceforth foreign buyers, who wanted subsidized long-term credit, had to formulate their price offers in non-sterling currencies. This was a belated recognition of the harm that had been done to the post-war UK economy by a stupid export incentive that no doubt enriched many foreign buyers of British goods but did little to help the UK balance of payments.

government had bullied them into signing fixed-price sterling contracts.

Before the 1967 sterling devaluation the Russians managed to obtain fixed-price sterling contracts for the purchase of UK machine tools to be supplied over a number of years. This was hailed in enthusiastic press comments as a marvellous accomplishment by British industry. The Russians were later to chuckle over the bargains which they had picked up and paid for in devalued sterling while the manufacturers, who had fallen victim to the export mythology, were saddled with export obligations which involved them in heavy losses; some even had to pay the supreme corporate penalty – they became insolvent. The collapse of Rolls Royce is attributed directly to the ambition of its directors to appear at press conferences and there hold forth on the marvellous long-term export sales which they had negotiated. Later on the British taxpayers learned that the foreign buyers had been given contracts that allowed for only a small price adjustment on account of cost-escalation in the period between placing the order and its execution many years later.

The following will help to give some rough numerate perspective to the interest subsidy: during 1972-76 British exporters were given access to credit with 6-7.5% interest, which was about one-half of the interest they would have had to pay for unsubsidized borrowings to finance loans to domestic customers. The most subsidized credits were for exports to the Comecon countries, and this policy – until Margaret Thatcher became leader of the Conservatives – enjoyed bi-partisan support.

The Heath administration in 1972 extended a £200m credit to the USSR at 6%. (The British economy luckily escaped having to honour it, because political obstacles halted the utilization of the credit.) In February 1975 Prime Minister Wilson returned from Russia with a flourish. His political fortunes at home were low but he knew that his prestige would rise amongst the electorate if he could wave the export flag. This he did. He told the public that thanks to his talented efforts the Russians were persuaded to show their love for Britain by kindly accepting a long-term UK credit of about £1 billion. Amidst the fanfares it was never officially disclosed what horrible interest charges were to be imposed upon the Russians, but unofficially the government let it be known that the USSR would be saddled with the hefty interest of 7.1-7.5%! As enthusiasm for Wilson's magnificent achievement rose, the news was leaked that the USSR did not want only cheap credit but intended, at the end of the long credit period, to repay some of the sterling loans in the form of Russian goods that they were unable to sell commercially outside their country and which British firms were expected to market. Was Margaret Thatcher unkind when she described it as a 'pretty good agreement – for Russia'? The soundest comment was made by a Liberal Member of Parliament who asked the elated Prime Minister: 'Is it not ironic that we are borrowing from the Shah of Persia and extending credit to the Soviet Union?' This inexperienced politician obviously did not understand that the export mythology centres on the physical dispatch of goods to foreign lands and does not dwell on the net benefit which exports confer on the balance of payments.

The export obsession reached its peak in the UK and other countries in relation to shipbuilding. At the end of the war British shipyards were swamped with orders and long delivery dates were quoted. UK shipowners found it difficult to have their ships constructed in domestic yards because, in large part, these were busy supplying modern ships to foreign, competing, shipowners. In the sixties, British yards were once again ready to build for their traditional British customers but by that time UK shipping companies had little reason to place their orders in UK shipyards. The generous subsidies and tax rebates and cheap credits were not available for orders from UK-resident companies but reserved only for foreign shipowners. On the other hand, British companies were welcomed as buyers in France, Germany, Japan and Scandinavia where they were accorded favourable export treatment. As a consequence, in the sixties, three-quarters of the ships ordered by British companies were built in foreign yards. British companies were also encouraged, indirectly, to have their ships built abroad thanks to the folly of the indiscriminate investment grants and investment allowances. These fiscal devices were intended to induce UK-based businesses to acquire capital goods including ships: they applied irrespective of whether the assets were manufactured domestically or imported. As a result British firms were subsidized for *importing* investment goods; this economic insanity attracted foreigners who rushed to buy UK-registered companies in order to collect grants and subsidies from the British taxpayers as a reward for ordering ships to be constructed in non-British yards.

Only in a hallucination was it possible to perceive that either the UK or the German balance of payments would benefit from the stratagem that was forced upon Royal Dutch Shell. The German and British Shell companies needed new tankers and both German and British yards were capable of supplying their needs. Because Germany pursued, in many respects, a similar export-mad policy as the UK, Shell (Germany) did not find it feasible to build in Hamburg, and Shell (UK) had to shun constructing ships in Glasgow. Being a multinational company, it succeeded nevertheless in licking the cream offered by the German and British taxpayers respectively. Shell (Germany) ordered its tankers in Britain (and collected the export presents of the UK), whilst Shell (UK) had its tankers built in Germany (and collected the magnificent export incentives which Bonn made available).*

TWO UNCOMFORTABLE SURMISES

The export of Brazilian bricks is of course an economic obscenity but it does not detract from the generalization that most international trade is of benefit to all the participants. The Jamaican export of bananas in exchange for the import of Scottish cars raises the living standards in both economies above the level at which it would be if Jamaica assembled its own vehicles and bananas were grown in glasshouses on the Clyde. There is, however, considerable doubt as to whether this general approbation for cross-border trade applies to all the import/export transactions of the industrialized countries during the many years of post-war full employment. Were the billions of pounds of credit-subsidized UK exports to countries of the Comecon, Latin America, Africa and Asia all an unmixed blessing for the British economy? When the country's

---

* This ridiculous situation was seen, after many years, to be so scandalous that the British government ultimately reversed its policy. Did it abolish the subsidies to foreigners for building ships in Scotland? No, but it made the taxpayers' export incentives also available to British companies which placed orders in UK yards. Later the government even closed the loophole that had enabled foreign-owned, UK-registered, companies to collect investment grants on ships constructed outside the UK.

productive capacity was stretched to the full, foreign customers in receipt of cheap, long-term credit sometimes ousted potential buyers of British exports who were prepared to pay in cash and needed no open or hidden subsidies. More ominous still is the suspicion that certain imports, which came into the UK in return for (or as a result of) some of Britain's exports, were less valuable than the goods that would have been manufactured for domestic requirements had British resources not been otherwise engaged. Fewer exports might have induced a reduction in imports. Might this not have proved helpful in raising, however slightly, the living standard of the British people?

The other concluding iconoclasm concerns the factors that make for successful exporting by companies and their sales representatives abroad. The textbooks emphasize that firms do well in foreign markets if they sell a technically excellent article, have a ready supply of spare parts, can point to a proven record of honoured delivery dates, etc. Marketing specialists put on top of the list the art of salesmanship and only whisper about the role of corruption in export promotion. A countervailing thesis, in Chapter VII demonstrates that state-interventionism in various shapes and forms is the most significant factor which determines the profitability of given exports. Only rarely are all exports in receipt of an identical subsidy. The size of the subvention often varies in accordance with a particular market or product group. Even in English-speaking countries the state is known to have discriminated in favour of one company's exports by giving it special favours denied to others. Mention has already been made of the perverse export incentives that are sometimes furnished by domestic controls. Finally, and some say most importantly, the change in the external exchange parity of a currency usually has a profound impact upon export profitability.

Uppish sales executives, who sweat it out in foreign hotel rooms, write irate letters to the press bragging that the country owes them gratitude for an export growth which is due to their selling activities. They are not likely to thank me for pointing out that the actions of governments, for good and for ill, have an influence on the volume of exports and their profitability which is considerably greater than anything that the most dedicated merchandisers can accomplish in distant lands.

Chapter VI

THE IGNORANT PUBLIC

"Tell me, please, Comrade Khrushchev, why did you pass a law changing the values of our currency? Didn't the government do that in order to raise prices?" Zverev, Kosygin, and I were proceeding from the fact that costs and revenues had grown many times over, and that it was very complicated to work with such figures. It complicated book-keeping. We decided to multiply the ruble by ten, so that something which had cost ten kopeks would now cost one kopek and what had cost a ruble would now cost ten kopeks. This currency reform was simply a matter of convenience; it did nothing to raise the price of products. The person I was talking to was not convinced: "I don't care what you say – the prices went up." I told him that was ridiculous and worked out the figures with him. [4]

HONEYDEW

There are professors of economics who regard the public as stupid, incapable of logical thinking, and generally irrational so far as their discipline is concerned. Of course few say so. (It might spoil their chance to run for a political office, make broadcasting authorities less inclined to invite them to perform and might even provoke vocal protests during their academic lectures.) In a presidential address to the Royal Economic Society, MacDougall explained why economics could never achieve the certainty of the natural sciences; it was due to 'human behaviour [which] is complex and changeable, fickle and sometimes perverse'. [17] No inhibitions held back the eminent Chicago professor who put into print some of the most vitriolic strictures that have ever been visited upon economic ignoramuses: 'The one thing clear now is that crowds "think" very little, if at all, in the sense of impartial analysis or criticism. And this is notably true under the condition of a political campaign, and one of the results of modern technology is to give the governing process much of the character of a continuous campaign, the first principle of which is to create the crowd-mind. Anything that appeals to the crowd-mind must be simple and romantic.... It cannot be expected to show anything but contempt for sound economic theory.' [14]

This chapter contains a few examples which illustrate illogical thinking and behaviour by non-economists relating to subject matters of economics. As if there were not already enough of such irrationalities, economists sometimes add to the list by describing certain behaviour as irrational, which does not deserve to be so styled. Irrationality generally characterizes the choice of means to achieve given goals – not the goals themselves. Outside observers do not always have the competence to diagnose correctly the rationality of the conduct of persons, the nature of whose goals they do not know. It may appear that their behaviour is directed to achieve objective A, whilst in reality objective B is aimed at. Thus people may be condemned as irrational when they disguise the fact that their conduct is targeted to reach objective B and not the manifest objective A. Misunderstandings of this kind lead to unjustified denunciations of irrationality, especially when economists are called upon to deal with investment and marketing problems.

Why do multinational companies choose given locations for their plants? Why do they select particular towns for their regional headquarters? Over a period of fifteen years I have interviewed many corporate decision-makers to find out the motivations for such choices. It must be remembered that these large companies can afford to pay for the best technical and economic advice. Indeed, all those I have spoken to have been at pains to say that their decision was arrived at because it was the optimum location for profit-maximization. When, however, I probed further, other motivations were reluctantly mentioned and I could not help but discern that it was these which sometimes tipped the balance. Similar conclusions were arrived at by several academic investigators in the English-speaking countries. Sargent Florence found cases where factories had been located in certain cities 'to please the wife'. [100] America's leading management journal reports: 'One

(US) company picked a village in Scotland for its factory because the president's wife, who was with him on an (exploratory) trip, remembered the lovely roses in front of the cottages, as a rare bit of sun burst forth.' [101] A professor of business administration at Harvard has this to relate: 'the president, in response to a question as to why a factory was constructed in Spain, said "my wife speaks Spanish, loves Spain, and now we are able to make several trips a year to visit the operation".' [102] These are not observations on idiosyncratic conduct by stupid executives, whose actions ought to be castigated as irrational. They only appear irrational because 'profit-maximization' is thought to be the objective, but they are in fact rational in relation to those other objectives which the executives really aim at and yet are too ashamed to acknowledge openly.

The journals of Western consumer unions – for example, *Which?* in the UK and *Consumer Reports* in the US – have had a surprisingly weak impact on the buying patterns of the (intellectually derided) masses. This may be due to the fact that they see it as their primary task to disseminate information which aids the so-called rational buyer. (These logical creatures are assumed to make their purchases in relation to the quality and price of competing brands.) I was once told that some editors of *Which?* feel frustrated because the results of their research are not acted upon by the vast majority of British consumers. To my informant's regret, housewives pay more heed to the contents of paid advertisements than to the objective messages of the unbiased Consumers' Association. If only the public cared to listen, it would learn that, per penny, soap X furnishes more cleansing potency than other soaps. The Consumers' Association's thorough examination of expensive slimming apparatuses indicates that these do little to help obese victims lose weight. *Which?* has explained *ad nauseam* that, therapeutically, unbranded anti-headache pills are no less effective but much cheaper than many branded medicaments. Obviously, if a person's sole or main aim is to clean himself, lose weight and fight headaches – at the least monetary expense – he would act irrationally were he not to follow the advice of *Which?*. But salesmen, merchandisers and advertisers do not sell exclusively soap, medicines and slimming aids – they offer potential buyers also honeydew, sexual gratifications, friendship, prestige, and the fulfilment of other yearnings. Soap X, recommended by the Consumers' Association, merely helps the user to clean himself whilst the allegedly inferior brand Y is used for washing *and*, in addition, promises to bathe the buyer in a fragrance that stirs romantic hopes. It is, therefore, often inapposite to condemn as irrational those creatures who ignore the best-buy recommendations of the consumer unions.

The marketing departments of large corporations not infrequently treat with contempt their in-house economists. They are accused of propagating the view that sales and profits can be enhanced by price reductions and quality improvements. Economists have also been reproached for advising that in promotional campaigns emphasis ought to be placed on the technical superiority of the company's products. There is some substance in this mocking caricature though students of modern economics are told in their textbooks how some articles, which failed to penetrate the market when first offered at $1, later became - repackaged and renamed - best-sellers at $3. It would be offensive to suggest that business economists are wholly unaware of the curious buying habits of the man-in-the-street. Yet they have a vested functional interest to portray the consumer in the 'rational' image of the Consumers' Association. Once one drops the assumption that teenagers buy soap in accordance with its price and putative cleansing qualities, what role can economists usefully play in advising marketing strategists? Companies may arrive at the defeatist conclusion that psychologists, priests and sociologists are better judges of consumer motivations and consequently will prefer their recommendations to those of economists.

A POT-POURRI OF IRRATIONALITIES
The following are a few instances of genuinely irrational concepts and behaviour. Some are blatantly ridiculous and on a par with a belief in fairies and witches. Yet, it is foolish to belittle their significance. Our fellow-citizens vote for politicians who are astute enough to espouse many of these irrationalities.

Rapacious employers
The myth, that most corporations are highly profitable (at the expense of their employees and consumers), is prevalent in many countries. In the spring of 1976 the Confederation of British

Industry commissioned a survey in which employees were questioned on what they believed British company profits to be as a
proportion of turnover. ('How much profit does an average company make before tax out of every £100 of goods it sells?') Previous
research has shown that the public-at-large thought that profits
were 40%! This sample, however, was regarded as slightly more
sophisticated and indeed proved so. The shop floor employees'
average response was 31% whilst that of the managerial staff was
20%. The actual figure is about 10%. How can one evaluate the
political consequences that flow from this stark over-estimation
of profits by most of the public?

Material living standards

Post-war Britain has accustomed itself to regular price rises. Any
rational observer can recognize the discernible signs of persistent
inflation. What is not rational is the belief held by many people, at
times the majority of the population, that the price rises substan-
tiate an (imagined) deterioration in their living standards. This
prevalent irrationality has been encountered by politicians of all
parties whenever and wherever they meet their constituents. The
easily ascertainable truth is that in every year between 1953 and
1973 average pre-tax and post-tax incomes rose faster than the rate
of inflation; in every single year of this 21-year period consumers'
expenditure in real, i.e. inflation-adjusted, terms was higher than
that of the previous year.

The polling organizations in many Western countries have in
their files a great mass of, mostly unpublished, material which
throws light on the irrational beliefs of the man-in-the-street. This
evidence is particularly illuminating when the public is asked the
same question at regular intervals. Over a considerable period the
British Market Research Bureau has questioned* a cross-section of
the public: 'Are you and your family better or worse off financially
than a year ago?' The relevant facts of 1972 are that the
cost-of-living index rose by 7.1% over 1971 whilst the GNP went

---

* When pollsters ask the public to forecast the course of inflation or their
own living standards one can be charitable about outrageously erroneous
predictions. Similarly, when people are polled to give their impressions
on the economy in general, one must obviously make allowances for their
ignorance of economics. But this survey asked people to state *past*
happenings in their *own* households.

up by 11.8%, pre-tax wages and salaries by 11.7% and consumers' expenditure by 11.3%. There can thus be no doubt about the solid material improvement which occurred in that year. Yet the twelve monthly surveys of the Bureau in 1972 show that only 29% of the British public thought that they were better off in that year. In October 1972 only 21% responded by saying that their living standard had risen over last year's, 12% said that they were standing still and more than two-thirds (67%) considered that their situation had worsened over the preceding twelve months. The Roper surveys indicate that the same irrationality is also prevalent in the US. A September 1978 poll reported that Americans felt 'worse off economically today than . . . five years ago'.[163] In fact US post-tax, real, disposable incomes were 8.4% higher in the first quarter of 1978 than in the corresponding period of 1973. But the public suffered from the money illusion in which they perceived more clearly the rise in prices than the actually bigger rise in their incomes.

Gold is not gold

A coin weighing one ounce troy of 22-carat gold is an indestructible article with a ready market. Bought legally or otherwise, it is a universal refuge of last resort from inflation, devaluation and taxation. A few acquire gold coins for their ornamental value or as pieces for a coin collection. Of course, for these purposes it matters whose face is on the coin and in what year it was minted but for the overwhelming majority of buyers the value of gold coins is linked directly and solely to the value of the intrinsic gold content. To comprehend the gold coin irrationality it must be stressed that the gold coins (worth billions of dollars), which are held in Asia and the Middle East, have not been bought for their aesthetic attractions but are seen by their owners to be nothing but stores of value. (They are often the poor man's substitute for bars of gold.) Because the inferiority of women is ingrained in the cultural pattern of several Eastern countries, coins engraved with the face of female monarchs are not as favoured as coins with the countenance of male kings. It is not just a question of preference but of price. Gold dealers in the West have learned to accept as a fact of life that, in Egypt and India for example, King Edward VII coins can be sold at a slightly higher price than coins bearing the portrait of dear Queen Victoria *though the intrinsic gold content of both* is identical.

Counterfeiters, who are known in the trade as 'imitators of sovereigns' and are now particularly active in Italy, naturally cater for this rife irrationality by producing mainly Edward VII coins and shunning the manufacture of Victorian coins.

The causes of inflation

In June 1974 an opinion poll [94] enquired what, in the public's opinion, generated the current British inflation; respondents could state several important causes. 64% of the recorded answers mentioned 'decimalization', 62% 'joining the Common Market', and 11% 'metrication'. When asked which single item had been the most important cause of the rising prices, 29% opted for 'world price rises', 22% for 'joining the Common Market' and 21% for 'decimalization'.*

In the month in which this survey was made, the UK's retail price index was 17% up on the corresponding month of the previous year. Three popular irrationalities 'explained' the causes of this rise.

(a) Most of the British public believed – this is definitely known also from several other sources – that the switch from imperial to metric measurements *would* lead in the future to higher prices. 11% of the respondents said that it already had had an important impact on the 1974 inflation. This was clearly nonsensical because the metrication process had hardly started and practically no consumer goods in the shops were in metric units. Even if it were true that metrication does raise prices – and there is no objective evidence for such a conjecture – it could not have accounted, in June 1974, for more than an infinitesimal portion of one percentage point of the 17% inflation.

(b) In February 1971 a decimalized sterling replaced the pound-shilling-pence currency. Popular opinion would have it that traders and manufacturers used that opportunity to round up prices unfairly. Even if one assumes that this took place on a large scale, the impact on the price level could not have been greater than two percentage points and, in any case, it would have been a once-for-all

---

* A mere 11% of the respondents in the cited poll thought that the 'government's economic policy' was an important factor and only 1% gave it as the single most important explanation for the inflation. How convenient for the politicians!

statistical phenomenon more than three years before this public opinion poll was conducted. Yet a very large number of the interviewees attributed to this 1971 event a decisive role in causing the ravaging 1974 inflation. This irrationality was still bandied about in 1977. Even the financial columnist of a serious newspaper continued to lend it support: 'Today is the sixth anniversary of the day we debased our currency by the disastrous switch-over to decimal currency. Of course, many other setbacks – such as the Arab oil price-war – have contributed to our appalling inflation since 1971. But undoubtedly the decision to base the decimal money on a pound instead of a 50p or 10s unit has been a *major* [my italics] element in the soaring rate of price increases. The cold figures from the Central Statistical Office show that since we went decimal, the Retail Price Index has increased by about 120%.'[149]

(c) Britain joined the Common Market in January 1973, seventeen-and-a-half months before this survey was made. There was and is much substance in the proposition that joining the Community will raise considerably British prices above the level they would otherwise be. In June 1974, however, this could only be a prognostication. When the UK joined, a five-year transitional arrangement provided for the Community rules to be applied gradually to the UK's domestic prices and tariffs. Except as a very minor cause, it was intellectually impossible for even the most fervent opponent of Britain's EEC membership to maintain in June 1974 that Britain's entry into the Common Market had already kindled the roaring fire of a two-digit inflation. Yet 62% of the interviewees thought so.

Soak-the-rich!

Britain's major political parties have unanimously condemned as unpatriotic the distribution of high dividends by profitable companies.* On occasions they enacted laws making it illegal to

---

* A socialist Chancellor of the Exchequer (James Callaghan) could not conceal his contempt: 'Company shareholders sat in their nests squawking for higher dividends and waiting to be fed.' A Conservative Chancellor of the Exchequer (Harold Macmillan) was more avuncular: 'If dividends were small economically, they counted psychologically . . . companies which had shown restraint in their dividend declarations had done the right thing by their country.' The subject is discussed in greater detail in *The Ensnared Shareholder*.[92]

increase dividends beyond a statutory ceiling.

Dividend restrictions have nothing to do with curbing company profits. Demagogic politicians who know this nevertheless are delighted to play to the gallery where the audience thinks of dividend controls as sticks with which to beat the wicked rich. It is a myth, albeit a minor one, that today's upper-income groups in the STC countries are the main beneficiaries of corporate profit distributions. A weightier irrationality is the pervasive belief that higher dividends make the rich richer. If only the electors of the United Kingdom – in which socialist and non-socialist governments alike are fond of imposing statutory dividend restrictions – would know the relish with which many of the wealthy families welcome the law limiting dividends: sometimes it is as gratifying as an effective tax-avoidance scheme. In 1978/79 a British company, making £100 profits per share and declaring no dividend, paid the Revenue £52 in tax and swelled the company's coffers with £48 of retained profits. If there had been no law limiting dividends, the biggest possible dividend (out of the current year's profits) which could have been declared would have been £71.64 per share. Gross dividends are cut down to size by the varying tax rates which apply to different classes of dividend-recipients. Charities and low-income individuals, not liable to any personal income tax, are left with a disposable dividend income of £71.64; the taxpayers, liable to the standard rate of income tax, obtain a net dividend of £48; the rich, liable to a 98% marginal tax rate, receive £1.43 per share. This should be enough to finance their expenditure on caviar and the upkeep of several yachts. It will be readily understood that the rich much prefer to do without this puny post-tax cash and yearn for a no-dividend policy in which the value of their shares rises commensurately with the retention of undistributed profits. Tax-wise, the rich gain by selling some of their shares – after the price has risen thanks to the profit retention – because capital gains are taxed at only a 30% flat rate.

If one honestly and logically sought to redistribute the national income by soaking the rich, one would not advocate dividend restrictions but instead pass a law compelling companies to distribute all their profits. It must not be thought that Treasury officials (and socialist politicians who understand the working of the tax system) are unaware of the plain fact that dividend limitations are liked by many of the rich. Yet so strong is the irrationality, underlying the popular concept of what the declaration of high dividends is supposed to signify, that no post-war British socialist politician has dared to decry this sacred cow *in public.*

What does revaluation mean?

On the eve of the German general election in 1969, the country debated hotly whether the mark should be revalued. The outgoing government was a coalition of Christian Democrats and Social Democrats; the Minister of Finance (Herr Strauss), who supported the former party, was opposed to revolution whilst the Minister of Economic Affairs (Dr Schiller), who was a Social Democrat, was strongly in favour. Several public opinion polls established that the majority of the electorate was against revaluation. This was quickly and unscrupulously exploited by the Christian Democrats who waged an electoral campaign in which they made political capital out of the contention that the Social Democrats, elected to power, would revalue.

Economists, who advised against revaluation, warned that growing unemployment would ensue from a dearer mark. This theme was also taken up by several German industrialists who feared that revaluation would squeeze the profit margins of their exports. Other economists, who supported Schiller's position, argued that revaluation would generally improve living standards. One aspect of revaluation was not debated amongst those versed in economics: all agreed that a higher exchange parity for the mark would spell *less* inflation for Germany because the prices of imported goods would drop and this would have a favourable impact on the retail price index.

Some think that in 1969 revaluation was the single most important *current* electoral theme. Many Germans voted for the Christian Democrats on the rational ground of wanting to support a party which was opposed to revaluation. However, the rationality of many Germans' voting behaviour was clouded by the publication of opinion surveys which showed that numerous opponents of revaluation had been imbued with the irrational belief that revaluation spells inflation and would bring about a rapid rise in the domestic price level.

Is Ernie impartial?

Premium Bonds, the British government's savings certificates which exploit the public's gambling passions, bear no interest. Instead, tax-free prizes – the highest is £100,000 – are awarded by a monster computer nicknamed Ernie. Premium Bonds provide the government with £1.4 billion of cheap money; the annual cost of the administration and the prizes is equal to 5-6% interest. The officials, who are charged with promoting the Premium Bonds, encounter several deep-seated objections. There are people who, on religious and moral grounds, do not wish to partake of the 'proceeds of a squalid raffle' (as the former Prime Minister Harold Wilson once put it). [95] Others think there ought to be more prizes. But what really upsets Ernie's propagandists and administrators is the implicit irrationality of the many gamblers who assert that Ernie is not truly impartial. No one has as yet seriously suggested that the Chancellor of the Exchequer arranges for his wife's nephews to win the top prizes but there is a prevalent belief (expressed in many communications to the authorities and the press) that the computer has prejudices. His electronic brain allegedly dislikes women and treats gamblers who are resident in the North of England with less favour than those living in West London. There are hundreds of thousands of Premium Bond holders who are genuinely convinced that bonds with given numbers and letters draw more prizes than bonds with other designations. No one should doubt the sincerity of those many irrational buyers of Premium Bonds who believe that a batch of one hundred single £1 bonds stands a greater chance of winning than one £100 bond. The responsible civil servants have written innumerable letters to the newspapers to refute these charges against the computer. Nevertheless, the irrational suspicions have survived for more than twenty years since Ernie first appeared on the scene.

GARLIC AND METRICATION

During the last war it was rumoured that pilots in the Royal Air Force were being issued with a special ration of garlic and carrots to sharpen their visual faculty in night-flying. This was factually inaccurate but at the time was as widely believed to be true as in 1974 people supposed the then current inflation to have originated in the switch-over to metrication and decimalization. Though both these fanciful beliefs are equally irrational they do not have the same social purport.

Following the wide circulation of these rumours, British ophthalmologists must undoubtedly have been asked by many wartime patients whether visual perception during the nightly blackout could be sharpened by eating garlic and carrots. The profession cannot have been unduly perturbed by having to answer such fatuous questions. Ophthalmologists could afford to laugh about people's unfounded faith in garlic and carrots because this pervasive irrationality did not lessen the deferential respect with which laymen continued to regard them as ocular experts.

Economists, unfortunately, have no such luck. Their professional standing, and their competence to make plausible predictions, are circumscribed by the irrational convictions and conduct of non-economists. When the public behaves irrationally and thereby demolishes beautiful prognoses drafted by economists on the assumption of rational conduct, the whole economic discipline suffers derision and all its practitioners are condemned as incompetent. By now economists are used to it.

We shall be discussing in the next chapter how politicians have an edge over economists in that, if they choose to do so, they can shape their plans in accordance with the identified irrationalities of the electors. When they are sufficiently unscrupulous, politicians may knowingly pursue policies which are not for the common good but only serve as expedient responses to the irrational beliefs of their voters.

Ophthalmologists do not need to pay attention to irrationalities whilst politicians may actually flourish by sponsoring the irrationalities of those whose electoral support they are canvassing. Can economists not also build irrationalities into their professional system? To accomplish this, one must first persuade 'economists to think of people as people, whose actions are largely determined by their emotions and not by cold or rational calculations of benefits and dis-benefits'.[89] It is attractive but impractical advice and no panacea for the problems which beset the beleaguered camp of economists. They dare not drop the assumption of rational behaviour for otherwise they have little to contribute professionally. Economists are not so stupid as to be unaware of the existence of irrationalities but, with a stiff upper lip, they are constrained to overlook them.

Chapter VII

IT IS POLITICS THAT MATTERS

General Motors has annual profits greater than the total revenues of 48 of the 50 States. Its annual revenues... are greater than the GNP's of all but nine nations in the world. The question in Washington and elsewhere is whether the company will soon be wealthier - and more powerful - than the US government itself.

H. Unger[23]

HAROLD LASKI AND GENERAL MOTORS

In 1946 I had the exhilarating experience of attending in a crowded auditorium the lectures of Harold Laski, who had then just finished a stint as chairman of the Labour Party. Older readers will recall what a bogeyman the good professor was in those days, especially in the US. As the intellectual leader of a neo-marxist strain in British socialism, he was also disliked heartily by the City of London and the sturdy bosses of the big unions. When the head of the Labour Party, Prime Minister Attlee, proposed to take large slices of the economy into public ownership, Laski prognosticated on how the British bourgeoisie would behave if these nationalization proposals were actually implemented. He argued that a social class does not give up power without a fight. His spellbound students were told that there was a distinct possibility of the rich sabotaging the socialist measures which were about to be enacted by parliament. The brilliant presentations by the distinguished professor of political science were indeed persuasive. They certainly influenced me though I wondered at the time how the dreaded bourgeoisie would organize its passive, and perhaps even active, resistance. Would the chairmen of the big corporations meet in a

secret conclave* to decide upon an agreed strategy? No doubt
youngsters in 1979 listen with similar starry-eyed awe to stories
about the unassailable strength of the private sector and the fierce
determination of the wealthy to resist the further encroachments of
socialism; they have even less justification to believe in such fairy
tales than my generation. In no developed economy in the post-war
years has there been any organized effective resistance to nationalizations, socializations, expropriations and punitive taxation. The
near-100% top marginal income tax rates in Britain and Sweden
have of course been denounced by their victims in fiery speeches
and some have recoiled in anger by emigrating to Switzerland.
That is all they could do as individuals. As a socio-economic group
the rich were forced to acquiesce – albeit angrily.

The captain of a very large corporation enjoys vicarious prestige,
personal fame and access to political leaders. The German
Chancellor does not usually pick the proprietor of a small Bonn
garage as his luncheon guest and is more inclined to invite the
chairman of Hoechst. If the great-grand-daughter of the founder of
the Ford empire were to win a tennis tournament, her picture is
more likely to appear in the newspapers than if my daughter
carried off the trophy. Should he request an interview, the head of
ICI stands a good chance of being received by the British prime
minister. To that extent, individuals (and members of their family)
associated with big organizations clearly have more influence than
poor citizens. But though it appears on the surface a plausible
proposition, it is untrue that in our age the vast turnover of
General Motors confers upon it the power to make the US
government do things which increase the profitability of American
business in general and of General Motors in particular. Were the
chief executive of General Motors to contact the President of the
United States to 'demand' that the Federal Bank lower the interest

* Today, with hindsight, we know how preposterous was the suggestion
that the captains of British industry might formulate a course of effectual
political action. (Most of them, in any case, are salaried employees,
because in our age there are few large family-controlled concerns.) The
Confederation of British Industry, in the sixties, invited the state-owned
corporations to join it. Some did and this helped to defray the
Confederation's expenses but it also signalled that the organization did
not expect to take up a unified political position.

level, he would be listened to without any assurance that his request would be met. The occupant of the White House, who is thinking of his re-election campaign, does not fear General Motors executives. He would be more impressed by a threat from leaders of the Automobile Workers Union to sway their members' votes.

Investment subsidies for a given project, a protective tariff, the prohibition of a strategic takeover bid by a foreign company – sometimes corporate requests for such state interventions, though motivated by self-interest, can be shown also to be in the national interest. If the allegedly powerful leaders of famous corporations are wise, they will recognize that in the public relations perspective of politicians they have a sensitive repute. Sagacious executives will therefore desist from publicly voicing the view that the solicited state interventions would benefit both their own companies *and* the public at large. This forbearance is judicious because politicians of the left and the right are wary of complying with demands or suggestions from famed company executives lest they be seen to be the handmaidens of the big corporate battalions. The chief executives of companies are best advised to maintain a low profile. Far better to have the case argued by consumer organizations, trade unions and municipalities. As a shrewd industrialist once told me: 'When I needed a state subsidy, I arranged for the shop stewards to bully the Minister of Industry. They achieved more in one hour than I could ever have accomplished. After all I am known to be wealthy and in a recent newspaper profile it was actually said of me that I am economically powerful.'

Many businessmen, particularly those who would not lower themselves to stand as candidates for elective political office, fancy themselves as competent to run not only their own commercial empires but also the country. Some years ago twenty-four prominent chairmen of the UK's largest corporations formed the Industrial Policy Group to teach the politicians what to do. With two exceptions, none had been active in the hurly-burly of street politics but, as moneyed élitists, they sought to enlighten the political élitists. Many of the things they said and published were highly commendable. Their proposals were intellectually meritorious but politically irrelevant. The Industrial Policy Group's recommendations were brushed aside by both the Labour government and the Conservative opposition, because these powerful men had failed to comprehend what makes politicans run. It was unkind but true to say of these top British managers that they were an 'uninfluential group of influential businessmen'. [15]

In the major industrialized countries, with one national except-ion,* large corporations – *by virtue of their size* – do not 'manage' political parties or civic leaders. The contrary is true. Increasingly, companies have to put up with the vagaries of external decision-makers. As the range of the state's interventionism is widening, politicians are becoming (indirectly) responsible for the level of profits in the private sector. This mars the populist concept of General Motors being mightier than the US government. It ought also to deflate the self-delusions of those chief executives of corporate giants who still exaggerate the objective importance of their managerial commands upon their companies' profits.

When future historians describe the political dominance of the state over the private sector in the last third of the twentieth century, they ought to reserve a place of honour for the Reverend Nicholas Stacey. He understood the link between politics and economics and set forth a strategy with which the non-nationalized segments of society can exploit the discretionary powers of the politicians. (The story deals with a charity but its maxim applies with equal vigour to profit-making manufacturing and trading enterprises.) Stacey is neither a political scientist nor an economist. He is a clergyman of the Church of England and was the Rector of Woolwich until May 1968, when he was invited to become the Deputy Director of Oxfam, a British charity that collects money and goods (through thousands of volunteers) to provide material succour to developing countries. After he had been in office for two years, Stacey urged the executive of Oxfam to revolutionize its

---

* Until recently the twelve biggest Japanese corporations, singly or acting in concert, exercised a decisive influence on the political decision-making process which they were able to slant to enhance their own corporate interests. The politicians of Japan used to take orders from the big Japanese companies in a way that corresponds to the marxist view of how General Motors orders about the President of the United States. In the very recent past, however, things have changed and ministers in Japan have become more conscious of the power of the electorate. They are shaking off the tutelage of the commercial octopuses and are now paying more attention to the electorate's real and imagined grievances than to the entreaties of the once domineering corporations.

approach to the expenditure of the collected donations. He asked whether charities, such as theirs, should 'content themselves with raising money knowing that, however great their efforts and however generous the public, it will make only the smallest dent in the problem? Or should they also attempt to influence governments in whose hands much of the solution of the problem lies?' He therefore proposed that Oxfam be transformed from a charity (that *only* disburses aid) into a political pressure group. The new activities were to be financed with part of the donations received for Oxfam's avowed aim of helping the poor abroad. Stacey told the Oxfam leadership that the sum of £20m by which the British government, at a time of financial stringency, cut its 1966 overseas-aid programme was greater than the total of all Oxfam's expenditure since its inception in 1942. Stacey went on to say that a reversal of the government's cuts, let alone an increase in state-financed overseas aid, would make a more practical contribution to the developing countries than any direct expenditure by Oxfam which would be made possible by a doubling or trebling of its collections. Put crudely, Stacey put forward the unassailable arithmetic case that when £5m of Oxfam's funds are used to buy food and blankets for the poor, this relieves less poverty, distress and suffering than when £5m are spent on political propaganda which results in the government increasing its overseas programme by, say, £25m.

Stacey resigned when the Oxfam leadership rejected his approach. Why they did so has never been spelt out. There is reason to believe that members of the Oxfam council wanted it to remain a charity which received only freely-given, personal gifts. Some of Stacey's opponents also may have thought it unethical* that the state should use its coercive powers and, through taxes, extract funds for overseas aid from all citizens regardless of whether they supported, opposed or were indifferent to the cause. In

---

* Throughout history there have been religious, political and charitable organizations that refused to accept donations from sources which they regarded as morally suspect. The Board of Foreign Missions in 1905 was rent asunder by the donation of $100,000 from John D. Rockefeller. It was called tainted money, and a leading Congregationalist minister said: 'Can any man, can any institution, knowing its origins, touch it without being defiled?' [145]

his single-minded dedication to overseas aid, Stacey brushed aside such scruples. In the next section we shall note that just as budgetary allocations by the state for overseas aid are quantitatively more important than the personal, voluntary efforts of Oxfam collectors, so too the politicians' bounties and penalties are more significant than the talents of executives in making or marring the fortunes of companies.

EXTERNALITIES

In one sense senior civil servants, chief executives of large corporations and directors of nationalized bodies have much in common: they do not risk their own money when making decisions. Sociologically, the president of Union Carbide, the director of a French nationalized bank and the commissar of the Russian aluminium trust are brethren-in-arms. All of them find that their managerial supremacy is restricted by 'externalities'. The most significant of these are political but there are also other kinds. The first externalities that plagued economic planners as they came out of the Garden of Eden were physical events such as earthquakes, droughts, floods.* Another group of externalities are also divinely inspired: the discovery of natural resources. I have great affection for the Dutch people, some of whom work harder than other Europeans. Yet, their rising standard of living in the seventies was largely the result of a foreign exchange bonanza generated by large finds of gas, and has therefore little to do with national diligence. Norway is about to achieve the biggest *per capita* GNP of Europe; this will be unconnected with high labour productivity but will be a consequence of the Almighty's capricious act of placing low-sulphur oil deposits around her shores. Similarly, British society will benefit greatly from the windfalls of the North Sea. This again owes little to managerial acumen; the magnitude of the UK pool of petrodollars will be no different whether a Maoist or a Conservative government rules in Westminster.

Both physical and political externalities in country A may have a

---

* The 1978 Annual General Meeting of United Biscuits was told by the chairman that profits had been adversely affected by bad weather in the US.

deep impact on profit-making in country B. Some Swedish companies grew in strength during the last war because they were based in a neutral economy which allowed them to have commercial relations with both Germany and the Allies. Japanese industrialists had no hand in starting the Korean and Vietnam wars, yet they incidentally made juicy profits out of them. The 1973 Yom Kippur war reduced the automobile manufacturers' profits in the subsequent two years whilst US coal companies[88] made mammoth profits as a result of the quintupling of oil prices. (Earnings per share of the Westmore Coal company rose by more than 1,000% between 1972 and 1975.) Prior to 1973, American investment analysts advised investors to sell their holdings in coal companies and buy into electronic corporations instead. The currently high dividends of American coal companies cannot be explained in terms of the skill of the managers or the efforts of the miners.

Multinational corporations, which set up subsidiaries outside their national boundaries, have to deal with the externality of what I term the Portuguese Pitfall. Everybody acknowledges the element of political risk in foreign ventures. From personal knowledge I can attest that in practice, however, when considering a particular national location, most corporate executives place (or at least used to place) much greater emphasis on such 'pure' economic factors as the level of taxation, the size of the market, industrial relations, exchange rates and the anticipated growth of the GNP. Renowned US companies have gone on record to say that they will not invest in a country like Britain where managers do not manage but go grouse-shooting and workers frequently down tools. During the sixties Spain was the European location most beloved by American investors because many US executives refused even to consider that there was any political risk to capitalism in a country where the iron hand of an authoritarian regime kept the workers in check. By the beginning of the seventies they already had second thoughts about Spain, Portugal then became the most favoured European country in the eyes of those multinational corporations which relied heavily on economic criteria; they were particularly attracted by the cheap and docile labour force that was firmly kept in place by a seemingly benevolent fascist government. The head of the international division of a US corporation once boasted to me about the excellent profits of its Portuguese subsidiary. According to him the outlook in Portugal was brighter than anywhere else because the US market was stagnating; Japan placed unofficial, but effective, restrictions on foreign-owned operations; Italy was on the brink of revolution; the UK was of course suspect because its workers were constantly on strike. I met this good man again on his return from a panic flight to Lisbon in 1975 after the violent overthrow of the government. He told me that the native manager of the Portuguese subsidiary was in prison though the company had been allowed to send him food parcels; the workers' council had taken over the plant; he anticipated a massive devaluation of the currency and the institution of controls on profit remittances abroad. This story is related with *Schadenfreude*. It is also intended to illustrate that radical political changes can topple in a short time an apparently sound 'pure economic' edifice. Such externalities, as by now multinationals with subsidiaries in most of Latin America, Africa and Asia are learning painfully, can quickly erode the profitability of operations however brilliant the executive in charge. These political externalities in foreign lands become fully transparent when assets are actually expropriated, but they can prove equally damaging in less obvious ways. New regimes may not formally confiscate the property of foreign companies. They can, however, wipe out their profits through ingenious tax laws, exchange controls, price regulations, etc. When this happens, some multinational corporations nevertheless continue to list in their global balance sheets the corporate assets in countries A and B which, though not legally expropriated, are in fact worthless because they can neither be sold nor do they in the meantime earn any profits. Alternatively, hostile governments may allow foreign firms to earn profits but not permit these to be remitted home.* In their accounting presentation of global profits parent compánies have been known proudly to report that they have earned $y in countries C and D, but 'forgot' to add in the report to their stockholders that these are arbitrarily 'frozen' profits which can therefore not be used for the payment of dividends.

---

* When the London-based multinational, Lonrho, published its 1972 accounts they showed net earnings of £6.5m, but no less than £2.9m – 45% of the total – were profits that had been generated in economies which did not allow them to be remitted to the UK parent.

Here is a sample of domestic externalities for which politicians are responsible. Sometimes purposely and sometimes unwittingly, corporate profits are affected when governments

    enact an Equal Opportunity for Women law
    nationalize the banks
    deflate the economy
    subsidize exports
    float the currency
    declare the first day of May a paid holiday
    amend the pollution laws
    raise the school-leaving age
    prohibit the building of factories in certain areas
    bail out the bankrupt railways
    withdraw troops from Suez and Vietnam
    establish a statutory annual vacation of eight weeks
    legalize the Closed Shop
    pay investment grants
    introduce import quotas
    put worker-directors on company boards
    prohibit the dismissal of employees with five years' service
    double the corporation tax
    institute dividend, price and wage controls
    forbid investments overseas
    start on a multi-trillion space programme
    control instalment credit
    allow the money supply to rise by 50% per annum
    protect local industry through an increased tariff
    lower the sales taxes
    decree profit-sharing
    ban takeover bids by foreigners
    send gunboats to Saudi Arabia to secure oil supplies
    expel foreign workers
    raise the interest level.

A rise in corporation tax is a *neutral* burden on all companies. Most externalities, however, have divergent effects. Even such manifestly non-discriminatory externalities as changes in the exchange rate of the national currency or fluctuations in the interest level affect companies differently in accordance with the proportion of their total output which is exported and the capital-intensity of their operations. Product-oriented tax externalities have been known to destroy the economic viability of otherwise sound commercial operations. A number of British factories had to be closed, not because of any managerial shortcomings but as a direct result of a sudden increase in VAT on television sets from 8% to 25%. Changes in the UK statutory conditions, under which instalment credit may be extended (minimum deposit and length of credit), have had far-reaching, positive and negative, effects on profits in the industries affected. This lesson was brought home to a US-headquartered company which had approved the purchase of expensive machinery for its Scottish subsidiary. On completion of the modernization programme the chief executive of the parent company crossed the Atlantic to admire the new facilities. The manager of the subsidiary acknowledged that the investments had doubled his production capacity and offered an opportunity to increase sales substantially; he also told his anxious superior that labour relations at the factory were excellent. His boss, however, was astonished to hear that whilst the replacement of the old machinery by more efficient equipment was obviously helpful, what really mattered was whether the Chancellor of the Exchequer would abolish the prevailing harsh instalment credit rules on the particular durables they were manufacturing. He did. Who is to get the credit for the consequent soaring profits? The international division at the parent company which had authorized the investments? The talented Scottish manager? Or the whimsical political decision-makers?

Western governments say that they are opposed to import restrictions but most of them nevertheless limit imports by indirect means. One such example was given by Arnold Weinstock, the head of the (British) General Electric Company: 'In the US that situation is to some extent dealt with by the requirement that suppliers to the American government should comply with what is called mil/spec, that is to say that the purchaser must have the facilities to inspect the manufacture of the object on the premises, and since the American government will only inspect things in the US, if you do not make the thing in the US you do not supply the American government. This means that 60% of the purchases of semi-conductor devices are sold at a very much higher price than the same thing could be bought for had they been assembled at

Taiwan or Singapore.... We have no such protection in this country.... ' [33] It is not clear whether Weinstock deplores the absence of this externality in the UK or decries its existence in the US. He wanted forcibly to make the point that it is this specified externality, and not the supposed technical and managerial superiority of US companies over their British competitors, which provides the main explanation why the manufacture of semiconductors is profitable in the US and (at the time) was considered commercially non-viable in the UK.

Price controls are a non-specific, general externality when they limit the profits of *all* companies to a given return-on-capital. In practice, however, they are frequently tailor-made for specific products. Governments are primarily concerned to keep down the prices of goods with heavy statistical weights in the basket which measures the cost-of-living index.* Investors in companies producing machine-tools and food products, respectively, will be penalized unequally, because the authorities squeeze much harder the profits of the latter. The dividends of inefficient machine-tool firms may consequently be higher than those of efficient, but severely price-controlled, food companies. Merchants selling furs may make more profits than traders who insist on making a living by selling margarine (which is in the index). The price control externality can sometimes be very refined. In 1973 UK bakers were ordered to freeze the price of bread but were allowed to raise the prices of rolls and buns by up to 25%.

Large companies do not instigate the depreciation or appreciation of national currencies – some corporations, however, have

* Governments love playing around with the index. Colin Clark, who was formerly Under-Secretary of State for Labour and Industry in Queensland, discloses a pointed instance. He tells of civil servants who 'have shown a marked tendency to make special use of their powers in order to bring down . . . prices of those particular commodities which happen to be included in the index number, while leaving the prices of kindred goods more or less alone. I remember myself receiving an urgent query from a price-fixing official as to which particular kind of jam was included in the index number, so that he could take special steps to keep its price down. This tampering with the index number by selective price control constitutes plain dishonesty.'[110]Colin Clark may rest assured that though Australian politicians have pioneered this cheating, they have long since been emulated in many other countries.

gained or forfeited more through this externality than they have earned or lost through their regular manufacturing and trading activities.

(a) The export of Volkswagen from German factories to North America was a highly profitable venture in the sixties. By the mid-seventies sales had slumped and whilst Volkswagen used to be the least expensive car sold in the US, it was now beaten by twenty-eight cheaper models of other manufacturers. The German car company was 'compelled' to start manufacturing in the US in 1978. This was not due to a deterioration in German labour productivity, nor was the decision to abandon exporting a consequence of higher transport costs or tariffs. The manufacture of Volkswagen in the US was an indirect result of the US and German governments' economic policies. This externality can be quantified: in 1960 the US consumer paid less than twenty-four cents for a German article with a one mark value; in the winter of 1978 (if he could still afford to buy goods exported from Germany) he paid fifty-four cents.

(b) The phenomenal ascent of the Swiss franc during the seventies dampened (through cheaper imports) the rise of Switzerland's cost of living and helped her banks to prosper. It is a tribute to most of Swiss industry that many of the export manufacturers managed to survive in the face of the political stance of their government which allowed the franc's external exchange parity to appreciate. Some firms, however, could not stand the pace; neither quality nor devoted merchandising were of avail in markets where imports, denominated in francs, had outpriced themselves. One such victim was the Juvena cosmetic firm, the directors of which explained to stockholders in 1976 why it was necessary to close down the British selling operations despite the 40% growth of UK Juvena sales in that year. The reason was embedded in an external factor over which the Swiss entrepreneurs had no control: the steep rise of the Swiss franc, and the *expectation* of further rises, made it commercially unattractive to import Swiss-made cosmetics into the UK. (Between 1972 and 1978 the parity of the franc rose by more than 200% against sterling.)

(c) Just as the reduced profitability of Swiss exports was not a reflection on the ability of Swiss executives, so the obverse windfall gains of British exporters in this period are not to be ascribed to any heightened managerial efficiency of British executives – their seeming successes were a sequel to the sharp depreciation of sterling. Between 1975 and end-1977 unprecedently large growth rates in UK company profits were recorded. When the totals are dissected, a clear correlation is found to exist between low or standard profits and companies (e.g. price-controlled bakers) selling only or exclusively in the domestic market, whilst singularly large profits were earned by UK corporations exporting big chunks of their output. Though British-American Tobacco, a corporation deriving most of its profits from overseas, had not been successful in increasing substantially its sales it, nevertheless, had made bumper profits because its foreign currency receipts were translated into sterling at a favourable rate. One commentator said acidly, 'Sterling's weakness continued to glamorise the profits of BAT.' Some immodest British company chairmen patted themselves on the back for the glorious profit increases they could report in 1977; they implied that it was really their personal achievement and neglected to attribute these adventitious profits to the externality of a declining sterling.

So far we have dealt with open and explicit externalities which corporations are powerless to do anything about; they are akin to what lawyers call Acts of God. In contrast, contingent externalities are formed by discretionary government decisions that can be influenced by corporations. These flourish not only in the developing countries but can also be found in some spheres of Western economies where ministers and civil servants have political-cum-administrative powers to advance the fortunes of individual firms. They may have scope to discriminate (within a given industrial branch) between giving aid to company A and refusing any to company B; company C may be penalized with a tough price-ceiling whilst company D is treated more liberally; exchange controls can be interpreted flexibly; state contracts may not necessarily be awarded to the cheapest supplier. Though we assume that in STC countries such contingent externalities cannot be affected by bribery, it is nevertheless a fact that state patronage can sometimes be actively solicited in other devious ways. A famous foreign corporation had plans to enlarge its existing UK factory; on advice received, it found that it would be more propitious for its relations with the government if, instead, a branch factory was opened in an (uneconomic) location where ministers had a political party interest to promote new industry. There are instances where governments want to see certain faltering firms kept alive, but do not dare to do so with taxpayers' money - large companies, which seek to put themselves in the good books of the political decision-makers, may magnanimously offer to rescue them. In several countries foreign and indigenous companies have formed joint ventures with nationalized corporations in the hope that this will give them an edge over competitors in gaining procurement orders from the public sector and perhaps also protect them from future nationalizations.

WHAT MOTIVATES POLITICIANS?

The scope of political externalities is more momentous in the last third of the twentieth century than it was in the days of Adam Smith. Since 1940 dictatorships and democratically-elected legislatures have been promulgating, at record speed, laws which regulate their citizens economic conduct. Simultaneously, the proportion of the GNP governed by the state has been growing. However, we are presently witnessing a countervailing social revolt which is strikingly changing the character of the parts politicians play in our society: the increasing political self-consciousness of the masses is attended by a decreasing respect for the putative wisdom of their leaders.

A few years ago a prominent London banker said in a letter to the press, 'Everyone would agree that to hold a referendum on which type of nuclear reactor we should choose for the new generating programme would be a farce. It is surprising that so few seem to realize that a plebiscite on our continued membership of the EEC would be just as absurd; the factors involved are just as numerous and complex, and equally beyond the knowledge and comprehension of the man or woman in the street.'[98] His was a patrician voice from the past when electors voted for educated legislators because only these could 'properly understand affairs of state'.

The decline in obsequiousness has diminished trust not only in professional politicians but also in the leaders of non-party (ethnic, occupational, religious) groups. Tammany Hall can no longer deliver votes on a plate, nor can the representatives of ethnic groups in the United States. In the 1974 Italian divorce referendum professing Catholics demonstrated that they had ceased to poll automatically in accordance with the instructions of their cardinals. British trade union officials and shop stewards are usually able to 'command' the dutiful following of the rank and file when voting takes place by a show of hands in some meeting hall. During the EEC referendum most of the UK trade union leaders advocated a 'no' vote, but as this issue was decided in secret polling booths the majority of the members defied them with equanimity.

The growing belief of the electors that they are as capable as full-time politicians of knowing what is good for the country has changed the art of governing in that the electorate must now *constantly* be wooed and .not just before elections. Above all, politicians can no longer afford to do things which they believe to be good for their constituents – they must *appear* to be working in their interest. Modern politicians are under unremitting, carping surveillance and no one who speaks in the language of the mentioned banker – 'we know best' – stands any chance of being re-elected.*

The intensified craving by politicians for popular approbation which prevails today explicitly in democracies is beginning to be an implicit feature in many dictatorships. The old-type dictators (*à la* Hitler, Stalin, Franco) wanted to be loved by the people, but their survival did not depend on receiving *active* support from the majority of the population. (As a Hungarian Communist chief once formulated it: 'those who are not against us are for us'.) If a minority actively opposed the regime by force, the dictatorships of the past could rely on the bullet and the concentration camp to crush the rebels. The winds of change that have eroded servility in parliamentary democracies are also blowing in non-parliamentary

* In his diaries[105] and public appearances after retirement, the Oxford don and former cabinet minister, Richard Crossman, cynically expounded how he had had to play to the gallery (in his constituency) in order to reach – and then remain at – the pinnacle of his political summit. He had been intelligent enough to realize that his career depended on the approval of (to him) largely unintelligent voters.

societies. Many modern dictatorships are wary of using the repressive methods that once served former despotic regimes so well. General Franco, at the beginning of his rule, could govern in the safe knowledge that if Spaniards did not like what he was doing, they either had to suffer it passively or take their punishment if they opposed him actively. A few years before he died, he lost his absolute power to govern. Though he was still not dependent on the outcome of any election, he already had to make concessions to extra-parliamentary opposition groups, because he no longer had the social (as distinct from the military) strength to mow down strikers and other law-breakers.

No constitutional change altered the Communist character of the Polish state in 1970 but the happenings of that year radically modified the manner in which the country was governed. It forced the governors of Poland to take some account of how the governed wanted to be governed. The 1970 head of the Polish Communist Party, Gomulka, obviously believed – on the Hitler-Stalin-Franco model – that his control over the repressive organs of the state sufficed to crush any active opposition to the policies he was pursuing. Most economists would probably agree that when he ordered a steep rise in consumer prices in 1970, he was doing the right thing to redress the price-distortions of the Polish economy. The people, however, did not see it in this way and, unlike politicians in democracies, the Polish Communist Party saw little need to persuade them and explain the wisdom of the new price policy. In the absence of a mechanism to throw out the ruling party at a free election, popular opposition could only express itself in violence. Rioting, looting and arson swept through Gdynia and other towns; the police and army are said to have left forty-four people dead. Shortly after this shooting rampage, the comrades removed Gomulka. His successor, Edward Gierek, was in his heart no more and no less bloodthirsty than Gomulka but he had become more sensitive to the man-in-the-street. In 1976 there was again a good reason why the government should order a substantial rise in food prices. Of course, there were no parliamentary deliberations and the people heard of it through curt announcements. Within hours some factories came out on strike and the railway lines outside Warsaw were ripped up. After only one day of rioting, Gierek did what Gomulka would never have considered. He gave a one-minute television broadcast to proclaim the ignominious withdrawal of the price increases, and the troops were ordered not to shoot any strikers. Gdynia of 1970 had carved something vital into the consciousness of the leaders of the Comecon countries: the deference of politicians to the short-sighted, selfish and unintelligent views of the masses is beginning to be a fact of life also in dictatorial regimes.

GALBRAITH SNEERS

In 1974 Enoch Powell was the parliamentary candidate of the Ulster Unionists – a regional, mainly Protestant, party – in the constituency of South Down. At one of his election meetings he spoke against state aid being given to an ailing Ulster shipyard, Harland and Wolff, the largest single industrial employer of the province. He maintained that if the enterprise could not survive on a commercial basis it ought, if necessary, to be closed despite the concomitant loss of 10,000 jobs. Powell knew that his party favoured state aid for this shipyard and that the overwhelming majority of Ulster electors would be appalled if the UK Treasury stopped subsidizing lame corporate ducks. Why then did Powell say what he did, thereby embarrassing his political colleagues and endangering his own chances of being elected? As one who rejects, on principle, state subventions for non-viable firms, it was natural for him to apply this maxim also to a company in a neighbouring constituency. Of course, he could have avoided mentioning the subject before the elections, but this he regarded as dishonest. He held that the electors were entitled to know all his salient views including those which would not be generally popular. Powell's approach to electioneering tells us a great deal about Powell; it is also of wider interest precisely because it illustrates, by contrast, how individual political candidates, who seek the approbation of voters, do not ordinarily behave. No national party, in government or opposition, would have dared to deliver such a brutal message which knowingly ran counter to a popular sentiment.

Powell proves that there are aberrant politicians who refuse to bow to the intellectual tastes of the masses. Their number is so small as not to blemish Rudolf Klein's socio-political generalization on the new 'relationship between public policy and public opinion. The deferential politician seems to be well on the way to replacing the deferential voter.' [62] In his brilliant analysis Klein demonstrates that modern politicians do not attempt to sell their ideas of the public good to the voters but instead seek to find out what people believe in order that they, as politicians, can then respond to it in the formulation of their political programmes. He discerns a tendency for governing parties first to gauge the feelings of the masses before proposing legislation – hence the significance attached to published and unpublished opinion polls.

Politicians 'consult' their constituents not because they believe them to be wise but because they genuinely fear them. Galbraith thinks that this 'fear' is bogus: 'Perhaps the oldest and certainly the wisest strategy for the exercise of power is to deny that it is possessed. Monarchs, including the most inimical of despots, long pictured themselves as the mere projection of divine will. This the established religion then affirmed. It followed that their behaviour, however scandalous, expensive and damaging to health, life, livelihood or common decency, could not be questioned at least by the true believer. It was in the service of higher will. The modern politician perpetuates the same instinct when he explains, however unconvincingly, that he is only the instrument of his constituents, the expression not of his own preferences but of the public good.' [16] Why did Galbraith make this unfair attack on politicians? He himself has tried to sell many of his economic ideas – and not all are unsound! – to politicians who have turned them down on the ground that *vox populi* would not approve. He attacks his political friends for making excuses that he condemns as insincere. It is relevant to mention that Galbraith has in his time been a civil servant, professor, author, journalist, broadcaster, food controller and now is perhaps best described as a preacher. In his multifarious activities he did not have to submit himself to the verdict of the popular franchise. He arrogantly denounces politicians (who do not readily buy his prescriptions) for asserting that the masses play a vital role in political decision-making. His long association with the Kennedy family, through which he was graciously appointed to some of his unelected illustrious jobs, should have taught him that whilst Joseph Kennedy could ignore popular sentiments when he accumulated his millions in clever speculations, his sons – as politicians – had to assume a servile posture even when dealing with people whom they detested socially and intellectually. Perhaps such conduct is not always honourable and palatable but that is the price which men must pay if they wish to succeed in politics. It helps to explain why many wholesome economic policy recommendations fail to be implemented. Instead of sneering, Galbraith ought to show compassion for politicians who would like to do what they think is in the public interest but desist when they sense the actual or potential disapproval of the electorate.

Chapter VIII

THOSE KNAVISH TAX-GATHERERS

Confound their politics,
Frustrate their knavish tricks!

Henry Carey

PATRIOTISM IS NOT ENOUGH

In the year in which the output of a national economy is $100 billion, the combined output of the private and public sectors is also $100 billion. The purport of this tautological equation is not always understood by the man-in-the-street, so that politicians can trade on his ignorance with impunity. The budget message, new taxes and changes in the money supply, can screen the truism that when the GNP remains unchanged from year one to year two, demands for more state expenditure can only be satisfied at the expense of the private sector.* The great political contest of our generation turns on how big is to be the proportion of the earnings of individuals that they may spend freely and how big the proportion over which politicians are to hold sway. Governments face this dilemma: they boast of their role in providing massive benefits but at the same time are desperately eager to camouflage that, to pay for them, politicians are forcibly taking away money from individuals and are thereby depriving them of means to finance personally selected satisfactions. This boils down to the *public relations exercise of obscuring the true proportion of the GNP which is controlled by the state and, more importantly, arranging for the transfer of resources to the public sector to appear less burdensome*

---

* We are assuming an economy in which the value of imports is equal to that of exports. This assumption is dropped in the last section of the chapter.

*than it actually is. The less obvious the transfer and the less painful
the operation, the better for politicians.*

Much energy is expended by politicians to hoodwink the public
into making the transfer look innocuous. The ideal situation is
when people are unaware that they, personally, are being deprived
of something. Politicians can also sleep soundly when electors
voluntarily give up part of their incomes by assigning it without
compulsion to the state. The extreme case is when poor and rich
citizens send in donations to the Treasury or provide in their wills
for certain assets to be conveyed to the government. There are such
patriotic men and women but, alas, their number is limited and
consequently politicians must frame laws or apply some fiscal
tricks to gain command over that portion of the GNP which they
seek to control.

In its crudest form the government can create a legal obligation
on each adult to work for the state x days per year without
remuneration; laws may be enacted which provide that the owner
of each lorry shall carry freight for nationalized corporations on y
days per year without payment. These feudal techniques are not
needed today for in a world of computers and money printing-
presses, there are superior, sophisticated means to achieve the same
objectives.

Fiscal economists debate the fairness, cost-of-collection, industrial consequences, etc. of given taxes. Without shame, and to the
consternation of some professors of economics, politicians do not
pay too much attention to these academic considerations. They
judge alternative ways of raising revenue by the criterion of which
technique *appears* to the majority of the population to be the least
beastly. The inflationary method of transferring resources from the
private to the public sector is much favoured because few of the
electors are conscious that this is a perverse form of taxation. There
are also other helpful techniques which conceal from the victims
that they are being deprived surreptitiously of part of their
earnings. Some fiscal ruses do not disguise the fact that people are
being taxed but only obscure the true burden of the taxes.

The appetite of the tax-gatherers extends beyond mustering
funds for the public sector. The state takes away from individuals a
larger portion of their incomes than is needed to finance the
collectivist state services, such as the police, nuclear power stations,

roads. The government also forcibly transfers resources from the private sector which are re-cycled into the private sector. 90% of the British population has its disposable income reduced by taxes which subsidize everybody's burial expenses and dentures. Companies complain that because of heavy taxation they do not have enough money left for new investments – the civil service machinery kindly returns some of their taxes as grants, loans and subsidies.

SEVEN TECHNIQUES

Some of the salient fiscal instruments employed by the modern state are set out below; they include a number of devious means. Readers from the other STC economies ought to be green with envy that the UK has a world lead in the tax-knavishness of its politicians. Many, though not all, of the cited examples are from the British Isles – today there is less effective control by the UK legislature over the transfer of resources from the private sector to the state than existed in the nineteenth century. The House of Commons is not always made cognizant of the true financial cost of given items of expenditure. Parliamentarians are asked to vote funds to cover the nominally small deficit of the National Pencils Corporation but are not told of the notionally large losses. They are not given an opportunity to debate the government's secret edict which forbids the procurement officers in the whole public sector to purchase pencils from the cheapest sources but forces them instead to buy the low-quality products of the National Pencils Corporation at high prices. This is a surreptitious tax on the products of other state agencies which, without being regarded as such, subsidizes the uneconomic production of state pencils.

The Conservative administration of 1970-74 perfected the art of knavish tax-trickery in two related areas. They played around with the prices of most nationalized corporations, ordering a few to earn exorbitant profits in order to cover the losses of others. Overall, however, they sold many of the products and services of the public-sector corporations at a loss in order to manipulate the cost-of-living index.* The other crime of the Heath-Barber government

---

*The Labour politicians, who succeeded the Conservatives in 1974, were equally naughty by driving in the reverse direction. They generally made

was more atrocious still. Whilst publicizing their cuts of open (direct and indirect) taxes, they did not simultaneously reduce the state's share of the GNP. They easily resolved this incongruity through inflation. Enoch Powell once again reacted as an iconoclastic politician. He favoured a drastic reduction in public expenditure which would have enabled the government to reduce the weight of the tax burden. Powell argued that until the state's role in the national economy was radically scaled down, it was improper to tax people by the dishonest technique of inflation and he called for an increase in honest, open, taxes. Powell called upon Tony Barber, the Chancellor of the Exchequer, 'to put back on to us sufficient taxation to be sure that no gap opens between what the government spends and what it receives'. [121] The next day's newspapers reported this perverse call for higher taxes from a leading member of the house of Commons. The public failed to comprehend that Powell did not actually propose an increase in the tax burden: he advocated the replacement of the opaque inflation-tax by honest taxes. The Chancellor certainly understood the message but turned down Powell's plea. Barber must have believed that the administration would be less hurt politically if, instead, it transferred resources from the private sector to the state by means which the voters did not identify as painful taxes. Was Tony Barber a more astute politician than Powell? Some called the Conservative Chancellor a knave whilst others praised him for responding expediently to the voters' ignorance of what constitutes a tax and what does not.

Direct taxes

A direct tax on income is the most honest and transparent method of raising revenue. If the state's ambition is to control 50% of the GNP and an income tax is imposed to yield an amount equal to 50% of all gross (personal and corporate) incomes, this would be

---

the nationalized corporations raise their prices to such an extent that they could act as (unofficial) tax-gatherers. This was denounced by the chairman of the National Consumer Council who compared the state-owned companies with mediaeval barons because as state-protected monopolists they 'can charge more or less what they like ... no taxation without representation is a principle not yet fully accepted in the nationalized industries'.[99]

meaningful even to economic illiterates. That is why politicians regard it as such an unpalatable tax.

Indirect taxes

When revenue is raised through indirect taxes (VAT, customs duties, excise imposts), this too is an honest method of raising revenue because parliamentary approval must first be sought to fix the rates. Indirect taxes, however, are not quite as blatantly transparent as direct taxes. Consumers are not always fully aware what proportion of the retail price ends up in the hands of the tax-gatherers.

Surreptitious taxes

Income and corporation taxes lower the disposable incomes of individuals and companies. Indirect taxes openly raise the prices of goods and services. Through the machinations of wily politicians the state can lower disposable incomes and/or make goods dearer also by other means, some of which are exemplified in the coming pages. Politicians love clandestine taxation techniques because the public and parliament can rarely evaluate them in quantitative terms.

(a) With cunning skill government departments – sometimes even in STC economies – have been known to demand (and receive) goods from private suppliers at 'political discounts'. In some developing countries import licences may sometimes be granted only to applicants who undertake to sell part of the imports to the public sector at below-cost prices. In several countries the subsidiaries of foreign firms are bullied into making available to the government a given proportion of their output on favourable terms. The companies – which have been 'taxed' in this tortuous manner – are expected to recoup the losses, incurred through their forced deliveries to the public sector, by charging private-sector customers compensatingly higher prices.

(b) Statutory anti-trust bodies, in most parts of the world, force companies within their orbit to scale down the prices which they would otherwise charge. Monopolistic firms in the private sector are thus frustrated from earning super-profits whilst monopolists in the public sector may actually be encouraged to do so. Just as a nationalized corporation can be ordered by its political masters to operate on loss-making lines, so managers of state-owned enterprises can be instructed to pursue the opposite course, i.e. to exploit their monopolistic position to make super-profits which flow to the Treasury. In 1976 and 1977 the UK Treasury successfully collected a surreptitious tax by the good offices of the British Gas Corporation which – without, of course, specific authorization from parliament – acted as an unofficial tax-gatherer. Wielding a heavy, brutal stick it left the captive customers of gas no alternative but to pay for the gas (plus an unknown tax) what the monopolist told them to pay. In the 1975-77 period the Treasury similarly ordered the telecommunications division of the British Post Office to exploit its monopolistic standing to raise the telephone charges to such a level as to generate super-profits. The government thus obtained revenues which were not voted upon in the House of Commons and was saved the bother of tabling proposals for taxes that needed parliamentary approval.

(c) There are two main types of export tax. The first is enacted openly with prescribed rates; it is intended to be an orthodox revenue-raising instrument. The second – ordinarily found only in developing countries – achieves the same fiscal objective but by a circuitous route. Producers of staple commodities are prohibited from selling abroad on their own initiative and a state-controlled marketing board is appointed as the sole national exporter. If there is little domestic demand for the commodities in question, then the captive producers have no choice but to sell their goods to the export marketing board which buys from them at low prices and sells in foreign markets at high prices. The resultant super-profit is composed of the ordinary trading surplus plus the proceeds of (an indistinct) export tax.

Governments may have reasons for seeking to ban the export of certain goods. This they can achieve by imposing such a heavy export tax as to voluntarily induce potential exporters to sell their merchandise at home. (Clearly the aim is not to raise revenue through such a tax.) Alternatively, the government can impose a physical export ban. In either case the authorities are penalizing the (frustrated) exporters for the benefit of domestic buyers who are thus enabled to collect good bargains from resentful vendors. When the price of scrap metal rose sharply in Continental Europe, UK steel producers had to pay commensurately more for domestic scrap because had they not been prepared to do so, the owners of the UK scrap would have sold their merchandise abroad. Salvation came to the British steel industry when the Department of Trade banned the export of scrap which compelled British scrap merchants to sell within the UK at prices below those prevailing in the foreign markets that were now closed to them. This produced a subsidy for domestic steel producers which can be quantified as being the difference between the actual price paid for scrap and the price they would have had to pay in the absence of the export ban. The cost of the subsidy was defrayed by the owners of UK scrap whose notional losses can be measured as being the difference between the price at which they had to sell scrap within the UK and the higher price they could have obtained abroad.

(d) The man-in-the-street has a naive view of how state subsidies work. He imagines that the government imposes a tax on certain people who are obliged to send cheques to the Treasury which in turn sends out cheques to the designated recipients of the subsidies. The cost (to the national economy or the taxpayers or the consumers) of £100m of subsidies is seen to be equivalent to the £100m of taxes which supposedly finance them. The modern state machinery is too sophisticated to have to rely exclusively on such honest book-keeping procedures. Subsidies are not always in the form of cash grants from the Treasury and governments have a public relations incentive to select subsidies which need not be financed by fiscal imposts that have to be mentioned explicitly in the budget. By employing a variety of unorthodox (not strictly fiscal) measures, the cost of a £100m subsidy may be far above or below £100m. The export ban on scrap is a classical case of how political tricksters can bestow a subsidy on an industrial branch without the state having to send out any cheques. The same game can be played with imports as I shall illustrate in the following instances appertaining to coal, agriculture and ships.

Coal: It has been the earnest wish of many British governments to smother the coal miners with financial kindnesses. Many of the hefty coal subsidies are registered in the budget books but some are unregistered. I once heard a Minister of Energy, Tony Benn, declare on television – with obvious pride – that he had 'stopped the import of coal'. [122] This was when coal could be imported into the UK at prices lower than those set by the state-owned monopolistic National Coal Board. In fact Benn did not score a complete success and some cheap coking coal did come from Australia and Poland but to the extent that he was successful in preventing British consumers from buying cheap foreign coal, he collected an indirect tax from them without any specific fiscal authority from the House of Commons. What is significant is not his objective to help the coal-mining industry but his tactical choice of *how* to pay an additional subsidy to the miners. Had he not prohibited the import of coal, the National Coal Board would either have had to cut its prices in order to make it unprofitable for the consumer to buy imported coal or it could have retained its prices and lost part of the domestic market to the cheaper coal imports. In both circumstances its deficit would have gone up *visibly* and the state aid to the mining industry would have had to be increased by an amount that could have been discerned from studying the government's expenditure figures. As it is, Tony Benn (and some of his predecessors) found a way to avoid this particular tax-subsidy from being intelligible to the public. How many British consumers knew that they were paying a specific coal-tax? No one, not even the Department of Energy, could say for certain what was the value of this vague, but nevertheless real, subsidy.

Agriculture: The old British system of subsidizing the agricultural sector was open and above board. With some minor exceptions, food imports were neither prohibited nor taxed and the UK housewife therefore paid the same low prices for both imported and British foodstuffs. British farmers could only compete with some of the imported foodstuffs by selling part of their output at below-cost prices. They were compensated for this by 'farm deficiency payments' set out in the budget. The subsidy to British farmers was paid out of general state revenue. Everyone knew how big the subsidy was and how big the burden on the rest of the British economy.

The agricultural policy of the Community is not only economically invidious but it also offends the cannons of democracy in that the total cost of subsidizing EEC farmers is not ascertainable. The Brussels subsidies to the agricultural sector are funded in two ways. One is through cash disbursements. Farmers are given subventions and the Community guarantees them certain minimum prices. The agricultural producer is largely uninterested in whether the housewife is able or willing to buy all his produce at the offered high prices. If she does not do so, the EEC will take off his hands the surplus and store or burn it; alternatively, it may be dumped in foreign markets – Russia is a favoured place – at prices below those paid to the EEC farmers. These billions of dollars of subsidies are an orthodox tax burden because they are financed through contributions from the member-states which in turn raise the money by asking their legislatures for the necessary appropriations.

The EEC politicians are clever. They know that these openly-financed expenditures on farm supports are not sufficient to sustain the level of agricultural output for which the farming lobby is pressing. A non-cash technique is therefore employed by the politicians which does not expose them to the opprobrium they would have to endure were the *whole* EEC agricultural subsidy financed by easily quantifiable, honest, tax methods. The Community's conjuring trick is to load a further burden on to the housewife by *prohibiting the import* of most (competing) foodstuffs. In theory there is no ban on foreign food but the same effect is produced by laying down 'minimum import prices' and imposing heavy levies on foreign-produced foodstuffs which reach the ports of the Community. (The import levies are not meant to earn revenues for the Community's treasury but are prescribed in order to make it commercially non-viable for most foreign farmers to market their products in the EEC.) The cornerstone of the Common Agricultural Policy, through its punitive levies, is to formulate such artificially high prices for the sale of non-EEC foodstuffs in the EEC, that no sensible housewife would buy imports in preference to local produce. Were there no import restrictions (and import levies), the EEC consumer would clearly buy less from EEC farmers at the high guaranteed prices and purchase instead the cheaper foreign food. If, however, the leaders of the Community then still wanted their farmers to be as coddled as they are today, they would have to hand out even greater *open* cash subventions. The beauty of the knavish tricks of the EEC politicians is that presently they can extract a hidden tax from the consumer (who is unable to buy cheap foreign food). They are thereby saved the embarrassment of having to go to their parliaments for authority to raise even more funds for the visible costs of the Community's agricultural subsidy.

Ships: The American farming lobby complain bitterly about Europe's closed door but the US government pursues a similar policy concerning shipping. American shipyards have production costs which are far above those of other countries. Big government grants are paid towards the cost of building ships in American yards and these, of course, are part of the Federal government's registered expenditure. When the legislators on Capitol Hill were told that unless additional subsidies were given some shipyards would have to close, they, as good politicians, were disdainful of raising taxes – open taxes – to finance them. This is why the Jones Act was passed. Without explicitly taxing the US consumer, the government managed to give American shipyards a surreptitious subsidy by restricting inter-coastal US shipping to vessels built in the US. How big is this implicit tax on the American consumer?

(e) Many of the hidden taxes and subsidies involve the transfer of resources from the private sector to the state. Sometimes, however, the technique is employed to hide from the public that nationalized corporation A is taxing its customers in order to provide subsidies for the loss-making, nationalized corporation B – the facts are to be obscured from the inquisitive eyes of the common people. Through placing procurement orders on a non-commercial basis, the potential profits of one state agency are cut to eliminate potential deficits of another. In this way members of parliament are not called upon to debate the necessity of providing a subsidy for a loss-making activity.

Forced loans

Governments can obtain resources from the private sector also through borrowings. In conventional budget thinking current outlays (salaries for policemen, milk for indigent children) should be financed with taxes collected in the same period in which the disbursements are made. Capital spending (on schools, bridges) is to be funded mainly through medium- and long-term loans. Few governments today still adhere to such a compartmentalization. Some, for example the USSR, use the proceeds of ordinary taxes to finance the acquisition of capital goods, whilst most Western countries have at one time or another in the post-war years floated government bonds to finance current state expenditure.

The state need not borrow only from willing lenders. Laws may be passed to compel the population to make loans to the government. In authoritarian regimes legislation may be unnecessary when the authorities can browbeat their citizens to hand over their savings. Nove [120] has told in detail of the unofficial rule that used to prevail in Russia whereby the equivalent of two weeks' wages had to be saved 'voluntarily' and the proceeds invested in state bonds. Though the authorities explained in their propaganda abroad that these were not compulsory loan subscriptions but patriotic gestures, dire consequences awaited the comrades who did not in fact comply with this saving edict. When, after the demise of Stalin, Malenkov came to power and sought to gain popularity, he slackened the official pressures to make people buy government bonds; within one year their sales had dropped by more than half, which is a good indication of the previous 'voluntary' character of this revenue-raising technique.

Compulsory loans to the state have been and still are a fiscal feature of many capitalist economies. During the war, British (and other) governments instituted statutory 'forced savings', whereby a given percentage of all incomes had to be handed over to the state as a loan. Nowadays, the technique of compulsory loans from the private sector is operated in some STC countries with greater finesse: laws are enacted which oblige institutional investors (pension funds, insurance companies) to hold part of their assets in the form of government securities. In addition, the state may assume powers - in the UK these have been delegated to the Bank of England - to demand of banks that they place at the disposal of the government some of their liquid assets at no, or a low, interest. Such decrees (in the UK) do not depend on the explicit approval of parliament; the banks are thus 'taxed' by means that are not spelt out in the annual budget message.

Voluntary loans

State borrowings from genuinely voluntary lenders cause no pain to the subscribers; this is therefore an ideal public relations technique of raising revenue. Nevertheless, one ought to look even this gift horse in the mouth. When the state can compel people to buy government bonds, it automatically has also the power to fix the interest rate which can be derisory or even zero. However, sales of government securities to willing savers can only be executed at the current market price for money. In a situation, in which the private sector is highly liquid and unwilling to borrow even when potential lenders offer funds at less than 1% interest, sales of new government securities impose no burden on the private sector. But if private corporations are in the market to raise new finance, then a demand by the state for new loan subscriptions from the public will affect them adversely. The more money the government seeks to raise, the higher the interest rate which it must offer to lure voluntary savers away from alternative investments in the private sector. The higher the government's interest rates, the more must the private sector offer. This bidding goes on, with the government calling the tune, until most firms have been crowded out. Compared with the private sector, politicians have two relative advantages in the tapping of voluntary savings. First, the interest rate which a private corporation can afford on investment funds must be lower than the anticipated investment yield, whilst a public sector corporation can always turn to its political masters when high interest charges threaten the viability of its capital projects. Second, the state needs to offer lower interest rates than private-sector companies because investors rightly assume that the government will never be insolvent.

Tax-exempt loans

Many Western governments proclaim the patriotic virtue of saving and in the same breath morally condemn savers for earning an investment income. To punish them, interest and dividend receipts are taxed at higher rates than apply to 'earned' income. Investors, liable to high marginal tax rates, think primarily in terms of net (i.e. post-tax) income. Wicked governments dangle a carrot before them: they are promised exemption from income tax, investment-surcharge, capital gains tax, etc. if they liquidate their private-sector investments to buy appropriate government bonds.

Is it a harmless fiscal trick when the government issues tax-exempt securities? Many see this as an innocuous game in which the government gathers fewer taxes but simultaneously pays out less interest than if it had issued bonds with interest on which ordinary taxes are collected. Whilst this is formally true, tax-exempt securities ought nevertheless to be treated as Treasury pawns in an obnoxious scheme which overcasts the presentation of the revenue-expenditure accounts of the government, making them less meaningful and economically accurate. When the US government allows municipalities to issue bonds which are free from Federal income taxes, and thereby reduces its own potential tax receipts, it in fact pays a subsidy to the municipalities, the quantitative dimensions of which are certainly not comprehended (and perhaps not meant to be comprehended) by the unsophisticated taxpayers.

Harold Macmillan, when Chancellor of the Exchequer, borrowed from the Communist states the fiscal skill of raising revenue painlessly by selling government securities, the interest on which is paid with tax-free lottery prizes. As Premium Bonds proved to be a magnet which attracted hundreds of millions of pounds of voluntary savings, the second Wilson administration found it politically expedient to improve this fiscal technique and make it an even more important source of revenue. In the name of economic sanity, Harold Wilson raised the top marginal income tax on investment earnings in the private sector to 98% and simultaneously arranged for advertisements to be placed in the press to proclaim a new tax-free Premium Bond lottery prize of £100,000. The following was the position in the financial year of 1978/9: a very rich man, if owning Premium Bonds, could regularly participate in draws that might net him a £100,000 tax-free prize; one of the alternatives to investing his savings in these government tax-exempt (gambling) bonds was to buy fixed-interest securities of Britain's largest and most reputable corporations which offered a gross yield of no less than 12%. In order to be left, after tax, with an annual disposable income of £100,000, he would have had to clip £5m of coupons. To earn £5m of gross interest, he first would have had to buy bonds at a cost of about £42m.

The printing press

When I taught a course on taxation in the early fifties, I listed inflation as a source of government revenue. A respected colleague, whose field of instruction was monetary economics, reproached me for poaching on his territory. We have moved a long way since those days and modern textbooks on taxation now give a prominent place to inflation though few emphasize even today that it is deliberately engineered by politicians. Inflation is not an Act of God and foreign happenings are a poor alibi for fiscal tricksters who print money.

Crude inflation-taxes were imposed by dishonest rulers throughout the ages. Monarchs enriched themselves by debasing gold and silver coins. After the Russian revolution the Bolsheviks robbed the remaining private sector by printing bank notes. Modern inflation-tax techniques are perforce more complex. Nowadays, the managers of central banks serve their political masters by the inflationary issue of Treasury Bills. The layman does not grasp how this inoffensive activity can drive up prices but his lack of understanding helps politicians to finance additional government expenditure without increasing visible taxes.

Printing money – to use a colloquial term – has the merit of causing the country's price level to rise only after months or even years. The inflation mechanism, which is fitted with a delayed-action trigger, is therefore a handy device for the dishonest transfer of resources to the state. With newly printed money the government obtains goods at prevailing prices as well as the services of employees in the public sector at current wages. By the time companies, which had supplied goods to the government, set about replenishing their inventories and wage earners spend some of their temporary savings, prices have gone up. The government, through its own actions, has induced a rise in prices and wages but, as it was first on the scene as a buyer, has benefited by acquiring resources on the cheap.

To owners of monetary assets (bank deposits, fixed-interest securities) a rise in the general price level, which lowers their purchasing power, is equivalent to paying a capital tax. Inflation is a useful means of taxing the ownership of monetary assets, and reducing the real value of the national debt, without formally instituting a wealth tax.

Legislators are busily engaged on debating whether the standard income-tax rate shall be 34% or 33%. Members of parliament can make a name for themselves by voting against a government proposal to put up the VAT on sausage skins. There is indeed effective parliamentary control over such trivia, but this is often of little concern to the politicians in power. In the last resort they can always increase the inflation-tax; in many countries they need no explicit parliamentary approval for such a dastardly deed. This, to politicians, is perhaps the most attractive aspect of the inflation-tax.

FOREIGNERS CAN HELP

This chapter began with the dogmatic assertion that, with a constant GNP, the public sector can only grow when the private sector is reduced commensurately. The section on the 'seven techniques' depicted how the transfer of resources is implemented honestly and deceitfully, through domestic borrowings and taxation. Politicians in many countries can thank their lucky stars that what has so far been described holds true only in an economy with no surplus or deficit on its international transactions. When help can come from abroad, politicians are then not restrained by the straitjacket of their country's GNP. If resources are obtainable from foreigners by begging, borrowing or robbing, the public sector can expand without the painful transfer of resources from the domestic private sector. To put this in a more concrete form, a country's current living standard can be improved not only by working harder but also when a way is found to import more than is exported. It certainly worked for the people of the United Kingdom (from the beginning of 1974 to the middle of 1977).

During the first two years of the second Wilson administration, which commenced in 1974, the country experienced an average annual inflation of 20%, a sharp drop in industrial output, and the quintupling of the price of imported oil. To balance the books on external transactions, it would have been necessary to lower radically the exchange rate of sterling and/or have import restrictions and/or push up exports – all of these measures, in the short run at least, would have reduced quickly the existing living standard. The Labour government, despite a drop in the GNP, also increased the size of the public sector and extended the provisions of the Welfare State; in a closed economy all these things would only have been possible following a massive transfer of resources from the private sector.

When historians are allowed to open the record books of 1974, more will become known of the sagacious-cum-expedient advice rendered in those days by a member of the cabinet, the ex-financier, Harold Lever. He is said to have shown much political horse-sense. Lever helped to persuade the Labour government – not that his colleagues needed persuasion to sanction such a palatable recipe – that to resolve the impending balance of payments difficulties *and* allow the public sector to grow, it was unnecessary to have politically disastrous cuts in consumer spending and welfare benefits. Why not run instead a large deficit on the current account balance of payments? Indeed, the government accepted his advice and billions of dollars of imports were brought into the country without being paid for by exports. The Shah of Iran, the International Monetary Fund, the West German government, the purveyors of expensive Euro-dollars – all were called upon to help the Labour government build socialism and run a big deficit on the balance of trade. By Christmas 1977 the UK government's foreign currency debts (including those incurred before 1974) had reached a staggering total of $35 billion.

Not everyone agreed with this politically convenient Lever solution. The begging for foreign funds was humiliating and the interest charges on the Euro-dollar market were burdensome. There were those who said that it was unwise to mortgage the future and some preached that a country should live within its current means – these were lone voices. Chancellor of the Exchequer, Denis Healey, explained it all: 'My impression, and I suppose we all derive our views from contact with our constituents, is that the British people would prefer to maintain the highest possible standard of living at the expense of borrowing at low rates over a reasonable period rather than incur the sudden and dramatic fall in living standards which would be involved if we did not succeed in getting this borrowing.' Healey was satisfied to attribute the Treasury's foreign currency borrowings to the will of his constituents. Perhaps intuitively they understood that without the help of foreigners the growth of the British public sector would have entailed an even bigger drop in their personal disposable incomes. Healey, however, had a different reason for implementing Lever's strategy. If the UK had really balanced the books in 1974, the consequent decline in its popularity might have swept the Labour government out of power.

It is very difficult to explain to non-economists that when a government borrows from its own citizens to finance public sector expenditure, it ordinarily takes away resources from the private sector just as if it had collected taxes. The man-in-the-street thinks that the sale of government bonds *at home* yields the state the wherewithal to distribute lollipops to today's citizens which will only be paid for by the next generation. Healey knew, of course, that in a closed economy you cannot eat a cake in 1975 and pay for it in 1985. (I hope to verify in Chapter X why politicians are therefore so obsessed with the timing aspect of their actions.) The Labour Party politicians embraced lovingly the proposal to borrow from foreigners, because revenues procured in this way can indeed by enjoyed today and are only repayable when the government, responsible for the borrowing, has gone. This makes cadging from foreigners the politically most rewarding tax-gathering device.

Chapter IX

THE RECTITUDE OF INVESTMENTS

There is nothing that produces jobs for economists like government controls and government intervention. And all economists are therefore schizophrenic: their discipline, derived from Adam Smith, leads them to favour the market; their self-interest leads them to favour intervention.

Milton Friedman

INVESTING IS NOBLE

In the ethos of capitalist and communist societies, investing – like exports, monogamy and the love of cats – is regarded as being 'in the public interest'. Company chairmen boast to their shareholders about increases in investments. The social virility of national economies is often gauged by the proportion of the GNP which is devoted to non-consumption. The reverse side of the coin, saving, was once a Puritan virtue and preachers suggested that it was good for the soul. Today the passion for investing is fostered because of the putative economic benefits that accrue from capital goods. Hence British prime ministers have been advising the Queen that peerages should be offered not only to meritorious exporters but also to deserving entrepreneurial investors.

In Chapter X attention is drawn to the curious, voluntary behaviour of persons who are prepared to save by deferring the consumption of $100-worth of apples even though they are aware that these savings will provide them later with only $90-worth of apples. However, when economists and politicians deliver sermons on the virtue of saving, they do not ordinarily think of such peculiar subjective time preferences. What they have in mind is that human happiness can be enhanced by foregoing the consumption of $100-worth of apples because the resources thus released will be utilized to produce $100-worth of machine tools, which (in the course of time) will generate more material enjoyment than is derived from $100-worth of apples. This seemingly attractive proposition begs two questions that are particularly pertinent when the state compels people to save. First, even when one is certain that the foregone pleasure of eating today $100-worth of apples means the availability of $120-worth of apples tomorrow, are there not many individuals who would derive greater pleasure from munching today five apples rather than six apples in the future? Whilst the first question is an immeasurable conundrum, the second one can sometimes be quantified: do $100 of capital goods always lay enough golden eggs ultimately to produce goods worth $120 or more? Future increases in the material output of a country depend only in part on how much is invested in the present; they also hinge on how fertile the investments prove to be. British politicians have mouthed glib generalizations on why the UK has been lagging behind the post-war growth of other industrial countries and have often attributed this to an insufficient expenditure on capital goods. To a degree this is true, but a much greater failure was the channelling of a sizable portion of the UK's savings into investments which were less fruitful than those undertaken by her main competitors. The size of the investment volume often matters less than where and how savings are invested and the degree of utilization of acquired capital goods.

It is in society's interest that the suffering from deferred consumption should at least be alleviated by the selection of fertile investment projects, those which lay the largest number of golden eggs for each dollar saved. *The bigger the indiscriminate state support for investments (through, for example, subsidies and grants for any type of capital expenditure), the greater the likelihood that resources will be invested in projects with a low fertility or no fertility at all.* Nowhere has this been more pronounced than in the socialist fatherland. Wilczynski has shown that the system by which the Russian central government used to provide investment finance (through non-repayable grants) proved highly wasteful. To the managers of the state enterprises, capital became a 'free' input; they were under no obligation to charge realistic depreciation in arriving at the prices for their goods. This squandering of resources finally led the USSR to change course in the sixties when enterprises were instructed to make provision for interest payments to the suppliers of capital (the central authorities) and were ordered to calculate higher depreciation charges. [123]

No one rose in the British parliament to protest when that good socialist John Diamond (at the time Chief Secretary of the Treasury) drawled out, 'All honourable members, without exception, are anxious to encourage investments'. [29] He did not mean by 'encouragement' the sort of thing parents do to help children learn to read or wipe their nose. Diamond religiously believed that the state should increase taxes on personal incomes and consumption in order to bestow cheap credits, cash grants and various subsidies on patriotic investors.

To be infatuated with investments is not a British disease but the folly has been greater in the UK than in any other Western economy. Despite the post-war balance of payments difficulties, this love for investments was not restricted – banish the xenophobic thought! – to the buying of capital goods made in the United Kingdom. Provided the assets were new, they qualified for the taxpayers' subsidies even when they were imported. I once advised a firm in Tokyo, which planned to set up a plant in Wales, that it would be statutorily entitled to a cash grant on the Japanese-manufactured machines that it was planning to install. Japanese are much too polite to call a Western consultant a liar to his face, but I felt that they did not believe me. They sent a delegation to London which returned to confirm that the Department of Industry would hand out this, unexpected, bounty. I later received the impression that they thought the British were mad.

In Chapter V reference was made to the stratagem by which foreign companies bought control of UK-registered shipping firms in order to benefit from the luscious investment grants. A government spokesman later revealed that these foreign-controlled shipping firms had indeed proved to be good boys – they had invested a great deal of money in new ships. Such investment performance deserved a prize! £39m was handed over to them in grants – the only snag was that a mere £4m were a reward for building ships in Britain whilst £35m were a gratuity for acquiring vessels constructed in foreign shipyards.

The heresy is spreading that the installation of sophisticated machinery is not the only, or even always the best, way to make a society richer. Egypt's Aswan Dam was conceived to considerably increase indigenous food production by irrigating wide areas of arable lands – this objective has been achieved. The country's birth rate, however, rose at an even faster rate so that the *per capita* acreage under cultivation actually fell between the conception and completion of Egypt's biggest capital investment project. If only a portion of the resources spent on turbines and bulldozers had been lavished on a financially well-endowed programme of birth control, the average Egyptian would today be better off.

Rodents not only consume food but also contaminate it; they damage food packaging and storage facilities and transmit diseases. Post-harvest losses attributable to rodents and insects are estimated at 5-20% of the world's grain crops; the damage varies widely as between countries.[84] Although the US has less than one rat per inhabitant, the Food and Drug Administration nevertheless believes that rodents consume or contaminate 10% of the country's entire grain crop. The rat problem in India is much more serious; some estimates mention five to eight rats per inhabitant. There can be no accuracy in the proportions of India's grain production which is lost or fouled. Whether it is 20% or 50%, this is clearly an economic problem of the first magnitude. A concentrated extermination campaign would be costly but would bring more immediate material happiness to the Indian sub-continent than the buying of thousands of large tractors designed to increase food production.

It is more glamorous to build a dam and install an irrigation turbine than to spend money on family-planning centres and the extermination of rodent saboteurs. Equally, it is politically more rewarding to build a *new* school*, hospital or road than to disburse funds for the maintenance or improvement of existing facilities;

* In 1978 the National Association of Head Teachers released a statement in which it described how economies in education budgets have led to disproportionately large cuts in the amount of money for maintenance. Consequently many schools, including newly-built ones, were rapidly being turned into slums through lack of proper repair and maintenance. The Association's general secretary added that 'every private house owner knows that if he puts off proper maintenance work on his property, it will cost a lot more in the future.' This may be true but is irrelevant in this context. The glory of opening one newly-built school far exceeds the kudos which politicians can earn from keeping a hundred schools in proper repair.[106]

the former is called investing whilst the latter is registered in the budget books as current expenditure. Politicians want to be able to boast about investments in *additional* medical edifices. The works officers of the National Health Service have alleged that the British hospital authorities are 'tempted to reduce their expenditure on the maintenance of assets ... It was apparent that there was an excessive concentration on new construction and that this resulted in a failure to provide major policy direction on conserving the far greater bulk of existing buildings and services'.[99]

The leaders of many developing countries have been bitten by a particularly virulent investment bug. Until recently the Western paternalistic aid lobby was imbued with the conviction that above all the ex-colonial countries need machinery, big machinery, beautiful big machinery. The ministers and officials of the emerging independent nations welcomed industrial white elephants as pleasing prestige symbols. As a result of some re-thinking in the West the aid budgets were restructured; a smaller proportion was assigned to large, capital-intensive, projects. Several Cadillac-driven leaders of the developing economies protested vociferously: is the unwillingness of rich nations to donate the most modern investment goods not a sign of racial bigotry? Suggestions that it is often more sensible to utilize the aid funds to supply consumer goods, spare-parts to service already existing machinery, raw materials, etc., have been known to be dismissed with contempt. Whilst in the fifties the policy of concentrating on mammoth capital projects in the developing world was only in the experimental stage, there is now empiric evidence to highlight the foolishness of such an aid strategy. The flagship of Britain's overseas investment aid to India, the steel works of Durgapur, is still open for inspection. Indian economists are debating amongst themselves whether the other steel elephants, donated by the Russian and German taxpayers, have not been even greater commercial failures. (Horror stories came to light in October 1970 when an Indian parliamentary committee examined what had happened to some of the Russian aid funds 'invested' in non-viable, large, capital-intensive, ventures.) From many parts of Latin America, Asia and Africa have come reports which show that some of the donated modern machines are under-utilized; sometimes there is no market to absorb their potential output and sometimes the lack of foreign currency to pay for the import of raw materials and spare-parts makes it impossible to operate them. An instance of socio-economic damage to the fabric of an under-developed society, caused by intoxication with a capital-intensive investment, has been given by Owen in his study of an ex-colonial African country. A highly automated factory for the manufacture of sandals was opened and created employment for forty injection-moulding machine operators. The impact was to put out of work seven thousand native leather shoemakers, reduce the incomes of the indigenous producers of leather, glue, thread, polishes, hand-tools and carton boxes and make the country dependent on imported plastic machinery and pvc grains.[109]

STATE INVESTMENTS ARE EVEN MORE MERITORIOUS

If investing is a desirable exercise, then it follows that the state should help with subsidies. If subsidized investing in the private sector is a good thing, then capital projects carried out by the state are even more praiseworthy. Keynes imputes to the 'State' – he curiously writes it with a capital letter – the ability 'to calculate the marginal efficiency of capital-goods on long views and on the basis of the general social advantage'.[24] It is true that the modern state has the power to recruit financial resources to make investments which rapacious capitalists would shun* but this power is often not

---

* Khrushchev tells a poignant story: 'Stalin once said in my presence: "We've won the war and are recognized the world over as glorious victors. We must be ready for an influx of foreign visitors. What will happen if they walk around Moscow and find no skyscrapers? They will make unfavourable comparisons with capitalist cities." At Stalin's order, the skyscrapers were built. . . . The rent was so high (to pay for the maintenance of the buildings) that not a single inhabitant of Moscow could possibly afford to live in them, so Stalin decided to reduce the rent somewhat. . . . The whole thing was pretty stupid, if you ask me. You'd never find capitalists building skyscrapers like ours.'[4] Krushchev may be right about capitalists but the governments of some capitalist countries are as guilty as Stalin in spending public funds to invest in white elephants.

exercised wisely. Enterprises in the private sector are subject to the discipline of an economic calculus whilst there is no such constraint on civil servants who assume the role of entrepreneurs with taxpayers' money.

Keynes's implicit idealization of politicians as sagacious investment decision-makers rests on three crutches: investment projects with a long gestation period may not prove attractive to private risk capital; an investment which is socially advantageous is not necessarily very profitable; politicians opt for particular investment projects in accordance with their *general social advantage*. The third crutch is a sick joke. Keynes makes this preposterous suggestion to contrast the acquisitive wickedness of private entrepreneurs with the dedication of elected and unelected public servants. In real life, politicians frequently take investment decisions in relation to narrow electoral considerations.* 'Logrolling' is an American term to describe the action of legislators who vote for certain bills in return for a promise that state funds are allocated to vested interests sponsored by them. 'Pork-barrel' has become a phrase of contempt which denotes special payments, made from the public purse, to benefit locations represented by scheming politicians. The national interest, in the true sense of the words, does not always motivate the British politicians who hand out discretionary investment grants; companies owning factories which are sited in electorally sensitive areas may consequently receive subsidies denied to their competitors.

Keynes was wrong to sell politicians as wise and honest investment experts concerned only with the public interest. The opposite is the case. As they have a short political life, it is very

* The longest suspension bridge in the world, spanning the river Humber near Hull in North-East England, is expected to be opened in 1981 when this loss-making creature will become the biggest white-elephant bridge of the UK. There is an attempt now to whitewash the politicians who were responsible, between 1966 and 1969, for considering and then finalizing this disastrous investment decision. It is said of these innocents that they were misled by bad advice from non-political consultants. What a travesty of the truth! The responsible minister has since confessed that he and other colleagues in the cabinet were aware of the economic case against the bridge. Notwithstanding what they knew, they nevertheless gave the order to build it – 'in order to win the Hull by-election'. [105]

dangerous to entrust them with other people's money, especially to make long-term investments. The efficiency of current expenditure items can be scrutinized by parliament whilst the politicians who have initiated them are still in office. The public which is told that income tax is being increased to improve the quality of school meals can judge within a matter of months whether the additional tax burden is matched by a worthwhile benefit. However, a nuclear power station may, only twenty years after its commissioning, prove to have been a wise or unwise outlay of taxpayers' money.

Politicians need not bother about the spurious accuracy of the expenditure estimates of long-term state investments. This is why they hardly ever qualify their seductive propositions though it may be technically impossible to state an honest, numerate forecast. But even in cases where reasonably reliable costs can be ascertained, politicians often publish bogus prospectuses. The minister who fosters a white elephant is not likely to be in a responsible position when the initially announced calculations are seen to have been manifestly wrong.* Privately-owned corporations, particularly the smaller ones, have to cut their losses midway as they run out of funds because numerate projections, on which they had based their investment decision, are found to have been erroneous. Not so with state projects! Keynes could not have been more wrong: the longer the gestation period of a state-financed project, the less does the political initiator have to think in terms of marginal efficiency or overall social advantage. If the cost schedule turns out to have been wrong, his successor will pick up the bill for the additional expenditure. He can always put the blame on his predecessor. The ministers who made the original Concorde commitment were fifteen years older, and no longer ministers,

---

* Lord Beeching, a former senior manager of ICI and later the head of a British nationalized corporation, was once asked how governments arrive at decisions on long-term investments, the escalating costs of which are uncertain: 'One often finds situations in which, to a considerable degree, the government wants to be deceived; it is expedient to be deceived. You can always pass the buck afterwards and say: "Well, the other people told us that we were entitled to rely upon them" .... But it is convenient to proceed with some exciting project because somebody says that it will ultimately make money and you get all the credit for having supported this wonderful British venture. So there is a temptation to be deceived.'[33]

when the last R & D (research and development) invoices reached
the Treasury for payment.

DICTATORSHIP IS GOOD FOR INVESTMENTS
Chapter VIII commenced with the tautological assertion that the
combined output of the private and public sectors cannot be
smaller or larger than the GNP. It is a parallel truism that in a
given year a country's GNP is equal to the combined output which
is destined for consumption and investment. In an economy, with
no unemployed resources and zero growth and imports equal to
exports, investments can only be increased at the expense of
consumption and vice versa. This is blatantly transparent in a
self-contained moneyless society. Certainly Robinson Crusoe
understood that the logs he cut down each day could be used either
for consumption (heating and cooking) or for making tools and
building a new cabin. In our sophisticated money societies the
same principle applies but is not perceived clearly by the
man-in-the-street. Politicians deserve to be censured when they fail
to accompany their pleas for more investment with an explicit
warning that this entails less immediate consumption. Politicians,
when they have the power to do so, may raise the proportion of the
GNP designated for investment without the public fully understanding the impact which this has on its current living standard.
Economists describe euphemistically as 'forced savings' or 'involuntary investments' a situation in which the investment level is
higher than that which people would freely have chosen by a
voluntary lowering of their current consumption.

The more powerful a government, and the more oblivious it is of
the wishes of its citizens, the bigger its capacity to devote a large
segment of the GNP to investment. I am not saying that the
investment segment of authoritarian regimes is always bigger than
that of comparable democracies. My purpose is merely to introduce the hypothesis that dictatorships, if they so wish, can more
easily bring it about that people consume less and thereby release
resources for investment. Wilczynski [123] has illustrated this political element in his economic study of European communist
countries; Nove [120] has also dealt with the close connection
between political terror and a high rate of capital accumulation.
Various statistical investigations have established that between the

end of the war and the mid-sixties the investment proportion of the GNPs of the Comecon economies was double that of the Western industrialized countries.[28] Hanson says that this is the result of democracies 'being more vulnerable to public opinion;'[124] he concludes that the consumption pattern in the non-communist world is consequently 'more amenable to the wishes of the population at large than in Russia'.

If the impressive investment dimensions of the communist world in the fifteen to twenty years after the war were made possible by the repressive character of their brutal regimes, then the socio-political changes of the post-Stalin era may help to elucidate why the investment proportion of the GNPs of the Comecon countries has been declining in recent times. In the Siberian concentration camps they no longer crack the whips as often as in the days of Stalin. The communist politicians have come a few steps nearer to comprehending the populist influences to which the legislators of the House of Commons, the US Congress and the German Bundestag are exposed: when the governors seek consent from the governed they hear the clear message that politicians can enhance their popularity by providing more consumer goods. The new communist generation can no longer be exhorted to work with Stakhanovite fervour: it prefers personally-owned tape recorders to *Pravda* articles on the wonders of big irrigation schemes. The Poles did not riot in Gdynia because their communist government failed to manufacture enough bridges and turbines. They rebelled because they wanted more and better and cheaper consumer goods. Wilczynski has also adduced a pragmatic reason why today the communist rulers no longer pray quite so fervently to the investment god. He believes that the over-emphasis on investments has dampened the work effort of the communist toilers: 'Experience showed that depressing current consumption beyond certain levels tended to produce demoralization and alienation amongst workers in the form of absenteeism, a large labour turnover, pilfering in factories and on farms, damaging socialized property and even open riots.'

THE MORAL ARGUMENT
Though the problem of 'forced savings' is particularly acute in

dictatorships, it also exists in democracies whenever and wherever governments indiscriminately force their citizens to defer consumption irrespective of whether they are happy to do so or not. Marglin put it succinctly: 'Why do governments require citizens to sacrifice current consumption to undertake investments that will not yield benefits until those called upon to make the sacrifices are all dead?' [119] Why should the residents of Glasgow be taxed to provide London with a modern underground railway? Why should non-smokers be forced to lower their living standards in order that the state may have the wherewithal to hand investment grants to tobacco companies? Is it not morally wrong that old-age pensioners and teenagers alike are *compelled* in 1979 to reduce their current consumption because the government needs money for a nuclear reactor which is scheduled to come into operation in 1990 to beget benefits during the subsequent hundred years? (It is somewhat hypocritical of politicians to tell an eighty-year-old couple that their 'forced savings' are merely a deferment of consumption.) It is even more shameful that some donors of aid to poor countries insist that their charity shall be given primarily in the form of capital goods. Little and Clifford have drawn attention to this wicked attitude; they both belong to the UK aid lobby and do not object to the British public being taxed to assist the developing countries. Yet they are outraged at how some of the funds are spent by the political paternalists: 'Why, and with what possible justification, should we urge that the poverty-stricken should save more for future generations? Why should we prefer the poor to save what we give rather than consume it?' [30]

With the help of the seven fiscal techniques outlined in the previous chapter, the state transfers portions of the incomes of individuals and corporations to the coffers of the Treasury. When such transfers are arranged for the purpose of releasing resources for investment activities (under the auspices of the state), they lower the general level of consumption. *All* citizens suffer. However, there is no link between the compulsory investment load which an individual must carry in the present and the investment-fruits which he is either desirous or able to consume in the future. To some extent this is unavoidable as governments invest in community projects for which it is not feasible to charge a toll (e.g. prisons, flood barriers). 'Forced savings' become especially immoral when the state uses its coercive powers to reduce everybody's consumption in order to induce investments that could be financed with socially-just techniques. A large segment of the state's investment volume is presently channelled into projects where it would be fairer if only the users (of the produced goods and services) paid for the investment finance through a proper pricing policy. Furthermore, there is no moral justification for why the state should make all citizens consume less so that politicians might provide loans, grants and subsidies to investors in the private sector. (The Cardiff old-age pensioners were taxed so that a Canadian bubble gum manufacturer could receive his subsidy for a factory in Scotland from a benevolent British government sitting in London.)

There is a three-dimensional freedom for savers in a market economy. The first deals with the right of an individual to save only as much as he wishes to save. If 12% of the GNP of the Adam Smith country is accounted for by investment, this is not the result of any coercion; some individuals dis-saved, some saved nothing, some saved 15% (and others 25%) of their earnings. The second dimension is concerned with ensuring that the financing costs of an investment shall be borne exclusively by the beneficiaries of the investment. The means to build a nylon factory do not come from the 'forced savings' of oppressed Cardiff old-age pensioners but from voluntary suppliers of capital who are rewarded with interest and dividend payments that are incorporated into the price at which the nylon products are sold to willing buyers. The third dimension allows people to reverse savings decisions which they made in the past. In a capitalist society an individual who in year one had saved-invested 20% of his earnings can in year two reduce his current savings rate to zero and even dis-save by selling the Ford shares in which he had previously invested his non-consumed earnings. (Of course not all individuals can dis-save simultaneously; there is also no guarantee – even in 'normal times' – that a $100 investment is always redeemable for at least $100.) This freedom to opt out of past investments actuates fluctuations in the capital market, which is why Keynes was so disdainful of this individual liberty that capitalism offers. He was 'moved towards the conclusion that to make the purchase of an investment permanent and indissoluble, like marriage, except by reason of death or other grave cause, might be a useful remedy for our contemporary evils'. [24] We know that Keynes was violently opposed to the evils of capitalist speculation except when he speculated for himself, his friends or his college. Keynes, like some of our present-day socialists, had enough of an authoritarian streak in him to consider in his writings whether savers ought not to be deprived of the right to disinvest at their pleasure. Hence he sought to abolish the liquid investment market where willing buyers and sellers of capital meet. Keynes pleaded that the state ought to make it unlawful for people who bought, say, a fifteen-year bond to sell it before the end of the fifteen-year period. However, he ultimately arrived at the – to him sad – conclusion that unless a society is sufficiently regimented to prevent individuals from hoarding or lending money, it is necessary to retain an open, liquid investment market. Keynes recognized reluctantly that, in its absence, voluntary savers would be impeded from making new desirable investments. The right to reverse a previous investment decision 'calms (the saver's) nerves and makes him much more willing to run a risk'.

Keynes was aware that Communist countries dispense with the nonsense of free saving-investing but he did not live to see this ugly principle of 'forced savings' flourish, in peace time, in many Western democracies. There are politicians who sneer at the moral objections to 'involuntary investments' because they think that investing is so good for the people that, if necessary, it must be rammed down their throats. In the final section of the next chapter a countervailing force is described which makes many politicians think twice about the expediency of 'forced savings'.

Chapter X

TIME IS OF THE ESSENCE

I do not ask to see the distant scene,
One step enough for me.
Cardinal J.H. Newman

AMBIGUOUS PERCENTAGES

An economic policy proposal can often only be evaluated properly if one knows within what time-span its burdens are to be borne and its benefits to be enjoyed. Many charlatans set out to deceive a gullible public by deliberately obfuscating, or omitting to define, the pertinent time measurement. Though this chapter is concerned mainly with time as a *political* feature in decision-making, it is introduced by a number of eclectic examples which all underline the importance of meaningful time dimensions – unless, of course, there is an ulterior motive for not using them.

The councillors of an industrial city courted popularity when in year one, before the elections to the town council, they announced a 5% cut in municipal taxes which, they explained, would lighten the tax load without reducing the value of any service. The councillors could appear to be magnanimous because they had rejected the town engineer's urgent request for a $100,000 appropriation to repair the sewage installations. The merits of the tax cuts of year one were appreciated only in year three when taxes had to be raised by 15% with the prospect of remaining on this plateau for years to come. The city had become saddled with a bill for $2.2 million to build a completely new sewage facility as the existing one, not having been properly maintained, had broken down and could no longer be repaired.

$3 billion, equal to 10% of the GNP, are officially estimated to have been spent on the construction of new dwellings in year x. No one disputes the correctness of this figure but what does it mean for the welfare of the country? The statistics have nothing to say on this. Hence one does not know whether the houses will bring one hundred years of utilitarian happiness to their occupants or whether they are built to last only ten years. What is politically significant is that only after many years will the population have even the vaguest notion of the use-value of this $3 billion output in year x.

On a cold day in January 1975 the annualized interest rate on the Euro-sterling market jumped to 442%. It was reported in the financial press but the news did not filter through to the wider public which would have greeted this astronomical figure with incredulous astonishment. If only the current affairs producers of the US television networks had been more diligent and discovered the 442% rate, they could have replaced some of their scheduled foreign programmes with a sensationalized broadcast on how a 442% interest rate surely heralded the demise of the capitalist system in the UK. Financial experts, who were conversant with the real time-span of this 442% rate, saw no reason for panic. It was in fact the consequence of a bear squeeze organized by the Bank of England, and covered merely one overnight borrowing period. (The average annualized interest rate on the Euro-sterling market in that month was a modest 12.7%.)

The following is a crude but successful trick promoted by the public relations officials of several British trade unions. Carefully briefed, a striker stands pathetically before the television cameras: 'Why should the managing director of our company draw £15,000 whilst my mates and I only take home £75?' This disparity of 200:1 is meant to arouse public sympathy for the downtrodden strikers. Of course the first figure is before-tax, whilst the second is after the deduction of tax and other items. But the height of this planned demagogy is to contrast a yearly emolument with a weekly payment. Perhaps readers of this book will regard it as too coarse a propaganda stunt to be efficacious. There is evidence that many television viewers are in fact influenced by such phoney comparisons, which is why the stratagem is frequently employed.

On the eve of the second general election in 1974 the cost-of-living index in August rose by less than 0.1% over July. Denis Healey, the socialist Chancellor of the Exchequer, knew of course that this was a fluke; it had much to do with a seasonal drop in food prices and a reduction in VAT, which he had cleverly implemented before the elections and could have only a once-for-all statistical effect. Nevertheless, the 'miracle' had to be sold to the innocent electors. Healey declared that when the Labour Party took over from the Conservatives in March 1974 the inflation rate, on an annualized three-monthly basis, had been running at 19% but the socialists had been able to reduce this to 8.4%. As soon as the elections were over and Healey's party had won, the real dimension of the British inflation became clearly discernible: in 1974 and 1975 the annual rates were 16.8% and 24.2%. Healey, however, could now afford to be full of remorse in public. Overflowing with contrition he conceded that it had been wrong of him to have cited the 8.4% figure, which had been arrived at by annualizing the percentages of an untypical three-month period. Healey said how sorry he was to have unwittingly given the impression that the 8.4% rate pointed to a decline in British inflation whilst in fact he himself did not think so at the time. Precisely!

Devious forecasters know how to harness the time factor. A well-remunerated consultant to large European companies once shamelessly admitted to me in 1975 that he was happiest when his corporate clients asked him to predict given economic indicators for 1985 and 1990 but that he was reluctant to comply with numerate forecasting requests for the year immediately ahead. He was, and is, not the only one to adopt such a cautious - or cynical? - posture. There must surely still be alive some old people who can recall the religious fervour with which the first Wilson government's National Plan was released to a trusting public. It contained detailed forecasts on how the economy would develop in the following six years. Hundreds of pages told citizens what life would be like in 1970 as compared with 1964. The 1970 predictions were said to be based on *year-by-year* projections that had been calculated by the government's planners. Strangely, however, the British public was only given the annual average growth figures for the *whole* forecast six-year period. George Brown, the boisterous architect of this expensive statistical nonsense, hoped that the National Plan would yield his party big political dividends. As a clever politician he therefore did not reveal the projections for the *individual* years of 1966, 1967, etc. Had he done so, the National Plan would soon have been debunked as a hoax. Instead, he asked people to wait till the end of 1971, the earliest date at which the accuracy of his political-statistical project could be tested. George Brown had been in politics for a long time and knew there was little reason to fear that people would remember six years hence what had been published under his imprint in September 1965. There was also the chance that he might then no longer be the responsible minister. If he had that last consideration in mind then this was indeed an implicit prediction which came true.

When in 1973 the Conservative Chancellor of the Exchequer ordered the Bank of England's printing press to work overtime in order to stimulate euphoria generally, he shrugged off accusations that he was thereby kindling the fires of inflation. He was right of course if the time scale of his actions was measured in months – the bitter crop was not harvested till 1974 and 1975. The editor of *The* (London) *Times* is an adherent of the monetarist school which maintains that excess money supply (the increase in the money supply above the growth of a country's output) basically determines the rate of inflation.[118] To test this he compared the creation of excess money supply in given years with the price increases in those same years, but no correlation was formed; sometimes inflation grew faster and sometimes slower than the excess money supply. His faith in monetarism was only restored when he compared (over a ten-year period) the British excess money supply of years 1, 2, 3, etc. with the inflation of years 3, 4, 5, etc. The rates matched closely. So tightly did the cap fit that Rees-Mogg could show that an average annual 9.4% rise in the excess money supply during the years of 1963 to 1973 was equalled exactly by a 9.4% growth of inflation in the 1965-75 period. Such a two-year time-lag is worth gold to cunning politicians.

SPELL OUT THE TIME SCALE!
Time is often a weighty factor in the economic calculus – but not always. Time only plays this role when it is possible to choose between suffering now instead of later, benefiting today rather than tomorrow. These options do not always exist. The citizens of a besieged city cannot heed the warning that it is 'economically'

wasteful to eat seed potatoes rather than plant them when the alternative is death through starvation. British Leyland was approached in 1973, together with other automobile companies, to finance an expensive group study on the 1990 world demand for cars. British Leyland turned down the proposal and gave as a reason that it was in acute financial difficulties. The contingent benefits that would accrue from knowing about marketing conditions in the remote future had to be sacrificed because its available finance was needed for the payroll of the immediate future.

When a nation is involved in a life-and-death conflict ordinary time considerations do not apply. Everything is concentrated on the present. Goering ruthlessly cancelled all Wehrmacht projects which were unlikely to bear fruit until after the war. [107] During the Battle of Britain in 1940 Lord Beaverbrook, as head of the Ministry of Aircraft Production, was castigated by many for disrupting the orderly procurement of weapons for the army. He pirated scarce resources destined for the production of tanks and guns in order to divert them to aircraft factories. By thus increasing the production of aeroplanes, he helped to slow down the output of other war materials. Beaverbrook's justification was that unless the *air* Battle of Britain could be brought to an immediate successful conclusion, Germany would win and if that were to happen the army would no longer need tanks or guns.

The ships built in the war-time Kaiser Californian yards were of low quality. By peace-time standards they were not commercially viable. The value of a ship is ordinarily determined by the ton-years of its useful life. It is more economical – in terms of finance, materials and manpower – to produce one solidly-built vessel with a prospective twenty-year durability than ten ships which do not last more than two years. Yet Kaiser's decisive contribution to the allied war effort was his shipbuilding techniques which ignored the seeming waste of constructing vessels that would soon become obsolescent – the only criterion was that they should not break down before the war ended. Conventional time considerations applicable to capital assets were justly ignored when the order of the day was to produce speedily the largest number of ships.

Ordinarily, however, people do not face the predicaments of starvation, bankruptcy or war. They are more likely to be in 'normal' situations where they can make a rational time choice between two or more feasible options. Youngsters must decide whether it is preferable to leave school at sixteen and immediately earn money or whether to become non-earning students. In weighing up the merits of these alternatives they will set the notional loss of earnings between sixteen and twenty-one against the increments of consequentially bigger earnings between twenty-one and sixty-five.

In a poor, heavily populated, country with merely ten cancer specialists, only a small minority of those needing their services can in fact receive them. Should the authorities order these doctors to stop looking after patients so that, as full-time teachers, they might train one hundred students to become cancer specialists after completing a six-year course? This would cause much agony during the interim period though at the end of it the country would then have one hundred-and-ten doctors who could bring succour to all requiring cancer treatment. If the time perspective of the country's decision-makers is $6\frac{1}{2}$ years or less, this cruel proposal would clearly be rejected. However, if they think of the overall benefits which would accrue in a longer time-span, they might give it favourable consideration.

A less melodramatic, but in principle identical, time-dilemma is presented by the discoveries of finite quantities of oil-gas in the North Sea. Lest the author be embarrassed, I shall not give the source for the following: 'It is important that oil should be produced at the optimum rate for the maximum benefit of the economy.' Laymen reading this gibberish may suspect that it hides some erudite message from a learned economist. In fact it has no intelligible meaning, because it does not spell out the most important factor in the national debate on what is to happen to Britain's fuel resources: *over what period of time shall the oil-gas bounty be exploited?* The political decision-makers are faced with real options. Shall they bring much material happiness to those alive now and therefore deplete all the reserves within fifteen years? Or shall the enjoyment of the oil-gas be spread over thirty or perhaps one hundred years? This is essentially a political question and economists have few professional qualifications to help answer it. All of us, however, have the right to demand of the decision-makers that in propounding their fuel policy the time-span, over which the benefits are to accrue to the British people (and the investors in the oil companies), shall be set out clearly and unambiguously.

FIVE TIME PREFERENCES

When we say of an individual that his preference is for consumption today rather than tomorrow, this does not imply that he necessarily wishes to consume all his earnings today and save nothing. Similarly, when it is asserted of another individual that he tends to prefer consumption tomorrow, we do not mean that he is prepared to forego all current consumption and seeks to save all his earnings. It is rarely an all-or-nothing issue but ordinarily revolves around a marginal slice of income. To assume otherwise would be to behave like the celebrated acquaintance of a famous professor of economics. He was a poor tramp who had found a one-hundred-dollar note and made a bee-line to the nearest restaurant where he impatiently ordered one hundred dollars' worth of ham and eggs. [14]

a)   There are individuals who so value today's consumption that they are prepared to increase it by sacrificing tomorrow's consumption. These are extremists who, in a given year, aim to consume more than they earn currently; they cover the difference by borrowing. The availability of instalment credit for durables caters for the demands of such people. Less pervasive is borrowing for holidays. Whilst most families temporarily reduce their living standard by regularly putting aside money for a future vacation, others are not prepared to lower their consumption beforehand and consequently borrow. This means that having taken a loan of $200, they must pay $250 (to cover also interest) in the post-vacation period and reduce their consumption accordingly.

b)   A less extravagant mode of preferring today's consumption to that of tomorrow is to spend in the present all one's current earnings and past savings. Nothing is put aside for the future however luscious the fruits of saving promise to be. Unilever used to have a pension scheme with both employers and employees contributing a percentage of the wages; the pension, at sixty-five, was based on the joint contributions of both sides. The fund manager explained the company's generous policy when an employee resigned before reaching retirement age: '. . . an employee leaving service (before he became entitled to his full pension). . . was given the choice between taking paid-up pensions derived from the *whole* of the employer's contribution as well as his own . . . or of taking a return of his own contribution with interest. I will not go so far as to say that pressure is put upon him, but he is required to sign a statement on which detailed figures are set out so that he can see clearly that the return of his contribution is a far less valuable right than the paid-up pension.'[116] This means that people were given a choice between an immediate cash payment of £100 and an entitlement to deferred benefits worth £200 (plus interest). The time preference of the Unilever labour force for now-rather-than-later was so pronounced that 65% of the resigning male office staff, and 95% of the male works staff, opted to take immediately the smaller amount and thereby gave up their right to receive a much larger amount in the future.

c) Some people have a time preference for tomorrow which is conditional on the reward for giving up consumption today. When offered, say, 4% interest, they will not save but at 10% they are willing to defer consumption. For this category the prospective profitability of their invested savings is decisive.

d) There are people whose time preference for tomorrow is so intense that they are prepared to give up consumption today though their savings will not lay any golden eggs. This is sometimes known as the *pure* time preference for tomorrow. There are indeed rational grounds on which to defer consumption even if the savings yield a zero return. Prudence, the wish to leave one's mistress an inheritance, the attainment of independence through owning capital, miserliness – all are possible motivations.

e) The extremists of (d) belong to this category; their time preference is the very opposite of those in category (a). They are anxious about having a nest-egg in the future and, if necessary, will exchange a foregone consumption of £100 today for £90 consumption tomorrow. Robinson Crusoe was one of them. Although he knew that mice would gnaw at his inventory, he was so bent on accumulating a reserve that he went short of food to put some grain aside for a possible emergency. In the language of economists, he saved at a negative rate of interest. There were times when the Swiss government penalized foreigners for putting their franc-denominated savings into Swiss bank accounts. The banks were not allowed to pay them any interest but were under a statutory obligation instead to charge foreigners interest for the privilege of looking after their money. Some foreign depositors consciously preferred to forego the pleasure of spending now 100 Swiss francs on buying caviare in order to accumulate capital in Switzerland which tomorrow, after paying the negative rate of interest, would be worth only 90 francs.*

ROY HARROD AND THE STUPID PUBLIC
If each citizen would declare to which of the above categories (a, b, c, d or e) he belongs, we would know of the personal time preferences of all the individuals of a given society. However, we would still be completely in the dark about the actual consumption-investment pattern of that society. The desire of a majority of the population to opt for a current consumption volume which exceeds their current incomes will be thwarted when there are not enough individuals, on the other side of the barrier, who are willing to match this desire by deferring their own consumption and lending funds to eager borrowers. In addition, as was pointed out in Chapter VIII, the modern state has ways and means to frustrate its citizens' wishes by inducing 'forced savings'; the government may promulgate compulsory subscriptions to state loans; the authorities may pass a law forbidding instalment credit; employers may compel their employees to defer consumption through payroll deduction for pensions; etc. Thus personal time preferences do not determine the division of the GNP into consumption and investment. Nevertheless, they are still highly significant, particularly to politicians who seek to ascertain the aspirations of their constituents.

---

* There were foreigners who, notwithstanding the negative interest, were happy with their Swiss bank deposits because they speculated on the franc ultimately appreciating in value against other currencies. Such unworthy creatures have no place in category (e).

Whilst it cannot be proved decisively, politicians are increasingly coming to the conclusion that *the vast majority of citizens prefer, in varying degrees, consumption today to consumption tomorrow.* Many economists assert that this is true *and* undesirable, which is why some of them portray the majority of the public as stupid animals. Many moralists have also reluctantly concluded that their fellow-citizens are uneager to save enough – hence they denounce them for being selfish in not considering the welfare of future genera-tions. (The Club of Rome wants our generation to ponder on the fate of mankind in a hundred years.) Many economists and moralists – sometimes they are the same persons – propose that, to remedy the ills which flow from the selfishness of the majority of the public, the state ought compulsorily to divert resources from consumption to investment.

When the ignorant public prefers consumption today to the future pleasures which await those who defer consumption, then – to cite Pigou's elegant phrase – its 'telescopic faculty is faulty'.[25] Feldstein gives a plethora of sources to back up his contention that 'economists have long believed that individuals irrationally discount pleasures merely because of their futurity'.[26] Sen is an academic economist who is not prepared to join in the economic discipline's onslaught on the putative illogicality of the public's preference for current consumption. Sen concedes that it may be perfectly logical but he still condemns the man-in-the-street for being guilty of 'rapacity'.[27] These accusations of selfishness are echoed in the writings of many other economic moralists. The most acrimonius comment has come from the pen of Roy Harrod. Those who do not save voluntarily as much as Harrod thinks they ought to are culpable of 'rapacity and the conquest of reason by passion'. This meek academic denounces with venom his fellow-citizens' alleged weaknesses: 'We may be dead at the future date and not rate the welfare of our heirs as highly as our own. The desire to use the money now is reinforced by animal appetite. Greed may be thought to be as appropriate a name for this attitude as time preference, though less dignified. Time preference in this sense is a human infirmity, probably stronger in primitive than in civilized man.'[34]

Economists, who negate the political philosophy which would accord to each individual the liberty to decide what proportion of his income he shall save, are busily drawing up blueprints for the enforcement of 'optimum'* rates of non-consumption. How to design these is the subject-matter of many learned articles on both sides of the Iron Curtain. The 'optimum' debate centres on the twin issues of the size of the investments to be undertaken directly by the state and the amount of force that governments ought to exert to make the present generation sacrifice itself for the coming generations. There are not many living economists who do not somehow favour state interventionism to augment investments. A few are prepared to limit the government's role to merely 'influencing' the saving propensity of individuals. (They have in mind Pigou's modest proposals to achieve this by abolishing taxes that militate against capital accumulation and giving tax exemptions to savers-investors.) The majority of modern economists, however, do not believe that the state should play around with kid gloves. They demand that governments, having set an 'optimum' consumption-investment schedule, should use their iron fists to make the public comply. Of course, this is to be done for the good of the ignorant, selfish citizens who do not care enough about the welfare of their yet unborn sons. What if the 'optimum' rate blatantly contradicts the personal time preference of the public? We ought to be grateful to Harrod for spelling it out: '... on the assumption ... that a government is capable of planning what is best for its subjects, it will pay no attention to pure time preference ... '

THE POLITICIANS HAVE THEIR WAY

Sages in university cloisters design schemes to force people to save against their wishes and sermonize about the duty of politicians to compel the selfish masses to reduce consumption. In the end, however, it is the politicians who must do the dirty work. Albeit many of our rulers agree privately with the sentiments of Harrod and his colleagues, they find themselves unable to translate them into practice. However strenuously politicians may deny it, they usually have no choice but to pay court to the infamous time

---

* In academic literature this 'optimum' concept is connoted either, as Tinbergen [32] did, the 'optimum rate of saving' or, as Horvat [31] described it, the 'optimum rate of investment'.

preferences of their electors and consequently give priority to policies that yield short-term results.*

Some politicians do not even have the constitutional authority to make important decisions, particularly those of a long-term character, until they have obtained prior, explicit, consent from the electorate. The ministers of the Swiss government lack the independent power to rule effectively because the people have to be consulted at frequent referendums. The Swiss seem to be getting progressively bored with their form of democracy: whilst until 1960 usually 60% of the electorate participated, the voting proportion in many of the referendums since has declined to about 35%. This dependence of the executive on the outcome of referendums is so weighty that it deprives the Swiss government of the capacity to take decisions on its own, even on matters which in other political democracies are regarded as relatively unimportant. In June 1976 a government proposal to grant an interest-free loan of 200m francs to a United Nations agency for aid to poorer countries was defeated. (The Swiss electorate obviously felt that the 0.14% of their GNP, which was already being contributed to international aid, was more than enough.) Many local politicians in the US are similarly restrained from independently implementing certain public expenditure because it demands the prior consent of the taxpayers in a plebiscite; this is especially so when bonds are to be floated to finance infrastructure investments. The municipal councillors of Chicago, for example, are weak creatures in that even the building of new hospitals must be ratified by the electors through a referendum.

Legislators in most other democracies have clearly more power than the Swiss and Chicago politicians, because they only face their

---

* Though the selfish time preferences of the electorate leave their main impact in the shaping of government policy relating to long-term investment, they may also affect politicians' decision-making in other areas. T.E. Smith believes that the time preferences of the majority of the population are the main cause for the unwillingness of the leaders of the Third World to give birth control the attention it deserves: 'Decisions to restrict immigration may pay immediate political dividends in terms of the possibility of reducing unemployment and of providing a larger share of the cake . . . for indigenous people. Decisions to attempt to control the natural rate of growth of population through fertility reduction cannot pay immediate political dividends.' [108]

electors after three to five years. Yet even this relatively longer
time-span makes it often unattractive for them to take a long-term
view of big issues. Many strong politicians come to power
determined that they will not be immersed in current issues only
but will also find time to reflect on long-term policies. The original
intentions are no doubt sincere but are almost invariably drowned
by the cold reality of having to think of the next electoral contest.
Magruder, of the Watergate infamy, proposed to Nixon that
regular meetings be held by the administration's top officials
who were concerned with the President's long-term goals. When
Nixon was inaugurated this was thought to be a marvellous
idea, yet top summit meetings of this kind never material-
ized: 'The White House was simply too geared to day-to-
day events ... for anyone of importance to think two or
three months ahead. The important people were the ones who
were on the firing line, not those who were pondering the
future.'[113]

It was an innovation in Britain when Prime Minister Heath set
up a Think Tank in the cabinet office, which was to submit to the
government, at semi-annual meetings, long-term proposals. It was
a conscious attempt to supplement the known preoccupation of
ministers with short-term affairs. Two American political scientists[114] were allowed to interview top British civil servants to
discover whether the institution of the Think Tank had indeed
wrought a beneficial change in the time considerations of the UK's
political masters. They uncovered what no doubt they had already
theoretically discerned before coming to London: British ministers – so their chief civil servants reported – constantly think about
'getting themselves re-elected'. When the staff of the Think Tank
was asked by the ruling politicians to deal with issues, they were
almost exclusively 'attractive issues'; the authors define these as
matters that could have an immediate impact on the active political life of the ministers. The Heath government did not show
interest in issues, however fascinating, 'that might go on at a later
date'.

Strong supporting evidence has since become available with the
publication of a revealing book by Peter Walker, who was a
prominent member of the Heath administration: 'The basic
weakness of our present society is that by its very nature our party

and parliamentary system encourage the use of temporary expedient at the expense of the long-term solution.... Looking back upon the Conservative government of 1970-74, one of my regrets is that we did not as a cabinet find the time to stand back from the day-to-day pressures and talk over the long-term strategy we wished to pursue.* We would all have benefited if periodically we could have spent two or three days together discussing the longer-term objectives....'[97]

A similar spirit had pervaded the 1964-66 Labour government. In January 1965 the Chancellor of the Exchequer (Callaghan) wanted the government to adopt some realistic measures that were likely to prove unpopular. This was at a time when the Labour government was about to lose its majority in the House of Commons and therefore had to consider that it might soon have to face the electorate. Crossman reported this of a cabinet confrontation: 'Callaghan said that we must end illusions and tell the people honestly that expenditure was exceeding economic growth and that this could not go on. George Brown replied that too much probity would destroy us; if we took Callaghan's advice we should be ruined. We now had to make a short-term calculation and dispense with the assumption that we were going to stay in office for three or four years.... So our whole tactic had to change. We must now have nothing but short-term tactics and prepare an offensive designed to put the blame back on the Tories.' [105]

Politicians are very concerned with two public relations aspects of government expenditure: the transfer of resources from the taxpayers to the coffers of the state should proceed as painlessly as possible and the actual expenditure should lead to the maximum of *immediate* happiness. Within the confines of a given departmental budget, the Minister of Education has some discretion in varying the respective allocations for investments and current educational items. He will, however, remind himself that the gestation of some investments may be five years, which is too long a period to make

---

* The Permanent Secretary of the Department of Trade and Industry was asked by a parliamentary committee how governments arrive at decisions. Well versed in English understatements, he replied, 'If I were rash I would say that all governments tend to look at things in the short term but that would not be entirely fair; short-term pressures do however loom pretty large'. [33]

them politically very useful either for himself personally or for his party. A disingenuous politician weighs on the political time scales new school buildings versus higher subsidies for school meals, better teaching equipment versus higher salaries to appease the teachers' lobby. The Minister of Health has to deal with a similar set of options. Taking a long view it might be desirable to allocate a very large part of his budget for investments in new hospitals and expensive surgical equipment. He will, however, be tempted to consider the politically attractive alternative of gaining immediate popularity by abolishing prescription charges and giving liberal pay rises to the employees of the state medical services.

A government announcement to build a bridge delights the electors in the favoured region. Consulting engineers have prepared two schemes for the political decision-makers: at a cost of $100m a bridge with a durability of twenty years can be built whilst an expenditure of $120m would make it possible to erect a bridge with a durability of forty years. If one thinks in terms of welfare spread over forty years, then the $120m expenditure is obviously a better economic proposition, but if my description of what makes most politicians run has any validity they will be sorely tempted to opt for the $100m scheme.

State-owned corporations obviously suffer more than the private sector from anti-investment political expediency. When governments have to cut public expenditure, the axe first falls on the (previously agreed) capital budgets of the nationalized corporations. Nigel Lawson, a member of the House of Commons Expenditure Committee, explained why: 'I do not think it is so puzzling that there is a concentration on capital (expenditure cuts) because it is politically easier to lay off building than to lay off people.'[19] We have it on the authority of Richard Marsh, the erstwhile chairman of British Rail, that 'none of the five-year investment plans the Railway Board has produced has remained intact for more than six months because of the conflict between the short-term problems of government and the long-term objectives of the Railway Board'.[115] In 1974 Marsh asked twelve major material suppliers to the railways what price reductions they would make in return for five-year supply contracts. Substantial reductions were offered and the resultant savings would have amounted to tens of millions of pounds. Yet, because capital expenditure is a political football, no fixed orders on a regular annual basis could be placed by British Rail. The Treasury officials would not allow this, for they knew that budgetary allocations for capital goods, as distinct from those for wages, are always subject to political revision.

In October 1975 the Chancellor of the Exchequer, Denis Healey, made himself unpopular at his party's annual conference. He said among other things, 'Investment is not a soft option. The most difficult thing in a democracy is to persuade people to consume less now in order to be able to produce more and have more jobs in the future. But unless we are prepared to do that, all we say about industrial regeneration is claptrap.' The sentiments were certainly not novel. They were only remarkable because they were professed by an astute politician when actually holding office. I am sure he meant what he said and intended to act accordingly. He was soon put to the test. A few months later, in February 1976 and again in December 1976, the economic situation demanded severe cuts in public expenditure and, with difficulty, he persuaded his cabinet colleagues that they were indeed necessary. From the published details of the global cuts, it is clear what had happened during the cabinet deliberations. Only very few current expenditure cuts were agreed to by his colleagues. Instead, most of the government departments and nationalized corporations were instructed to reduce severely their capital spending. Farm subsidies, school meals and most social expenditure items were left untouched – the Healey programme centred largely on building fewer schools, hospitals, prisons, fire stations and entailed a curtailment in the procurement of new machinery for the state-owned corporations. At the end of the day Healey behaved as politicians almost invariably behave when they ponder on what the electors would really prefer.

Though, in theory, the dictatorships of the Comecon world are immune from the populist forces to which Healey had to succumb, increasing attention is now nevertheless being paid in those countries to the time preferences of the people. It was noted in Chapter IX that investment (as a proportion of the GNP) has been declining sharply in Eastern Europe. In September 1976 things came to a head in Poland. In the wake of growing consumer unrest, the government was forced to announce publicly that henceforth top priority would be accorded to agriculture, food processing and consumer goods at *the cost of industrial investment*. Prime Minister Piotr Jaroszewicz told the discontented comrades that massive industrial investment could not continue at the pace of the preceding five years; he cited figures to prove how the growth of investment had already been halted. [150]

Though they are mutually inconsistent, the thesis outlined in the preceding chapter and the conclusion of this chapter are both facets of the same major dilemma which politicians have to live with. Many of them sincerely believe it to be in the public interest to reduce consumption in order to raise the investment level. They also have the know-how to handle the fiscal and monetary instruments of the state machinery to bring about 'forced savings'. When faced with the choice of expending public money on either new investments or keeping existing capital goods in good order, politicians aim to opt for the glory of the former. But, irrespective of their personal inclinations, politicians sooner or later encounter the stark electoral reality that increased support for investments runs counter to the cursed time preferences of the people on whose votes they depend. It ill behoves those who practise their craft without being elected to it by popular franchise – stockbrokers, journalists, television commentators, academics, business executives – to denounce politicians as being either stupid or cowardly. The majority is neither. What bears constant repetition is that politicians know better than others that they can only survive by being re-elected. Unlike many of their critics, politicians comprehend the pivotal significance of the time factor in economic decision-making.

Chapter XI

THE WEAKNESSES OF
STRONG CORPORATIONS

We are big, but bigger we shall be,
We cannot fail for all can see
That to serve humanity has been our aim.
                    IBM company anthem

THE SELFLESS CORPORATE AUTOCRATS

Standing on a soapbox, of course it feels good to point to the glaring inefficiencies and 'uneconomic' performances of state-owned enterprises but it is spurious to make the boastful claim that privately-owned corporations are *automatically* more efficient. Despite the weighty impact of political externalities, the managers of non-state firms clearly have more effective managerial powers than their confrères in charge of nationalized companies. It does not follow, however, that (even when free to do so) the chief executives of modern corporations conduct themselves like the profit-maximizing entrepreneurs who figure prominently in economic textbooks.

The same motor that propels politicians in office also drives business magnates – they all love to do something impressive, are enamoured of big capital-intensive projects, and aim at building a mighty empire by enlarging and diversifying the activities of their department or corporation. Above all – unlike the majority of nineteenth-century capitalists – the modern tycoon seeks the affection of the man-in-the-street though this can often only be secured at the expense of his company's shareholders, employees and customers. When, probably between fifty and sixty, a loyal company man has reached the top rung of the corporate ladder and is appointed chief executive officer, he may cease to be motivated by the prospect of higher emoluments. (He will still press his board of directors for a substantial salary increase but this is mainly for the purpose of attaining a higher status amongst his country's executives.) As additional money for his own pocket ceases to be an important element in his life, he turns to the exercise of power, even when it is sometimes only the power of a paper tiger. The chief executive seeks fame; he wants to see his name regularly in the papers. Hence he will want the company of which he is the head to do socially acceptable things and make charitable contributions. He may also dream that the opportunity will arise for him to announce at a press conference that his engineers have perfected a new technological process which will help to eliminate some harmful pollution effects. Perhaps he is preparing for the day when the television cameras will focus on him as the entrepreneur who has inaugurated the world's largest aluminium processing plant. The Company Acts of the Western world place a statutory obligation on company directors to optimize profits for the benefit of those who have subscribed the equity capital. This injunction, however, is frequently ignored when the personal (non-material) interests of the chief executive clash with corporate profit-maximization. Peerages are rarely given in the United Kingdom for managing an efficient, profitable enterprise – if the chief executive wishes to become a Lord, he had better manipulate his company affairs in a manner which appears to be consonant with the current social sentiments of the community. A businessman in the United States, striving to be invited to a musical soirée at the White House, will not have improved his chances if wide publicity is given to a shut-down of one of his factories with resultant mass redundancies – even though the exercise helped to raise his company's overall profits. Perhaps the height of vanity is to cultivate the image of a 'good guy' when appearing on popular television programmes. The viewers will not be charmed by a giant corporation's chief executive who boasts of having raised the return on capital. So much better to be able to tell the interviewer that the company has just appointed a young, black lady to the board; this will prove how progressive he is and how much he favours youth, the non-Caucasian races and women's liberation.

Many US executives refuse to sanction company illegalities, even when they thereby harm their corporation, because they either disapprove on moral grounds or are not prepared to endanger themselves by taking such personal risks. The 1974-77 Washington disclosures perversely sustain the proposition that those chief executives of big corporations, who chose to violate the law, were often motivated more by the lust for power than by personal material self-interest.* The Church Committee and other investigatory bodies uncovered sordid cases in which the top managers of world-famous corporations initiated or approved deceptions, bribery, corruption and the falsification of accounts. This raises two fascinating issues which are unrelated to the intrinsic immorality of the plots. The first points to the arrogance of those chief executives who believed that their misdeeds would not be exposed and, if by chance they were, would not lead to the punishment of the wrongdoers. The second is sociologically more alluring. Most of the American company illegalities were targeted to increase sales, obtain government subsidies, bend the price controls and thwart hostile edicts from administrative agencies in Washington. The objectives did not include the attainment of financial rewards for the executives who implemented or authorized the transgressions of the law. Why did a high-ranking legal executive launder the money of his employer and then personally carry the dirty funds across several national borders? It was to enable his corporation (under duress) to make an illegal contribution to the Nixon campaign. The courier did not expect to receive a yacht. He endangered himself because he wanted to further the fortunes of the corporation which had made him a vicariously influential and powerful member of the business community in his state. The Spanish inquisitors tortured their victims to glorify God; diplomats the world over practise deceptions and utter lies for the sake of their country; these corporate criminals broke the law to aggrandize the companies for which they worked. (Some of the executives may have hoped to derive non-material prestige through their association with a growing corporate enterprise – in this sense, therefore, they were not pure saints.)

The modern company executive who has reached the top is a

---

* Some of the guilty executives, who were selfless economic criminals, received their punishment from an unexpected quarter. Idealism is not always appreciated – hence a few were dismissed from their jobs by ungrateful boards of directors.

strange animal. At times he uses disreputable means to increase corporate profits whilst on other occasions he charts a course which deliberately leads to reduced profits in order to enhance the public good (as he sees it). Before dealing with genuine conduct of this kind, one must first deal harshly with those many acts of sham Social Responsibility which public relations officers sell as idealistic corporate conduct. When a firm spends money on clean lavatories, spacious employee dining rooms and air-conditioned offices, it is nonsense to call this the 'welfare-inspired generosity of a good employer' – more often than not it is a sound policy to increase labour productivity by improving the conditions of work. Sweden's Atlas Copco was once praised for meeting a 'social responsibility challenge' by developing a silent air-compressor. An investigation of this noble deed reveals that the company had far-seeing directors who anticipated that some countries would soon legislate to outlaw the traditional noisy compressors. Indeed Atlas Copco was quickly rewarded for its business acumen when such laws were introduced and consequently it gained the market shares of competitors who had not prepared themselves for this eventuality. One may admire Atlas Copco without attributing to it Social Responsibility. A survey of British corporate charity shows that some contributions, declared to be business charity, are just hidden marketing expenses. One firm admitted that when a big customer is known to be greatly interested in a charitable cause, it may publicly make a donation because 'by means of such a donation reciprocal business may be expected'.[111] Courtaulds has stated frankly that its donations are governed by the consideration that the 'object of charities may be of some direct or indirect benefit to the company or its employees'.[125] An American manufacturer of razor blades sponsors cricket competitions; whatever its directors may say, they are not thereby discharging a Social Responsibility to Britain's national game, because their sole motivation is to gain 'free' commercial publicity whenever the media reports the matches for the Gillette cup.

Leaving aside such unauthentic corporate benevolence, there are numerous ways in which leading company executives exercise their discretionary powers to do things that are not intended to benefit (materially) their stockholders or employees – this has been called 'disinterested philanthropy'. Corporations may give away their goods or sell them at (genuinely) reduced prices to the government, local authorities or 'worthy causes'. Westinghouse proved its patriotism by making atomic reactors for the US government at a nominal profit. [126] Firms have practised inverse racialism by according employment priorities to members of certain ethnic groups, thereby rejecting better qualified candidates from the majority strata of the population. Companies have cleansed their profit-maximizing souls by establishing manufacturing facilities in areas of high unemployment though this brought neither them nor the national economy any material advantage – it was meant to establish the public image of a 'caring' company. Large corporations have been known to operate at a loss in developing countries – with no foreseeable profit prospects – because of their duty (their well-publicized, self-proclaimed, duty) to help the poorer nations. Big firms have been known to regard it as their 'social duty' not to put up prices even when the demand for their products, at existing prices, exceeded the supply: they thereby created a black market.*

There are curious instances of outright philanthropic contributions. A famous firm, which is a market leader in alcoholic drinks, has directors who regard rugby as a game that merits subsidies from their (unconsulted) shareholders. British Petroleum is implicitly censuring the UK legislature for not making sufficient state allocations to art; hence the company policy to sponsor British art exhibitions abroad. United States Steel once had a chief executive who was not satisfied with making speeches about free enterprise and manufacturing steel; he authorized the use of company funds to aid 'selected art museums and symphony and opera societies and otherwise encourage the cultural aspirations of the American

---

* Berle gives a telling example of how social damage was caused by corporate do-gooders in the name of Social Responsibility. In the immediate post-war years there was an acute shortage of automobiles in the US but the three big manufacturers decided that they would nevertheless not adjust their prices upward to a level which was high enough to equate supply and demand. Their motivation, as later publicized by the firms' press officers, was to avoid 'exploiting' the public and not to make super-profits out of shortages. The low list prices produced an effective excess demand for automobiles. The result was that as soon as the cars left the factories, middlemen bought up some of them and made bumper profits from reselling at a premium.

people'. [127]   There is hardly a deserving cause – from the renovation of a cathedral to the building of a dispensary for dogs – which does not have a multinational company amongst its major contributors. Those firms which spend funds in this way, and make sure that everyone knows about it, are accorded 'high generosity ratings'; those who lavishly subsidize art and sport earn the accolade of being 'the most enlightened business firms'. A shadow is cast by cynics on this Social Responsibility. A US investigation concludes naughtily that 'many company officials derive considerable satisfaction from the contribution they, in the name of their company, are able to make'. [134]   A similar sour note was struck by that pink daily paper of the City of London which is hardly hostile to business executives. It reported the donation by ITT of a substantial amount of money to the Western Orchestral Society of Bournemouth. The press officer explained why this was done: 'The support from, and participation in, the cultural activities of Bournemouth was an integral part of ITT's philosophy.' [151]   But why Bournemouth? Journalistic detection evinced that ITT's chairman, the autocratic Harold S. Geneen, was born in Bournemouth! Another respected British publication had this to say of the disinterested philanthropy by one of the UK's largest insurance societies: 'Talking of rowing, I must confess I was not totally convinced of Ernest Bigland's explanation of why the Guardian Royal Exchange Insurance Company so generously sponsored the world rowing championship at Holme Pierrepoint last year, as well as backing a film for TV and the cinema. The...managing director said that insurance and rowing both demand "blood, sweat and tears". I am afraid I suspect impurer motives. Bigland was a keen oarsman when he was at . . . School.' [135]

Individuals are charitably or uncharitably inclined but it is tendentious claptrap to assert that a company *per se* is generous or practises Social Responsibility. A corporation is a dry legal entity, registered in accordance with the company laws and there is no moral substance to the assertion that it has a soul. When executives disburse company funds for exalted purposes that have no connection with the business activities of the firm, they do something improper – at the expense of their stockholders, employees and customers. Where donations are tax-deductible, they also deprive the government of corporation tax revenue. Many of these non-profit exercises are a slur on parliamentary democracy by unelected persons who seek to shape public policy though nobody has appointed them as guardians of the common good. They say that their companies finance exhibitions of modern art and the training of hockey players because the elected representatives of the people have failed in their duty to authorize funds for these purposes. By autocratically disregarding the wishes of his company's stockholders, employees and customers, the chief executive of a rich corporation is frequently powerful enough to give away other people's money for charitable objectives selected in accordance with his personal whims. It is not entirely a selfless exercise because non-material benefits await the executive who basks in the glory of the Social Responsibility of his 'generous' company.

BIG IS BEST

To direct his company with Social Responsibility is by itself not enough to guarantee the chief executive an invitation to shake the hand of the Queen or the President. Unless his good deeds are also publicly noted, this ambition will remain unfulfilled. The bigger his corporate arena, the more will he attract attention and therefore the greater his chance to shine in the national limelight. The top executive, who seeks public recognition and honours (and not the satisfaction of managing a highly profitable enterprise), will be personally motivated to make his big corporation even bigger.

What is newsworthy 'bigness'? To be the largest employer in a given area or industry is clearly of journalistic interest. To be appointed as the manager of the world's most extensive potato-crisp factory deserves a picture in the tabloids. But the corporate bigness which interests most chairmen and presidents of growing companies is the size of the turnover or the volume of total sales, because it is that which really makes executives famous. Just as pop stars wish to get into the higher echelons of the record-selling charts, so company executives anxiously scan their corporation's place on the statistical ladders of – to cite the three best-known English-language company charts – *Fortune* (US), *The Times* (UK) and *Vision* (Switzerland). When a press officer issues a release to boast that his company's rank has gone up from last year's sixty-fourth place to fifty-nine in the present pecking order, the reference is to the most beloved of all publicity-earning business indicators: the overall size of the company's global sales.

Economists judge managerial excellence by the return on capital. It is not the size of the company earnings but the rate at which the invested funds have laid golden eggs which measures true profitability. The return on capital may indeed be the most significant economic indicator by which economists evaluate the performance of a management team but it is a criterion which is almost irrelevant to the purpose of gathering wide personal publicity for the chief executive. The ego of the top managers is bolstered by the announcement of big profits, measured in billions of dollars, which hit the headlines. A company with absolute profits of $100,000 and a sensational 40% return on capital will not have this news reported. On the other hand, wide publicity will be given to the whizz-kid who announces at his first press conference that the company he had recently taken over now has earnings in excess of one billion dollars. (Only investment analysts will pay attention to the fact that this great achievement was brought about by lowering the return on capital from the previous 14% to 9%.)

Apart from bestowing personal benefits upon its corporate chiefs, the big corporation also enjoys other advantages. To have on the payroll more than 100,000 employees puts a sword into the hands of the directors with which to smite the government if and when the company runs into severe difficulties. When in the wake of the Yom Kippur war hundreds of British companies, each employing less than a thousand people, were facing bankruptcy, none of their directors could personally plead his case with the prime minister. Yet, British Leyland with more than 200,000 employees was assured that its problems would be repeatedly discussed in cabinet. The taxpayers' purse was opened widely to keep it alive; it is a fact of life that, in this context, 200,000 is a great deal bigger than 200 multiplied by 1,000. Multinationals, which are large employers, have learned to exploit this in many host countries. In 1975 two US multinationals, with a bad managerial record in their UK subsidiaries, came begging to the government asking for assistance. They threatened to liquidate their UK plants and throw many workers out on to the street if the British taxpayer did not supply financial aid or if the government did not buy out their inefficient subsidiaries. Litton Industries only employed 3,000 employees in its typewriter factories whilst Chrysler gave employment directly to 30,000 and indirectly to another 40,000. Being big, according to the number of employees, is an asset not only for the chief executive's access to television, but also when it can pave the way to the purse of British (and other countries') ministers of finance. Litton was small enough to be given the no-go, whilst big Chrysler was granted a mixed aid package of £163m in order that most of its workers would remain employed – at least for the time being.

Being big also allows a board of directors to featherbed unprofitable activities. Unlike in small companies, loss-making operations of large organizations are often not identified as such. But even when their existence is known, the rotten branches are not chopped off at once. The chairman of EMI knew what he was talking about: 'All large companies tend to hide poor performances behind their profitable operations.' [36] My professional experience has taught me that it is much easier to persuade a big company to start a new product line, plan an additional investment or make a new acquisition than to convince the directors to cease doing something which is blatantly unprofitable. Outside consultants are often perplexed when no action is taken after they have demonstrated how overall profits can be raised by throwing out the bad apples. Not only does bigness enable a corporation to bear losses of one of its branches with impunity, but there is sometimes a managerial incentive not to increase profits by giving up non-viable sales. The wicked comment has already been made: the prestige of many executives is determined by the bigness of the total – profitable *and* unprofitable – turnover for which they are deemed responsible.

It may not necessarily be a good thing for the national economy, but, from the standpoint of the individual corporation, bigness is a definite advantage for empire-building. In the pre-war years many big companies became bigger by expanding horizontally, i.e. buying up their competitors. Anti-trust legislation today impedes such a development. One alternative is vertical integration whereby, for example, a textile manufacturer buys a fibre-making plant and acquires textile retailers. This form of expansion is still less frowned upon than horizontal growth, but is also becoming subject to public criticism, particularly in the US. A new growth trend is to buy up companies which make products that, though physically and technically different, compete in the market place with the output of the bidder. Thus match companies have acquired manufacturers of cigarette lighters, oil companies have bought coal mines, and razor-blade firms have taken over enterprises fabricating electric shavers.

These three trails to growth have an economic rationale. This cannot be said of the main avenue along which, in the post-war years, big firms have expanded: diversification for the sake of diversification by acquiring companies the products of which have no conceivable connection with the bidder's products, manufacturing capacity or customers. The successful producers of cough pills haughtily assume that their managerial geniuses will be equally good at directing the making of paper underwear. Here are a few Anglo-Saxon firms, which have bought up existing companies in completely unrelated fields:

Telecommunications	*ITT*	cosmetics
Newspapers	*Thomson*	oil
Fertilisers	*Fison*	scientific instruments
Tobacco	*Phillip Morris*	seafoods
Paper	*Bowater*	commodity trading
Car dealers	*Lex*	hotels
Textiles	*Textron*	plywood
Television	*CBS*	toys
Tobacco	*Imperial Tobacco*	sheep-breeding
Betting	*Ladbroke*	real estate
Entertainment	*Loews Theatres*	pet foods
Stationery	*Ryman*	coffee-making machines
Contraceptives	*London Rubber*	wine shops
Tobacco	*Reynolds*	plastic packaging
Hotels	*Grand Metropolitan*	milk products
Paper	*Reed*	vineyards
Car accessories	*Gulf Western*	films
Tea	*Brooke Bond*	hydrofoils
Tobacco	*American Brands*	pumps
Footwear	*Sears*	shipbuilding
Tobacco	*Liggett and Myers*	breakfast cereals
Sugar	*Tate and Lyle*	furniture

Whatever else is in dispute about the merits of the growth policies of the corporate giants, there can be no argument about the strength of the big company to carry through acquisitions (good and bad); this is a pronounced advantage which it enjoys over the medium-sized company. It applies in all three financing areas: borrowing, printing, and using retained profits.

It is a sad, unpalatable, fact that banks are more eager to lend $100m to a big firm, which has $25m annual earnings (and a return on capital of 9%), than they are prepared to make a loan of $10m to a smaller firm with $3m annual earnings (and a return on capital of 12%). This same economic injustice also prevails in the open money market. Unless a corporation is famous and has a big turnover, it will not be given an opportunity to sell its securities except on prohibitive terms. It is almost always easier and cheaper for big corporations to raise new money.

Unilever, as a public service, distributes educational booklets to schools. In one of them the company explains that 'in order to grow, a business must either invest money saved from its own profits or borrow the savings of other people'.[44] It sounds lovely but leaves out another financing technique, widely employed in the post-war years, which again favours the large organization over its pygmy competitors: big companies can pay for their acquisitions by printing new share certificates that the owners of the victim companies gladly accept in lieu of cash. Contrary to popular belief, big companies do not generally acquire inefficient firms. The return on capital of the victorious big bidders is usually lower than that of the victim companies.[35] Why should the stockholders of a profitable medium-sized firm, or the shareholders of a one-product company (irrespective of size), be willing to accept the freshly-printed share certificates of a relatively less profitable conglomerate bidder? The unsophisticated imagine that logic plus 'fairness' award a higher price to the share with an asset-backing of $100 and 12% return on capital than to the share with an asset-backing of $100 and only a 9% return on capital. The reality is vastly different. The shares of big companies are ordinarily traded at a premium over those of small listed companies. The shares of conglomerates are more highly valued by the market than the securities of comparable one-product companies. Shares of firms with a well-known brand name often have a distinct price advantage, as have the securities of big corporations which are headed by a chief executive with a go-ahead image. At the beginning of the seventies some disillusionment set in with high share valuations that were not justified by asset-backing or profit performance. However, during most of the post-war years many big and famous companies have had the cards stacked in their favour when acquisitions could be paid for with the bidding company's shares.

The alternative to borrowing money or issuing new securities is to decrease the payout of profits and employ the retained funds for expansion. Harry Pilkington is quoted later in this chapter as saying that when a company pursues such a policy, i.e. lower dividends in the present, it *ought* to enjoy the confidence of the investors. This pie-in-the-sky formula has not impressed stock-holders. When long-term investments are known to be financed in this manner (and particularly when the investments are said to be high-risk ones), the share price tends to drop. This has proved especially dangerous for medium-sized firms because the lower share price has enhanced the chance that a bidder will snap up the company. If executives of such companies, the equity of which is owned by outsiders, make excessive use of internal funds for growth, they may find themselves looking for a new job after a clever bidder has gained the favour of the ungrateful stockholders who approve of current high dividends and are disdainful of long-term, risky, investments. A big corporation, however, can more readily use this technique. ICI and General Motors may employ non-distributed profits for expansion without their stock-holders liking it, because it is highly unlikely that in consequence a takeover bid for ICI and General Motors would be launched successfully. The directors of the big battalions can afford to be nasty to their dividend-hungry stockholders without paying a penalty for it.

BIG IS BAD

It has always been recognized that the bigger an organization, the heavier the clay feet which stamp their impression on the flexibility of decision-making and the speed with which resolutions are implemented. Nevertheless, since the days of Adam Smith indus-trialists have sung a hymn of praise for large manufacturing units: the greater the division of labour, the higher the output per man. Hence a factory with ten thousand employees under one roof was idealized as being more efficient than a plant manned by only a thousand workers. In their passion for giant factories, companies have often disregarded that each production process has a point beyond which it is not economical to increase the size of the plant and/or the number of employees. More significant, however, is the growing perception that even where economies of scale are attainable through a bigger manufacturing unit, it is often desirable to forego these because of the social disharmony, higher incidence of strike and general human dissatisfaction which are associated with a large-scale place of work. Many companies in the Western world are therefore consciously opting to manufacture in several smaller plants, deliberately giving up the technical advantages which accrue from producing in one large plant. The Cummins Engine corporation has gone on record that in future it will restrict the number of employees in each factory to 2,500, because the ensuing peaceful atmosphere, as compared with that experienced in a huge factory, is in its view likely to lead to higher productivity. The company has stated explicitly that this policy of negating the past craving for size entails the loss of certain economies of scale. Yet Cummins, and other firms, find it worthwhile to sustain such losses.

To cut down the size of manufacturing plants is a minor matter when compared with the more acute disease of bigness which afflicts mammoth corporations. Some critics have actually proposed that surplus funds should be returned to stockholders when further expansion only exacerbates the malady from which the big companies already suffer. How naive to demand this of corporate executives who press on with growth for the sake of growth! Their selfish striving for personal (non-material) satisfaction – to be derived from a big company becoming bigger – is even more deplorable because profitability often declines as companies swell in size. There is now overwhelming evidence from both sides of the Atlantic that the mad diversification-acquisition strategy of the post-war years has lowered the asset-yield of many big companies. The more fervently company executives have diversified, the steeper the fall in corporate profits! The latest data on the UK [43] illustrates how the shareholders of many bidding companies have been hurt through takeovers – but this was not due to the acquisition of lame ducks. The opposite was the case: big corporations usually acquired profitable firms which, however, soon became less profitable as they were

entangled in the bureaucratic net of the conglomerate. Nevertheless, the belief persists that the bigger companies, the greater the
economic benefits for their stockholders and the country as a
whole. The following five features suggest that this is but a popular
myth nurtured by leading company executives.

1) When a big company makes a socially unpopular bid for a
   competitor, its public relations officers may gently hint that the
   country – and mankind in general – would benefit from the
   merger, because mammoth corporations spend more on R&D
   than small firms. Let us praise bigness because, in the field of
   technical innovations, $1+1=3$ when two firms combine their
   research efforts. So it is said. The total R&D budget of a
   conglomerate with $2 billion sales is naturally larger than that
   of a single-product company with a turnover of $400m. The
   comparison, however, is often spurious because the multinational conglomerate has a number of product divisions and it
   is the research expenditure of single divisions that alone can be
   meaningfully contrasted with the R&D of medium-sized,
   one-product, firms. ITT's total R&D is certainly bigger than
   that of the largest cosmetics company in the world but the true
   comparison is between the perfumery division of ITT and an
   independent perfume company. There are also other grounds
   on which to debunk this R&D apologia for bigness. The
   comprehensive Kennedy-Thirlwall survey [128] substantiates that
   there is no correlation between technological discoveries and
   the size of a firm. In some fields 'diseconomies of scale in R&D
   set in at quite a modest level of firm size'. Furthermore, R&D
   expenditure per pound and dollar of sales is usually lower in
   big companies than in medium-sized ones. To top it all, there
   is no proof that market-dominating octopuses necessarily
   produce more fundamental technical inventions, and they are
   definitely not the quickest innovators.*

---

* When Glaxo sought to merge with other pharmaceutical giants, the
Monopolies Commission prepared a study of the thirty-six (by sales)
largest pharmaceutical companies in the world. One of the arguments,
adduced to justify the proposed formation of a mammoth British pharmaceutical corporation, had been that the prospects for a flourishing research programme would be enhanced if the merger was allowed to go
through. The report would have it that there is 'little relationship between

2) Once a complex organization has passed the $1 billion mark in
    sales, it becomes a ragbag of small and medium-sized compan-
    ies, divisions and independent profit-centres. Catherwood has
    aptly said that such a big corporation is then no longer a
    unified body but 'only a very loose federation of baronies
    where real decisions are taken'. [22] It has been said of General
    Motors that its operating divisions have more autonomy than
    entire industry segments of the Soviet economy. Young
    Americans, who are taught to idealize the dedicated corpora-
    tion man, are imbued with the notion that the single-minded
    directors of Ford spend sleepless nights scheming how to beat
    the competition of General Motors. Such caricatures are
    penned by ignoramuses who have no idea what really moti-
    vates the executives of big companies. Its top managers do not
    dream constantly of how to improve the fortunes of their
    employers. First and foremost they think of the performance
    of their own departments or divisions – and their personal
    promotion opportunities. Salesmen ought to beware telling the
    manager of division A that division B of his company has
    already bought, and is satisfied with, the goods he is trying to
    sell him. The intense personal-cum-divisional strains may be
    such that this seemingly persuasive sales argument can actually
    spoil his chance to sell to division A.

    The top boys at the headquarters of the big corporations
    clearly *attempt* to make all the parts fit into a harmonious,
    cohesive, pattern. Their main weapon is the central allocation
    to the various sections of funds for R&D, sales promotions, in-
    vestments and acquisitions. Armed with knives, and intrigue
    in their hearts, the leading executives fight one another to grab
    the fattest plums from the global company budget. Recent
    revelations about forged company accounts have unfolded how
    leading executives sometimes attempt to hide the truth from
    outsiders (tax authorities, exchange controllers, supervisory
    government bodies). Very little is known in public about the

---

the ranking of the thirty-six firms according to size and the number of
major pharmaceutical inventions produced: the largest firms were not
necessarily the largest producers of major innovations . . . the very largest
firms had been responsible for a less than proportionate number of the
major innovations relative to their share of sales.' [129]

managers of divisions, departments and subsidiaries of big corporations who submit to the chief executive tendentious, often mendacious, *internal* reports on their areas of responsibility. They lie about their sales and present fanciful profit projections in order that, during the head office's annual budget deliberations, they may obtain more financial resources at the cost of their 'competitors' within the company. This internecine fighting is not conducted on gentlemanly lines – it weakens putatively strong companies.

3) The most fragile facet of the, allegedly powerful, big corporation is its sensitive socio-political standing. Bigness attracts undesirable attention. We owe it to the company historian of ICI who discovered pertinent minutes of a company committee which show that the (then) directors of Britain's largest manufacturing company were conscious of this already thirty years ago. Meeting under the chairmanship of the finance director S.P. Chambers – later to become the ebullient chairman of the company – consideration was given in 1949 to the possible partition of ICI into several wholly independent companies. The idea of breaking up ICI was broached because 'if we are not careful ... ICI will grow too big to be manageable'. The other motivation for this heretical proposition by the perspicacious directors of ICI was that if their company would keep on growing, it might attract 'public concern'. [130] Today this fear influences the decision-making of many directors who dare not pursue policies that they regard to be in their company's interest because of possible adverse reaction from the public and the politicians. However autonomous the divisions of a big corporation, the company as a whole will be publicly chastised for the misdeeds of each of them. The repercussions from a labour dispute in a subsidiary involving only a few hundred employees can shake the industrial relations of the entire organization and affect a hundred thousand people. A big corporation cannot be flexible enough to give special bonuses in one department lest this become known and arouse discontent in the rest of the organization. I know of a large British business firm which 'voluntarily' desisted from fulfilling a profitable order for South Africa. The employees in the small plant, where the

goods would have been manufactured, were happy because they expected to be called upon to work overtime at premium pay. Nevertheless, the head office decided that the 95% of the corporation's labour force who had no direct interest in this contract, might be alienated and take strike action against their 'anti-social' employer. (A small UK firm whose owners had no such problem happily took on the order.) Thalidomide was a tragic mistake by a British pharmaceutical company; the public has never learned its name because all the publicity centred on the well-known Distillers company of which it was a small part. The Naders and the various anti-establishment groups that publish debunking pen-pictures of business firms obviously pick on famous corporations. Small and medium-sized firms are as guilty as big ones of cheating their customers. Yet their sins and misdeeds have no newsworthiness – the names of big corporations make headlines.

4) Nationalization programmes, all over the world, frequently leave out the small firms. Many restrictive government regulations refer only to the big corporate fish. To cite one example: price controls are sometimes imposed only on the products of the big corporations but even when they apply in general are monitored mainly in relation to the 'powerful' firms.

5) So far as economic crime is concerned, the big corporation suffers from two disabilities. The first is embedded in its bureaucratic structure which, as indicated in Chapter IV, leaves the company wide open to be cheated by its own dishonest procurement officials. The second arises when illegalities are carried out by executives to further the interests of the company; if these are discovered, then the whole corporate organization is exposed to a *social* odium from which smaller companies perpetrating the same crimes are ordinarily immune. The small company has little reason to fear the backlash of public opinion; it can also be more flexible in its arrangements to pay bribes and launder black money. Would the Church Committee have received the publicity it did if the investigated companies had not borne household names? The paradox of the big corporation, said to be so powerful, is that it is veritably weak when involved in deals that demand corrupt

payments. When the big corporation tenders and makes corrupt payments, this – if it is later found out – may spell damaging, protracted, publicity for all its other business activities. The 1974-77 disclosures illustrate that a number of big corporations took this risk and were harmed by the subsequent revelations. Many more large companies, however, took their punishment by not tendering and thus 'voluntarily' forewent sales opportunities.

THE TIME DEVIL

Three (connected) time preferences play prominent roles in the decision-making of the big corporation. They relate to the personal publicity ambitions of formidable chief executives, the impact on investments, and the aspirations of executives to progress quickly on the promotion ladder.

The chief executive of a big corporation

He attains fame by virtue of being the head of a large organization; he remains famous so long as he keeps the job. If he is wise, he will act in anticipation of the certain fate that awaits him on retirement. Men-of-Yesterday – whether politicians, chiefs of nationalized corporations, leaders of mighty trade unions, senior civil servants, or directors of huge multinationals – are no longer asked to come to a television studio to comment on Peru, Chinese cooking or women's liberation; even invitations to open garden fêtes gradually peter out. The chief executive can usually look forward to a five or ten years' tenure; if his quest is for public approbation, he must reap what he has sown *during his incumbency*. Unless he is unselfish, he does not undertake things the costs of which cast a shadow on his stewardship whilst the benefits will be chalked up to the credit of his successor. The founder of IBM understood this well when he had a plaque fixed to the wall in his office: 'Net profits happen this year, not ten years hence ....'[131] This remarkable man wanted to be judged in his lifetime by IBM's current profits. The same principle also applies to the company chairman who prides himself on his Social Responsibility. It is not much use to him personally if he allocates company funds for building a museum for modern art which will only be opened years after his retirement by the then head of the 'generous' company.

Long-term, high risk, investments

The big corporation is in a very much better position to carry these out than the small company, yet many large businesses are less adventurous than they could afford to be. This is the view of Jewkes who has spent a lifetime examining the behaviour of large companies: 'The small firm may have the will to innovate . . . but it may lack the power to innovate because it cannot find sufficient capital. The big firm has larger capital resources and thus possesses the power to innovate, but it may lack the corporate will to do so . . . .'[153] The time preferences of the executives of the big corporations account not only for their reservations on long-term investments but also for the manner in which big companies grow bigger. The corporate giant, on an expansion path, can opt either to lay down new plant for a product innovation or to acquire the existing corporate assets of an active business. To do the former is a time-absorbing process that may take many years to reach fruition. The ambitious knights of industry, however, want to advance quickly and obtain, perhaps within a matter of months, a higher ranking in the charts which is why so many turn avidly to acquisitions. In the sixties, in the UK, the 'typical giant spent more on takeovers than on net new investment in fixed assets'.[35] Many will find it incongruous that important inventions, turned down by big corporations that did not wish to take the risk, have been developed by small and medium-sized companies, the executives of which were unconcerned with the current stock exchange quote for their companies' shares (or, being unlisted, had no share price to watch).

For many years, Chester Carlson, the inventor of what is now known as xerography, failed to induce any corporation to invest risk capital in developing his ideas. Finally, the invention was acquired by the owners of a family-dominated company, Haloid of Rochester, which, between 1947 and 1960, gambled $75m on R&D, twice the amount that the company was earning from its regular operations during that period. As a result, Haloid could only pay a miserable dividend. It financed the development work with its retained profits and issued stock 'to anyone who was kind, reckless or prescient enough'. Many of its executives took most of their pay in the form of new stock; some liquidated their savings and mortgaged their houses.[154] Today Haloid is called Xerox and the original gamblers have become multi-millionaires. History will record that though hundreds of big US corporations had been financially strong enough to take the risk of losing $75m, not one chose to enter upon this precarious venture. It was a medium-sized company that took a seemingly irresponsible risk with the equity capital of its stockholders.

Pilkington Brothers is now a publicly listed corporation with widely dispersed shareholdings, and the present directors are highly sensitive to its current profits as they affect the quoted share price. It was different in 1952 when it was managed as a family concern by its energetic chief executive, Harry Pilkington. A young scientist had then conceived the idea of floating a ribbon of glass on molten metal. Two things were certain: its development costs would amount to millions of pounds and if Pilkington were to finance these it would be necessary to curtail, for a considerable period, the distribution of a large part of the profits which the company was generating on its current activities. However, this was not merely a question of postponing dividends now for higher dividends tomorrow – there was a distinct possibility that the money would go down the drain. Even when the pilot plant had already been built, it turned out unsatisfactory glass for fourteen months. Until a late stage in the initial development phase, during which over £4m was spent (equal to about £22m in 1979 values), it seemed probable that the process would not be a commercial success. By the time the float process had been fully developed, almost seven years from its inception, the R&D costs had swollen to £7m (unadjusted for inflation). A Monopoly Commission report was later to speak of the 'long-established dominance of the Pilkington family within the business'.[160] This is a euphemistic way of saying that Harry Pilkington made the economic decisions on behalf of the Pilkington family, the main stockholders; he either persuaded or bullied them into taking this gamble. Only the family-owned character of the corporation made it possible to avoid becoming dependent on external financial resources and to spend such a vast amount of risk capital in secret over a relatively long period. Now that Pilkington is no longer a corporation where decisions are made at a family council round the kitchen table – could the same thing happen again?

Harry Pilkington today has cause to be proud that his gamble paid off. The floating glass invention was later recognized as one of Britain's greatest post-war technological innovations – and proved highly profitable for the family shareowners. Harry Pilkington set out his corporate philosophy in a speech in Scotland after he had taken the floating glass decision but without of course revealing this to his audience. Preaching to fellow-industrialists, he urged that '... we must persuade our own shareholders to take a long view. Of two companies in identical circumstances making £1,000 profit, the one that pays out £700 and reinvests £300 in the future is worth less, not more, than the one that pays out £300, and reinvests £700 .... So often the open market for shares applies false values.' [132] He went on to scold Britain's sinful shareholders who looked kindly upon companies handing out big dividends instead of favouring (as he thought they should) companies which practise maximum profit retention; he said explicitly that in some cases firms ought to retain all their profits. Harry Pilkington, as the president of the Federation of British Industry, implicitly acknowledged how scornfully shareholders react to investments which are funded by cuts in dividends. In his homiletic address, Harry Pilkington made the hazardous suggestion that the captains of industry should ignore the public's prejudices and finance new projects at the expense of current dividends. In his sermon he neglected to say that whilst such a strategy was feasible in his own family-dominated firm, it would be challenged in other companies by shareholders and executives whose time preferences Harry Pilkington deplored.

The aspirations of executives to reach the top quickly

These give rise to perhaps the most obnoxious time problem of the big corporation.* In theory, executives of multi-product companies owe their prime loyalty to the corporate entity and not to the

---

* Not every office boy of a multinational corporation wants to become its president or chairman. Nevertheless, I advise every employee of an American corporation, who is made to lie on the couch of the company psychiatrist, to answer (when asked about his life ambition): 'I want to be the chief executive.' The employee may be aware that he stands no chance or he may be happy in his present position – not everyone wishes to reach the top echelon. However, it is perilous to make such damaging admissions. An employee who does not dream of the marshall's baton lacks drive and his loyalty is in doubt. The psychiatrist will give him a bad report.

managerial unit for which they are responsible. (The problem is even more complex in multinational organizations, see p. 213). In practice, however, the salaries and bonuses and promotion prospects of the budding managers are discussed at head office in relation to the profit performance of the section, department, division or subsidiary with which they are associated. If the young, vainglorious, executive wishes to attract the personal attention of the company's president, he had better concern himself less with the fortunes of the corporation as a whole and cultivate the profitability of 'his' bailiwick. Profitability is measured by standards which vary with given time dimensions. The man who seeks to become chief executive would do well to cut corners and opt for short-term profits. He must score quick successes in his assignments so that he can move up the ladder before he is too old to be given the first prize. The executive, avidly seeking to be moved on to a higher assignment after managing a division for three or four years, has a personal inducement to mortgage its future profitability if this helps to increase profits during the time he is in charge. An ambitious executive on the way up cares little for the long-term fortunes of the divisions he leaves behind. That this is not a caricature of the modern corporation is evident from the many control mechanisms that big companies are introducing to frustrate their ambitious young men from gaining unsavoury spectacular results. The chief executive of the big corporation often knows first-hand that in a large organization one has to climb over corpses to get to the top. The larger the company and the more numerous its autonomous divisions, the greater is the loss of economic efficiency engendered by this destructive quest of individual executives for promotion.

Chapter XII

THE DREADED DREADFUL MULTIS

I have long dreamed of buying an island owned by no nation and of establishing the World Headquarters of the Dow company on the truly neutral ground of such an island, beholden to no nation or society.... We could even pay any native handsomely to move elsewhere.
      C.A. Gerstacker, Chairman of Dow Chemical [155]

RIGHTEOUS OR EVIL?

Multi is a convenient German synonym for the multinational, transnational, world, cross-national, anational, transglobal, international, corporation. It is only fifteen years ago that the notion of the multinational company began to be aired in the popular media. At present several crusading bodies are seeking to protect mankind from this novel monster. They include the International Chamber of Commerce, EEC, United Nations, International Labour Office, OECD, US Senate Foreign Relations Committee, various international trade union organizations and (a late-comer) the World Council of Churches. Special chairs have been endowed at universities, innumerable seminars held, dozens of books and hundreds of academic papers and thousands of popular articles published – all to satisfy genuine interest in this modern socio-economic-political phenomenon. Demagogues and sensation-hungry journalists find it expedient to depict the multis as world-wide bogeys but staid politicians too find them a profitable target. During the presidential election campaign of 1976, Carter attacked the US-based multis before a television audience of tens of millions. Whether he really believed them to be as harmful as he implied is not important. His advisers must have told him that some derisory words on the multis would be well received and that anyone who castigates them is a 'good guy'. The Carter episode also demonstrates that one does not have to be a left-wing firebrand to be cheered for attacks on the multinational corporation.

The wicked multis are defamed on three counts: they are profit-making organizations (which of course is bad); they are big corporations (which makes it even worse); they either are, or deal with, foreigners (which is by far their worst attribute). Two graves are being dug to bury the multis. They are assailed as exploiters by *host* countries in which they operate and also face increasing hostility from governments, trade unions and public opinion in their *home* country. The two-dimensional enmity to the multis is well illustrated by the behaviour of a Scottish shop steward. This good man used to organize strikes at the local Chrysler factory and, when management refused to knuckle under, he would tell attentive journalists that Chrysler ought to get out of the UK; indeed visiting Chrysler directors from Detroit found scratched on the walls of their Scottish plant, 'Yankees – go home!' Then came the 1975 crisis when Chrysler unilaterally announced that it was packing up. That same shop steward now appeared before television crews to denounce Chrysler for not caring enough about the British proletariat; it seemed that the US multi no longer wanted to exploit the Scottish car workers. Hence the new cry: 'Damn the Yankees for threatening to go home.'

The supporters and opponents of the multis affirm that, by virtue of their cross-border ramifications, they are efficient and mighty organizations; both sides ignore the brittle bones of these international corporate giants. The continued existence of the multis is challenged by the universal attack on private enterprise in general and big corporations in particular – reinforced by xenophobia. Nevertheless, the adversaries of the multis find it expedient to present these fragile creatures as strong corporate vehicles. The socialist Minister of Energy, Tony Benn, once self-effacingly spoke of the powerful multis which 'come to see me ... I am very well aware that I am like a parish councillor meeting the emperor, enormous power – moving their capital, moving their techno-logy'. [112] It is pathetic how Benn imagines himself as David fighting Goliath. Those who sketch (most) multis as business organizations which are neither good nor wicked may expect to be rebuked twice. The enemies of the multis will suggest that it is a whitewashing description whilst the heads of the multis will be annoyed because their economic strength and contributions* to world peace are debunked as fanciful.

An energetic American, Eldridge Haynes, was the first to unfurl the publicity banner of the multis. For quarter of a century, until his death in 1976, he travelled throughout the world extolling the virtues of the international company to all and sundry – even to the top men in the Kremlin. Haynes passionately believed that the multis are a world force for good because, in his view, they are cohesive and powerful organizations. He summarized his faith in the mighty-cum-benevolent multis in this memorable phrase: 'No government *dares* [my italics] bankrupt the (multinational) corporation because that would destroy jobs, cause unnecessary shortages of goods and services, and rob the government of badly needed tax revenue.'[41] At the end of his life Haynes seriously considered that an island should be found where multis could be legally headquartered freed from the interferences of sovereign governments, national taxes and similar nonsense. The following excerpts are taken from a filmed discussion between Eldridge Haynes, Arnold Toynbee (the historian), Orville Freeman (a former Secretary of Agriculture in the Kennedy and Johnson Administrations) and Aurelio Peccei (the vice-chairman of Olivetti and Fiat).

Peccei: 'I know of one step – one small step that seems to me may lead toward something; it is to give the multinational corporation an international charter. It may be located in a real or symbolic territory, but it will give it a non-national identity.'

Freeman: 'Why not an island somewhere that could be the situs for the multinational corporation?'

Haynes: '... the Caribbean.'

Freeman: 'I'll buy that... I think this is exciting... it would constantly remind multinational corporate management that they really are world-wide, and

* The treasurer of General Motors speaks: 'Multinational companies help promote world peace and stability and enable man to use the world's natural and technological resources with maximum efficiency.... By transcending national boundaries, they are a source of hope to the world in solving such continuing problems as hunger, poverty and energy shortages.'[39] Amen!

that they should act and think so ... it would tend
to meet this religious fervour ... by dramatizing
the basic concept that here is a little island
somewhere which these great corporations call
their home. It might even be a member of the
United Nation as family ... '

Haynes: suggested that it might go to Switzerland but ...

Toynbee: said: 'I prefer an island; there are some ex-colonial
islands that have become independent and don't
know what to do about it. I think one of them
might be persuaded to lend itself as a kind of
Vatican City as a seat for the world's multinational
corporations.' [156]

The first academic High Priest of the multis was Howard
Perlmutter of the Wharton School, who in the sixties advanced the
sensational thesis that by 1985 two hundred big privately-owned
corporations would dominate the non-communist world and
control a large majority of all manufacturing assets. This caught
the imagination of unoriginal writers and politicians who have
repeated this forecast, sometimes in slightly different garbs*, as if it
were some divine revelation. Perlmutter's prediction is seen today
to have been an ambitious flight of the imagination but there are
still some who continue to cite it because they need the vicarious
authority of a professor of economics to validate their vaunted
claim that the multis are both dangerous and mighty.

Perlmutter did not just predict. He found the prospect enticingly
desirable. When 'monster firms will be represented in all countries,
war will not be possible'. Why? In his opinion 'the bombing of
suppliers, customers and employees of the same firm will not be
found desirable or permitted'.

What do the adversaries of the multis think? When marxists in
Venezuela kidnapped the local manager of Owens-Illinois, they
demanded a ransom and the publication of their proclamation, at
the company's expense, in several newspapers of the Western world.
One such advertisement [137] declared that as this US company

---

* Lord Banks told Britain's Upper House: 'It has been estimated that by
1980, 75% of the world's manufacturing assets will be owned by some
three hundred multinational corporations.' [136]

was a multi, it deserved to be punished because 'multinationals . . . plunder the country and submit the working class to overt exploitation having sufficient political and economic power to intervene barefacedly into all of the country's internal affairs'. The World Council of Churches echoed similar sentiments when, at its August 1977 meeting in Geneva, multis were denounced as the accomplices of 'repressive states, predatory local élites and racism'. Over the years some members of the House of Lords have been particularly virulent when speaking on multinational corporations; the noble Lord Davies of Leek, for example, called them 'rogue elephants. . . . Should we sacrifice it (i.e. sovereignty) to a group which has no international responsibility whatever, apart from a worship of the God Mammon?'[136] Somewhat more moderately, but in content equally paranoiac, was the assertion by the chief executive of the British Trades Union Congress (TUC) that the multis were 'big enough to influence currencies and economies . . . no single government could control these juggernauts'.[38] On the platform of a United Nations agency, Ralph Nader let the chips fly: 'A most serious international problem caused by "worldcorps" is the way they manipulate or play off nations, governments and rulers against each other . . . . Unions are especially frustrated by this playing-off of nations since striking an ITT subsidiary in Spain *simply* [my italics] means that ITT increases production elsewhere or lets the strikers cool their heels while its empire suffers little.'[138] In an academic study of multis it is said that their policies 'have contributed more to the exacerbation of world poverty, world unemployment and world inequality than to their solution'.[42]

WORKERS OF THE MULTIS – UNITE!

There is a bewitching charm in Perlmutter's bombastic forecast that 'the multinational firm could team up with world-wide unions to further neutralize the nation state'. Some of the international labour leaders – especially the ebullient Charles Levinson, who heads the Geneva-based International Confederation of Chemical and General Workers' Unions* – agree with Perlmutter's ideological

* This is one of sixteen international secretariats (organized on an industry basis) which were formed in the post-war years to exert unified

dream because they too want to abrogate national sovereignties. Those who depict the multis as cohesive, international bodies, which are mighty enough to ignore national governments, applaud Perlmutter and Levinson. The extremists amongst the admirers and detractors of the multis regard the prospect of international labour action as a logical corollary; to them it makes sense that national boundaries are ignored in collective bargaining. They expect Nestlé, for example, sooner or later to negotiate at its Swiss headquarters with a trade union delegation that speaks in one voice for Nestlé employees in various national locations. Levinson has the ambition to attain the authority with which to go to St Louis and, as the spokesman for all the company's employees, bargain with the chief executive of Monsanto. His present aim is merely to sign an agreement regulating the conditions of work in Monsanto's two dozen national subsidiaries but one day, he hopes, it will be possible to negotiate a world-wide corporate wage-scale.

The theory is impeccably sound: a multi can be wounded badly by synchronized strikes of its labour force in different national locations. Not for want of trying have there been no really effective (non-political) cross-border strikes. The Italian unions once called a successful one-hour solidarity stoppage in the Genoa and Milan plants of Nabisco to support their affluent brethren in the US who were in dispute with Nabisco's parent company. There have been other instances of co-ordinated international action by the employees of multis but these have been few in number and their impact has generally been insignificant. When Levinson and his confrères first aired the prognosis that multinational labour groups would soon regularly confront multinational employers, they struck a chord of sympathy and fear with the chief executives of several renowned US companies. (Some of these men had a contempt for the nation-state which equalled that of Perlmutter and Levinson.) The facts are easily established: however impressed

---

international labour pressure on multis. For particularly large corporations, e.g. Michelin, Dunlop, ICI, Unilever, separate world councils were constituted; the employee representatives from the different national companies of a given multi meet occasionally to exchange views on the common enemy and then plot unified action against their international employer. (These meetings of the world councils are said to be usually good fun.)

professors of economics, businessmen and labour leaders are with the logic of international labour action, concrete attempts at cross-border collective bargaining have until now proved abysmal failures.

There are two explanations. First, despite what the uncritical friends and foes of the multis assert, most international companies lack the putative power to disregard the national variations in the labour conditions of the countries in which they operate. Second, the manual workers who are employed by the multis are basically nationalist-minded even though they have an international employer. Famous labour leaders, who are known as fervent internationalists to mass television audiences, nevertheless have to side in real life with the backward nationalist feelings of the workers whose dues pay for their salaries. Victor Reuther and Leonard Woodcock, operating from their Detroit power base, organized and financed the 'world councils' of General Motors, Chrysler and Ford in the hope that through these forums it would be possible to arrive at an active co-operation between the (North American) United Automobile Workers and the employees of the US automobile companies in other parts of the world. When British car workers came out on strike against their US employers, Reuther and Woodcock did not just shrug this off as a labour action in a foreign country – they actually visited the picket lines and saw to it that they were photographed. The UK unions then politely hinted at a solidarity strike in Detroit but this was turned down with regret. When the shoe was on the other foot and General Motors' employees were on strike in Detroit, active help was required from Europe. The British car workers did help – they sent telegrams of warm support. If the dream of transatlantic collaboration between different national unions could not be realized, was there not more hope for common action amongst the European employees of the automobile giants? Ford's management was too wise ever to take it seriously but some journalists avidly reported the 'threat' said to have emanated from conspiratorial meetings where workers' representatives from all of Ford's European plants had pledged to help each other. The crunch came in March 1971 when a protracted strike in Dagenham stopped the operations of British Ford. The Belgian workers reminded the British Ford employees that Dagenham had not come out on strike in support of a recent stoppage in Belgium; hence Belgian help for Dagenham would be limited to messages of solidarity. The German Ford workers adopted a different line. They thought it right, on principle, to halt production at the Cologne plant to aid their British comrades – but, much as they wanted to, it could not be implemented because this would have meant breaking a valid German labour contract. (They did, however, offer to send financial assistance which the British unions turned down as an insulting, ineffectual, gesture.)

The TUC once called a special conference of British trade unions to deal exclusively with the fight against the horrible multis. The then leader of the TUC, Vic Feather, closed the convention with some doleful comments. He told the assembled labour leaders how much he, personally, believed in internationally co-ordinated action against the corporate monsters who were exploiting mankind. But, he added with sadness, it was not very important whether this conference favoured fighting the multis because he feared that their members would not be prepared to heed strike calls in support of the wage claims of trade unionists in other countries. Vic Feather cited a poll conducted amongst the employees of Chrysler's Canadian subsidiary who were questioned on their contingent willingness to walk out (and lose wages) to aid striking workers in Chrysler's other national subsidiaries. 53% said that they would consider this favourably if the strikers were in the neighbouring Detroit plants. When asked whether they would act likewise if the strikes took place in Chrysler's Mexican and British subsidiaries, only 9% and 10%, respectively, responded in the affirmative. The official TUC report on this conference says drily, 'It can be assumed that a similar pattern would apply in the UK to workers in relation to virtually all countries.'

A WORLD CONSPIRACY
The admirers and detractors of the multis are again of one mind: international companies of all nationalities have substantial common interests. If this is so, then clearly great importance attaches to the suggestion that multis *ought* to organize themselves as a pressure group. Eldridge Haynes, for example, confessed that 'individually, the multinational corporation has little influence'. But, he claimed, 'collectively . . . multinational corporations . . .

could . . . alter the course of history . . . Their economic leverage is so great that no nation state can afford not to listen to their collective voice.' [41] What Haynes may have had in mind is orchestrated agitation for free trade, the uninhibited right to invest and disinvest, the dismantling of tariffs and the abolition of discriminatory taxes. Perhaps the multis could become a strong force were they to speak with one voice but in fact the rationale of *individual* multinational corporations counters such a combination (except on an *ad hoc* basis for very limited objectives). It is doubtful whether multis of even one nationality have enough in common to join together in a purposeful trade association which acts as a political pressure group – it certainly would make no sense for a multifarious bunch of international corporations with head-quarters sited in different national domains.*

Multis are competitors and often dirty competitors. When the media alleged that ITT was intervening improperly in the internal affairs of Chile, some multis bitterly complained that – after Allende had expropriated foreign companies – ITT secretly sought to come to an agreement with the new regime and thus undermined attempts to establish a common front of US multis. This is not the first time that international corporations have laid a charge of 'betrayal' against fellow multis. The expropriation of the assets of one foreign company can at times be beneficial to another. The Peruvian government unilaterally confiscated the property of Standard Oil of New Jersey. The victim, the US multi, was not even capable of dissuading other American companies from investing in Peru. 'In October 1968, only days after the initial seizure . . . Occidental Petroleum (a rival US multi) went so far as to offer to help Peru develop the expropriated properties . . .'. [152] If ever the files of the Arab Boycott Office in Damascus are opened, it will be discovered that certain multis have been placed on the

---

* In one sense all multis are brethren – they are blamed vicariously for the sins of other multis. When Hoffmann La Roche, Litton Industries, Lockheed and ITT behaved in a manner which outraged public opinion, other – blameless – international corporations were tarred unjustly. The head of the international division of a US corporation once complained to me that because of certain things that ITT is supposed to have done in Latin America, he had to appear before a Senate committee where his company was subjected to – as he put it – humiliating questioning.

black list because other multis, their competitors, supplied (true or misleading) damaging information about them.

Do all multis subscribe to the view that direct corporate investments should be unrestricted? If one reads the literature in which multis are portrayed as either mighty bogeys or powerful heroes, the answer is a resounding 'yes'. When one looks at their actual conduct things look rather different. A multi of country C, which wants the freedom to invest in country D, may yet fight hard to stop a multi domiciled in D from investing in C. A multi of C, which seeks to build a factory in D, may even try to prevent fellow multis of C from being allowed to follow suit. French, Canadian, British, Australian and US international corporations have fought hard against multis from other countries coming into their home territory. Multis have even lobbied against 'foreign invaders' investing in host countries where they own manufacturing subsidiaries. In 1977 Hitachi wanted to build a plant in England; several international corporations – including (US) ITT, (Dutch) Philips and (British) Thorn – unitedly campaigned against this Japanese multi entering a territory where they were already established. The Swedish multis have flourishing subsidiaries all over the world and are vocally indignant about restrictions on foreign investments by unfriendly host governments – they are also in the forefront of the struggle against the right of Japanese corporations to manufacture in Europe. In 1969 General Foods announced its intention to make a $117m bid for Rowntree, Britain's second largest confectionery firm. Rowntree's labour representatives and managers, the trustees of its controlling voting stock and the city fathers of the company's home town, York, fought bitterly against the bid – not on the ground that the offered price was too low but because of the foreign nationality of the bidder. These employees, executives and stockholders of Rowntree were all associated with a British-based multi which itself had foreign subsidiaries and thought that it was morally entitled to make takeover bids outside the UK. (General Foods found the opposition so strong that it ultimately abandoned the bid.)

Do all multinational companies agree on the virtues of free trade? The answer again depends on whether one reads the textbooks or looks at their record. In 1909 International Harvester, one of the earliest US multis, wanted to establish a presence in

Russia. The company approached three Czarist ministers who were delighted. Their joy was somewhat muted when they heard of the international company's reservation. Would Russia give the US investor the 'protection and encouragement which is accorded in other countries'[45] to foreign investors? The Russian government did not ask International Harvester to spell it out for they well understood what was asked for. Russia had previously suspended customs duties on certain harvesting machinery and free trade consequently flourished; exporters from all over the world were taking advantage of the opportunity to sell on equal terms in the Czarist empire. The Minister of Commerce appreciated the plea of International Harvester and promised explicitly that if a factory was built the government would rescind its policy of free trade and impose a high tariff on harvesting machinery, thus effectively impeding the Russian sales of International Harvester's competitors. Seventy years later the same economic self-interest propels multis: they are adamantly in favour of free trade when they export but with equal ardour favour high tariffs on imports into a country where they have a major manufacturing facility. European and American executives abuse the Japanese for rigging the home market by severe investment and import restrictions aimed at keeping out non-Japanese multis. Sometimes the very same executives join delegations which vociferously demand of their government to impose punitive tariffs on 'unfair' Japanese imports. We owe it to Philips of Eyndhoven, one of Europe's oldest and strongest multis, that published evidence is available to illustrate this ambivalent attitude. In the summer of 1978 the major British subsidiary of the Dutch multi circulated a polemical booklet to the political decision-makers of its host country.[164] In it the case was argued strongly that the authorities should take selective steps against the imports *and UK investment plans* of certain foreign multis which are a threat to British industry (including the already established enterprises owned by non-British parent companies).

Apart from the ludicrous humbug, this ambiguous behaviour of the multis exemplifies the true character of international corporations. The internecine fights between multis can only come as a surprise to those who see these corporate vehicles as actual or future members of a conspiratorial world-wide trade union. ICI, Hoechst, Mitsubishi and Monsanto can never be *permanent* members of the same international pressure group. They are competitors in the market place and also in their commercial-cum-political relations with foreign governments.

TEN DEBILITATING HANDICAPS

Not all who comment on the multis attribute to them the political power to twist the arms of governments – some restrict themselves to pointing out that the economics of treating the whole world as a corporate arena makes the international corporation more efficient, and therefore more profitable, than national companies. Below we are setting out ten factors which counter this seeming economic advantage enjoyed by the multis. There is no way of quantifying whether the 'handicaps' are more weighty than the benefits which are enjoyed by corporations leading a transnational life.

Global integration

Some international companies, e.g. Woolworth, have fully autonomous subsidiaries that serve exclusively the country in which they are located. They are self-contained in that the buying and marketing is in the hands of local managers who rarely have to consult their foreign masters. These are best described as holding companies with a world-wide investment portfolio. The true multis have a different *raison d'être* in that they take pride in international mobility. They buy and sell in all parts of the world, shifting – in theory at least – capital, managers and output from one national location to another. Though they have factories in different countries, the output of a plant is not destined primarily for the area in which it is located. Ideally, each factory produces one product range which is marketed throughout the world but few multis reach this sophisticated plateau. Most international companies manufacture identical products in several of their factories in various territories. But even in such semi-autonomous situations there is some global integration in that all factories receive certain inputs from common suppliers. R&D, which is usually carried out in the laboratories of the parent company, is utilized in the multi's operations everywhere. The purpose of these exercises is to attain (world) economies of scale through global corporate interdependence. However, in the process a fragile organizational structure is erected in which the snapping of one link can affect adversely the whole chain. The higher the degree of integration, the greater the global damage that may be caused by earthquakes, revolutions, protracted strikes or hostile government actions happening in *one* part of the world.

Social stigma

In Perlmutter's love songs for the multis stress is laid on the ability of international corporations to tap the labour markets of the whole world and then move about freely the recruited specialists and managers. This is only a half-truth because in the cold nationalist reality, in which multis must operate, governments often refuse to grant labour permits to foreigners; such restrictions by the host country may oblige a multi to engage inferior indigenous personnel. Furthermore, difficulties can arise when native employees are reluctant to accept orders from 'foreigners' sent by the international head office.

Multis offer travel opportunities and (often) higher emoluments than national corporations. One would have thought that this was a natural magnet which attracts the best technicians and junior executives. Many 'socially aware' intelligent youngsters scorn working for big companies and, in particular, fear the stigma that has attached itself to the multis which exploit the world. Jaques Maisonrouge, the legendary head of the non-US operations of IBM, is quoted as having told the American Chamber of Commerce in London that because of the widespread wrong ideas about multis at universities, there is a growing unwillingness on the part of idealistic youngsters to apply for jobs with international giants: 'he suspected this was why many good Harvard graduates had deliberately gone into smaller companies recently . . .'. [50]

National susceptibilities

It was pointed out in the preceding chapter that in big multi-divisional corporations the sins of one division are visited upon other, guiltless, divisions; conglomerates are thus socially more exposed than single-product firms or small companies. Multis suffer the additional disadvantage which emanates from their international ramifications. They must cover up at home the misdeeds of any of their foreign subsidiaries. Abroad, multis are enjoined to be sensitive to the national susceptibilities of the public in their host countries. Many international firms attempt to hide their foreign parenthood by operating under varying national labels in different countries. Not many are as lucky as Singer which has successfully fostered the illusion amongst its European customers that it is not an international firm; market research has established that, because of its convenient name, German, French and British housewives believe that they are buying products of a German, French and British company, respectively. In a rather moving way, Swedish multis have received this private advice: 'Even if it costs a little national pride we should refrain from raising the national colours over "Swedish" factories abroad.' Some multis find it propitious to appoint native managers to head their foreign operations. It is also not uncommon, though it hardly ever achieves the desired public relations objective, to name prominent local luminaries to the (usually) impotent boards of directors of national subsidiaries.

In 1977 Ford let it be known that it was looking for a European site suitable for a new engine plant. Several European governments showered seductive proposals upon Ford to induce it to select their country. The planners of the US multi finally chose Wales. The British authorities announced the investment at a triumphant press conference but Ford deliberately kept a low profile, because it had been advised that if it stated publicly the reasons for its locational choice, this might hurt national feelings in the countries which were rejected.

IBM could concentrate all its global production in only a few manufacturing plants and thereby gain meaningful economies of scale. Yet IBM deliberately foregoes these advantages and instead spreads its production over an (unnecessarily) large number of factories, situated in different national territories. Not all states which buy IBM computers can expect to play host to an IBM factory; to assuage their feelings, IBM goes out of its way to buy as many components as possible from suppliers in those countries.

The following are illustrations of what corporations have to endure when they operate simultaneously in several countries. The British subsidiary of a non-UK multi was referred to the Monopolies Commission; the local managers were convinced that the Commission would ultimately recommend that one of their company practices under attack be made unlawful. They therefore schemed to anticipate the publication of the Commission's Report (one year hence) by discarding the controversial practice immediately and thus avoiding adverse publicity later. The corporation's head office accepted the wisdom of such a step but nevertheless ordered the UK subsidiary to retain the *status quo* until forced to abandon it through a statutory edict. By coincidence another national subsidiary of this particular multi was defending at that time an anti-trust action in its country; the implementation of the intended action by the British subsidiary might have been used in the litigation against it. The chief executive of this multi took his international responsibilities seriously. He judged that something which was clearly good for the British market had nevertheless to be abandoned because of global considerations.

The Swiss pharmaceutical firm, Hoffmann La Roche, was to learn a bitter lesson after first suffering heavy losses. The company was involved in an acrimonious conflict with the British National Health Service about the prices of some of its products. Almost all other foreign pharmaceutical firms, in a similar predicament, had avoided litigation to escape unpleasant international publicity. Hoffmann La Roche, however, chose to brief lawyers and started a number of law suits. Whether the company or the National Health Service had a better case soon proved irrelevant. The Swiss multi also said that it was willing to abandon selling in the UK market; this may or may not have been a genuine threat but again was soon not to be the main issue. Hoffmann La Roche naively thought that it had stirred up a hornet's nest in only *one* country. As a result of the British litigations, details of its production costs and profit margins became public knowledge in the many countries of the world where the corporation was active. Other governments took an interest and, based in part on the facts disclosed in the British courts, took legal actions against Hoffmann La Roche on the ground that it had been charging exorbitant prices. Finally, the Swiss firm settled out of court in the UK but by then it was too late because the adverse world-wide repercussions had already taken their toll.

There is little doubt that when Chrysler announced in 1975 that it would liquidate its British subsidiary - unless the UK government extended the aid which it ultimately did - this was not an empty threat. Chrysler UK Ltd was in a precarious financial position and its net assets were not ample enough to satisfy all creditors and enable proper severance payments to be made to its tens of thousands of employees. Legally, the parent company in Detroit was not responsible for the debts of Chrysler UK Ltd which was a separate legal entity. Yet the head office of this automobile multi offered that, in case of liquidation, it would 'voluntarily' transfer millions of dollars to cover outstanding liabilities. Why this seeming generosity? Chrysler of Detroit had to consider the impact which a UK liquidation with unpaid debts would have upon its suppliers and employees in Mexico, Canada, Spain and the US itself. Multis cannot even bury a failing national subsidiary without incurring extraordinary funeral expenses!

My final example strikes a somewhat lighter note. The Guatemalan manufacturing subsidiary of Kellogg was 'requested' by the host government to adapt its promotional gimmicks to further educational objectives. The US multi obeyed by offering the young consumers of cornflakes plastic jigsaw pieces of a coloured map of Latin America. As behoves a loyal firm, manufacturing in Guatemala, it showed the Belize territory as part of Guatemala. (Belize, formerly British Honduras, is a sovereign country which Guatemala wishes to annex. Kellogg's cornflakes from the Guatemala factory are exported to neighbouring Belize.) Kellogg became involved in an international incident when the tendentious jigsaw maps were discovered by Guatemala's adversaries. Though Kellogg immediately stopped the export of cornflake cartons containing the politically offensive items, this did not save it from commercial embarrassment outside Guatemala. [139]

The moral shareholders

The traditional gadflies, who used to plague US corporations, harassed the wretched directors if the companies were not managed profitably. Nowadays, the annual general meetings are afflicted by stockholders who complain not about too few profits but about the immorality of multis earning profits in countries with governments of which the critics disapprove. The directors of mighty General Motors have had to justify themselves to irate shareholders about their wicked money-making in apartheid South Africa. When Angola was still a Portuguese colony, resolutions were tabled at Gulf Oil annual general meetings deploring the operations of the company in that area. [68] The UK has not been spared either. Scandalous things have happened at shareholders' meetings of, for example, Barclays Bank when do-gooders protested about certain profitable activities outside the UK which they regarded as morally reprehensible.

Foreign criminals

When they break the law in a host country, multis stand to lose more than indigenous companies. In some states judges discriminate between foreign and native transgressors, punishing the former more severely. In STC countries, however, there are no differential statutory penalties for corporate breaches of price regulations, exchange controls, safety laws, etc. Public opinion, however, is less tolerant when the guilty parties are the subsidiaries of foreign multis which will then also be exposed to homiletic reproaches from local politicians on the special duty that rests upon strangers to obey the law. The Governor of the Bank of England, in an address on multinationals, has depicted this handicap that they must sustain in host countries; especially noteworthy is the cynical phrase 'they cannot afford' which conveys a poignant message: '. . . the biggest companies have a reputation and a "good name" which they need to maintain. They cannot afford to engage in confrontations with government departments to the detriment of their good name as responsible organizations. Nor indeed can they flout public opinion indefinitely with impunity.'[37] This holier-than-thou behaviour, which is expected of multis, is particularly irksome when native competitors beat them at business by breaking the law. Taxation is a sphere in which multis can be especially vulnerable. Whilst companies have a statutory duty to pay corporation taxes, ordinarily they are not held responsible either morally or legally for the tax-compliance of their employees. (Indeed, it would be regarded as a dictatorial interference on the part of management if companies checked on the tax returns of their staff.) Until the end of the sixties most multis raised no objections to, and sometimes even connived at, the tax evasions of parent company employees who were assigned to foreign subsidiaries. The authorities of host countries now increasingly tend to hold foreign-owned companies liable for the tax-cheating of expatriates employed by them. There are instances where governments have exacted revenge from corporations for tax evasions of expatriate personnel who left the country before their misdeeds were discovered. Because the tax evasions of foreigners are seen to rebound on the companies which employ them, many multis are taking the unprecedented step of supervising the tax returns of their expatriate staff in certain host countries.

High wages

Multis are accused of exploiting the native employees of their foreign subsidiaries. Simultaneously, multis are accused by governments, unions and local industrialists of competing unfairly by offering exorbitantly high wages. Vic Feather, already cited for his dislike of multinational corporations, once told a meeting of the TUC how he had successfully browbeaten a horrible US multi: its un-British crime had been to pay a shorthand-typist more than was locally customary. Vic Feather proudly announced that he had compelled the foreign company to reduce the salary. Ford at Dagenham has had its knuckles rapped by British politicians when, as was its right, it remunerated its employees by more than the government thought it should. Heinz, after the 1975-77 UK wage controls had ended, awarded its operatives a 17% wage rise, as it was legally entitled to do; the executives of its British subsidiary were summoned to appear before a cabinet minister who lectured them on the impropriety of a multinational flouting the *spirit of a host government's aspirations* for a given wage level. The Australian, Prime Minister, Malcolm Fraser, on one occasion, denounced General Motors for being a bad corporate citizen of a country in which, he said, it had received 'special advantages'. What was its crime? General Motors had increased the emoluments of its Australian employees at the beginning of 1976 by an amount that Fraser personally thought was too high.

Affiliates only

To operate efficiently on a global basis, and with the least amount of friction, multis must own 100% of the equity of their subsidiaries. The United Kingdom is one of the few countries where multis are actually encouraged to own all the share capital of their British subsidiaries, and thus multis escape the disturbances which compulsory local share participation brings in its wake. In most parts of the world, however, it is now impossible to establish a new manufacturing operation without part, and sometimes the majority, of the equity being held by native shareholders. In the seventies, multis faced an additional challenge in many countries where previously 100% ownership had been permitted; they were instructed to divest themselves of the majority control of their existing foreign subsidiaries. In response, some foreign operations of stubborn multis were closed down. Other corporations reluctantly complied because, as a second best, they prefer to have foreign affiliates rather than no corporate presence in countries which proscribe wholly-owned subsidiaries. An international organization with affiliates instead of subsidiaries is but a pale shadow of the Perlmutter model in which the head office can shift resources from one national location to another.

Compensation

In eight out of the nine member-states of the EEC, foreign companies suffer no oppressive discriminations; they can also remit home their profits without restrictions and are free to disinvest whenever it suits them. This idyllic picture, however, does not prevail in most parts of the world. Multis have learned that the days of the gunboat are over. When they fall victim to xenophobia, they cannot rely on their governments to back them up, particularly in cases of subtle persecution. Nowadays, foreign investors are rarely molested by laws which take over their property without compensation. The host country has sweeter means and more progressive techniques at its disposal. It may allow a foreign corporation to sell its assets 'freely' but the government (and sometimes the unions) will not allow potential buyers to make a commercially fair offer. Multis are thus forced to sell 'voluntarily', at a derisory price, to a buyer designated by the government with payments often spread over a long period. When Gulf Oil was kicked out of Ecuador in 1976, it was terribly happy that the authorities immediately declared their preparedness to pay *some* compensation and not treat it as beastly as the Bolivian government had threatened to do when it expropriated Gulf assets.* Gulf Oil reacted realistically for it knew that had Ecuador not offered a single cent, President Carter would still not have bombed Quito. Instead, the State Department might have sent a diplomatic note, as it once did when a Latin-American republic threatened to

* When the Bolivian government seized in October 1969 the assets of Gulf Oil, which had invested some $169m during the preceding fourteen years in Bolivia, the Minister of Mines and Petroleum, Marcelo Quiroga, declared that not a single cent of compensation would be paid, because the corporation's past profits represent 'just compensation'. A year later, due to internal changes in the country, a new administration generously offered $79m. Gulf was to be paid this amount, interest-free, over a period exceeding *twenty* years.

expropriate a subsidiary of Owens-Illinois, stating, 'We are concerned'. When the governments of East Africa told the British multi, Metal Box, that they were about to take over its investments, did the British government break off relations with these fellow-members of the Commonwealth? No, but it increased aid to those countries which were driving out British companies. Most multis are too cowardly to scream in public when their foreign assets are threatened. Under the Nigerian indigenisation decree, foreign companies had to sell during 1977 a further quota of the equity of their Nigerian subsidiaries to bring native shareholdings up to at least 60% (instead of the previous statutory minimum of 40%). Unilever was offered (for the shares which it had to dispose of compulsorily) a price equal to two times annual earnings whilst on a normal stock exchange valuation the shares would have been worth ten times annual earnings. Did Unilever make a fiery attack on this insidious confiscation of corporate investments that belonged to the Dutch and British shareholders? The company issued a mild statement in which it said that the policy of the Nigerian government was 'most unfair'. Sometimes, when the sentence to expropriate all the property is commuted to stealing only half of it, the international corporation may actually give a cocktail party to celebrate the victory. That is what Kaiser Aluminium did in Jamaica where the anti-US prime minister originally wanted to acquire all of Kaiser's massive investments in his country; when the US corporation demurred, the Jamaican government – of course strictly within the law – ordered a tenfold increase of the current bauxite export levy. Not long after that, Kaiser saw the light. It 'voluntarily' signed away to the government 51% of the Jamaican subsidiary and all its 48,000 acres of bauxite land. Furthermore, it agreed to make in the future substantial annual payments to the Jamaican government; in turn the authorities magnanimously offered $25.5m in compensation. US stockholders were happy when the news came that they would receive some immediate indemnification – however small – for the investments which were being taken over. They were soon to be disappointed: Jamaica undertook to make the payments over ten years! The lurid accounts on the mighty multis should be examined in the context of the arm-twisting that they must today endure in even small, weak countries – how the mighty have fallen!

Internal fights

None of the listed external handicaps is as debilitating as intra-corporate squabbles – the most deadly enemy of the multis. Even when the parent company owns 100% of the stock of its subsidiaries, can the chief executive of the international corporation really pursue a tight global strategy as Peccei and Perlmutter, Haynes and Levinson, would have us believe? He will certainly try. If the overall tax burden can be minimized by moving profits from a Dutch subsidiary to a wholly-owned Irish company, orders will be given to that effect. If production costs are rising in Holland, serious consideration will be given to cease manufacturing there and, instead, buy from producers in Hong Kong and Taiwan. If one national subsidiary has surplus funds, it may be instructed to remit them to another (cash-hungry) national subsidiary. Currency manipulations are planned in the head office and the managers of the various subsidiaries will be told in what currency to invoice their sales and procurement orders. To a large extent all international corporations are intent upon following such precepts but their implementation depends both on externalities (over which the companies have no control) and on the obedience of their executives in the field. It was already noted that sullen managers of product divisions (in a multi-product national corporation) may make it difficult to achieve overall corporate objectives. In an international organization the resistance from the strong managers of national subsidiaries may be formidable enough to thwart the global strategy devised by head office.

The chief executive's function is clear. He is charged with subordinating the profit-making of single parts of the organization to the profit considerations of the company as a whole. He will want to inspire the senior personnel of the multi to see themselves working for the world company, *per se,* and not for its constituent parts. It follows that individuals with given area responsibilities are not to be evaluated at head office in accordance with how well their area did. However, most employees do not believe that this is how multis actually operate; they are sceptical that the chief executive really takes such an overall international view. Consequently, executives in charge of national subsidiaries behave as if their personal standing within the multi is linked only to the performance of their bailiwicks. Being realists, they say that it is not the profits of the world-wide corporation which matter to them; they care only about the profits of the subsidiary within their managerial jurisdiction, for it is these which (at the head office) determine their prestige, salary increases and promotion opportunities. Consequently, when the multi's head office sends an instruction that the profits of the German company should be administratively lowered by the transfer of some of its business to the ailing French subsidiary, there will be protests and even sabotage. Economists, writing on the significance of the international corporation, have been remiss in emphasizing the importance and viciousness of corporate in-fighting.

And many more

Apart from those already mentioned, there are a host of other discriminations that have been introduced by host governments to 'regulate' foreign-owned corporations. According to the laws of several countries including the US, multis (controlled from abroad) may not engage in certain economic activities or acquire companies in designated industries. In a very large number of states, international corporations may not borrow from the domestic banks or float bonds to finance (in local currency) the business of their subsidiaries. The right to remit profits to the parent company is often severely circumscribed. Multis may be allowed to establish manufacturing facilities only if they give an undertaking that a given proportion of the scheduled output is exported – some international corporations are thus 'forced' by the laws of their host countries to export at a loss. The profits generated by (foreign) multis may be taxed more heavily than the earnings of indigenous companies. Multis may have to use high-priced, low-quality, local inputs to comply with a statutory 'minimum local content' requirement which applies to foreign-owned manufacturers. This by no means exhausts the list of prevailing handicaps that multis experience.

COCA-COLA LEADS THE WAY

Not because of but despite the sanctimonious outpourings on the saintliness of multis it is right to record that, on balance, they have been a factor for good. The fast spread of technological innovations, the supply of entrepreneurial capital to poor countries, the jerking effect upon conservative, indigenous firms which wake up when confronted with an efficient competitor on their doorstep – all these have helped to raise material living standards in the world. Yet even a positive evaluation of the impact made by international corporations does not point to a rosy future for them. Hostility to the multis is often embedded in ignorance and irrationalities. Though many politicians perceive this intellectually, they nevertheless adapt themselves to the anti-multi sentiments of the populace. Under such circumstances little purpose is served in 'proving' to the politicians of India, Nigeria and Tanzania that by driving out foreign companies in the name of socialism, they are making their citizens poorer – at a time when the Communist states in Europe are begging multis to invest and employ-exploit their people. Some nationalist leaders in developing countries have actually admitted that the expropriation of multis has damaged their economies. However they aver that, like the damsel in the Irish ballad, they would rather be 'poor but honest'.

The international company is on the retreat and not only because it meets with increased external enmity. It is no longer advancing because forced disinvestments and expropriations have engendered an atmosphere in which the – once very considerable – internal drive of Western corporations to expand outside their national territory is weakening. Multis are still making some new investments in the developed industrialized economies. However, an increasing number are disdainful of venturing into developing countries unless they can buy insurance against contingent losses arising from expropriations and anti-foreign discriminatory measures. Some large companies, such as the dynamic British building corporation, Wates, are frank about their aversion to the uncertain conditions under which a multi must nowadays operate in many areas. In a considered board decision in 1976, Wates turned down lucrative approaches to work in the Middle East: 'We don't wish to become a multinational contracting company and neither do we want growth for growth's sake . . . .'[140] This stance is an extreme one but in consonance with the prognosis of the archangel of the US multis, Peter Drucker, who already in 1971 conceded: 'I'm not at all sure the multinational company will survive the next decade.'[40]

The reasons why big corporations, particularly American ones, were so eager in the past to spread their tentacles abroad help to explain their waning enthusiasm today.

(a) In the search for vertical integration companies sought safe access to raw materials which is why international corporations, until recently, dominated the extractive industries of developing countries. This is a sphere where today nationalist-minded politicians object most strongly to the presence of foreigners. Few countries presently allow multis to occupy the 'commanding heights' of their economies and are stripping foreigners of any remaining controlling interest in the extraction of copper, oil, bauxite, etc.* Iran and Saudi Arabia may still allow foreign-owned manufacturers of typewriter ribbons to survive in their countries – but oil companies, never again!

(b) Some corporations used to find high tariff barriers and heavy transportation costs insuperable obstacles to exports; hence they established manufacturing facilities in their major non-domestic markets. Today these two factors are no longer the quantitatively significant impediments to exporting which they once were.

(c) Multis went abroad to tap sources of cheap labour. This was certainly a decisive argument for European investments by US companies in the immediate post-war years but today this comparative advantage is being eroded fast. In the last ten years, unit labour costs in Europe have been rising more steeply than in the US.** The wheel is turning. When in the summer of 1977 a Dutch company, Koni (makers of shock absorbers), announced its intention of opening a subsidiary in the US, the works council protested. It did so because the employees feared that with relatively lower American labour costs a newly-built plant in the US would be able to export to Europe and compete unfairly with the high wage-cost products of the Dutch factory! The cheap-labour advantage is of course still an enticing reason to manufacture in the developing economies but it is precisely in many of these countries where the danger of expropriation is real enough to make investors fear for the future safety of their assets.

* At the beginning of 1968, foreign companies still controlled most of the large extractive industries of Spanish America; nearly all of these have now been expropriated. [152]
** The Chase Bank predicts: 'By 1983 US wage costs will be lower than in virtually any European country!' [166]

(d) Edison was of the opinion that the 'national sympathies' of the German consumer made it necessary for his company to manufacture lamps in Germany rather than export them from America. He was convinced that, irrespective of who owned the factory, the fact that it was sited in Germany and manned by German operators would make the public treat the lamps as German products.[45] Xenophobic-minded people are nowadays less ingenuous. The output of the Sony plant in Wales is produced by British workers on British soil but to the anti-Japanese lobby they are still Japanese television sets. Modern anti-foreign passions can sometimes hit the international corporation harder when it manufactures in a foreign land than when exporting to it.

After Pilkington had perfected their float-glass process (p.190), they were faced with the choice of either building their own manufacturing plants all over the globe or offering the invention to foreign glass firms on licensing contracts. With some very notable exceptions, they opted for the latter.* A senior vice-president of Xerox, in charge of its R&D, has attacked this decision. Praising the invention as 'a great innovation, a magnificent concept, very original and technologically viable', he reproached Pilkington for not exploiting it themselves outside the UK: 'They have done it by licensing. True, it's an income-producing formula, but not nearly as effective in terms of economic growth as if they themselves had been able to dominate the entire thing, which they could have done.'[157] Was Pilkington's resolution conditioned by an ability to raise several hundred million dollars to finance the building of many manufacturing plants abroad or did they seek to avoid the responsibility of managing additional foreign manufacturing operations? Whether by necessity or design, Pilkington's policy decision foreshadowed how most multis will be functioning in the future:

---

* Pilkington is a truly international company in that the majority of its profits are generated abroad. However, only a small part of its foreign receipts is accounted for by dividends from foreign subsidiaries and associated companies; the bigger part is represented by foreign currency earnings in the form of licensing, service and technical fees plus direct exports from the UK plus indirect exports (e.g. the glass in exported British-made vehicles).

they will no longer be direct employers of labour abroad, nor will they own the equity of foreign companies. They will either export goods or forge links with local entrepreneurs in different countries who will pay them handsomely for their technological, marketing and production know-how.* If the brand name of a big company is a commercial asset, then – with quality controllers making occasional checks – the modern multi will sell franchise rights to native capitalists. Coca-Cola is the model of the forthcoming multi. This US company owns only 5% of the 1,300 bottling plants spread around the world whilst 95% are managed and financed by native proprietors. Coca-Cola is the most famous and defamed US international corporation; few of those who castigate it as an emblem of predatory US economic imperialism seem to be aware how little this company has in common with the traditional multi. If demonstrators against US intervention in Vietnam could not find a Coca-Cola plant to set ablaze, they chose the next best symbol, a Hilton hotel. However, they were equally wrong in choosing this target because, with few exceptions, the Hilton chain does not, outside the US, own the hotels which bear its name. The capital, the management and the staff are mostly recruited locally. The head office of the Hilton Corporation provides a global booking service and supervises the national hoteliers to ensure that their standards come up to the Hilton schedule. The Hilton profits are not generated by the *ownership* of foreign assets.

The Pilkington/Coca-Cola/Hilton ball-game, which I suggest will soon be played widely, has many obvious attractions. No longer can the exploited masses in foreign lands complain that their wages are too low because they have a wicked foreign multi as their

* One such corporate animal, a German company, is already prospering along these lines. As one of the big suppliers of footwear in Western Europe, it had the traditional options of either importing from, or establishing its own manufacturing operations in, low-cost countries. Being headed by a young chief executive, this firm decided to do neither. Instead, it gave production contracts to local capitalists (in Greece, Hong Kong, Taiwan and thirty-five other countries). The shoes were modelled by German fashion designers; the production proceeded under the technical and quality supervision of German engineers; the foreign output was sent to customers designated by German salesmen – not one foreign worker was on the payroll of this modern multi.

employer. Once they understand that their employer is a native capitalist, no purpose is served by adorning the factory with *graffiti* to tell a foreign exploiter to go home. If the employees are outraged at their conditions of work, they may still burn down the factories, bottling plants and hotels where foreign know-how is utilized through licensing agreements, but the multis will suffer little because they do not own the properties and machinery. In future, politicians will not be able to cheer up their electors by passing laws to expropriate the subsidiaries of foreign companies – there will be no more assets left to be taken over. Governments will also not have to worry that the international involvement of their big companies entails the export of capital because direct investments will have been replaced by licensing, know-how and patenting agreements. At present multis, which establish manufacturing subsidiaries abroad, are told by the unions that they are 'exporting jobs' – less will be heard of these accusations in the years to come.*

The demise of the old-fashioned multi will be a gradual process. Politicians still have a few years in which to think of another convenient bogey that can take the place of the current populist myths besetting the multinational corporation.

---

* Some unions are bound to object even to licensing agreements. Lucas was threatened with strike action by employees who alleged that the company was negotiating to sell a licence for electronic engine controls to the USSR. The shop stewards wanted the prospective deal to be stopped; they insisted that Lucas should manufacture this equipment in Birmingham and 'try' to export it to the USSR.

Chapter XIII

354,000 HOUSES MADE
MACMILLAN PRIME MINISTER

*It's quite depressing.... We think it's disgusting that people
are allowed to make money out of housing which is a basic need.*
                                                    Margaret Bruce

DOWN WITH THE PRIVATE LANDLORD!

When Winston Churchill offered him the housing portfolio in his
government, he told Harold Macmillan that this would 'make or
mar [his] political career'. Churchill's surmise turned out to be
correct. Despite his previous achievements, Macmillan did not
really come into the public limelight until he was put in charge of
housing – 'three of the happiest years of my life'. As the instant
hero of the Conservative administration he became a front-runner
for the leadership of his party. Without the acclaimed housing halo
around his political head, Macmillan would never have been in a
position to grab the prime ministerial prize in 1957.

The sections devoted to housing in Macmillan's six-volume
autobiography, from which I am quoting,[46] are astoundingly
frank. He delivers convincing proof to historians that his friends
and foes had been right to credit him with astuteness and political
acumen. The craze for numbers, the deft timing of policies and the
ruthless brushing aside of long-term economic considerations – all
these are documented in those parts of the autobiography which
sketch his role as a superb actor on the *political* housing stage. The
moral of Macmillan's fascinating housing tale is that a politician,
striving to earn immediate populist applause, must concern himself
with the welfare of his electors in the short term.

In no other sphere of post-war British life have electoral considerations had such a disastrous impact as in housing. In this area the differences between the political parties have been minute. Economists of diverse hues and political credos are agreed on the damage caused by the British housing strategy. (There are left-wing economists who idolize the egalitarian society and regard private landlords as loathsome, yet they too are scandalized by the economic distortions caused by cheap rents.) The impotence of the economic discipline is again demonstrated: neither public opinion nor politicians have taken much notice of its, almost unanimous, strictures on the calamitous housing interventions by the state. However, let no foreigner arrogantly chide British politicians on that score. A housing nonsense of one kind or another has thrived and is thriving in many other parts of the world.* Only in the communist countries is the housing stock fully utilized. Their rationing methods are inequitable by Western standards. This does not alter the fact that the limited resources of their housing domain are less wastefully deployed than is the case in some of the rent-controlled, non-communist societies.

Conservative and Labour politicians have been handing out housing lollipops to voters who, out of greed or ignorance, believe that they are receiving something for nothing. Nobody is left out; everybody receives some sort of present: tenants of private landlords, tenants in council houses (properties managed by the municipalities but financed mostly by the central government) and owner-occupiers.

The ethos of post-war Britain prescribes that housing should be cheap; it is also deemed to belong to a realm in which profit-making is dirty. There are indeed a number of activities where the attainment of profits is, or should be, treated as taboo: the manufacture of weapons in wartime, the disbursement of justice at all times, ambulance services for victims of car crashes, etc. But what have these in common with housing? Whilst the Conservative Party favours a free market in the sale of Majorca holidays, umbrellas and television sets, it has joined the socialists in

---

* A convincing case has been argued that the present socio-economic troubles of New York City can be traced to the mad rent controls which have destroyed its free housing market.

disapproving of capitalists who strive to make a profit from letting their properties.* All post-war housing ministers were agreed that a newly-constructed dwelling for letting should not be owned by private landlords but that the state should become the country's major landlord (through council housing).

What to do about these horrible people, the landlords who own properties that had been built before the war? Socialist *and* non-socialist housing ministers schemed to kill them off and in fact have been doing so through draconian rent controls. The statutory ceiling on rents was deliberately fixed at such a level as to make it unprofitable for anybody to remain in the business of letting houses or apartments. (My reference is to sane people who are prepared to obey the letter and the spirit of the Rent Acts.) The success of this bi-partisan approach is almost complete. Whilst in 1914 more than 90% of all families in the UK rented their houses from private landlords, this proportion is now about 10%. A tribute ought to be paid to the candour of the socialist Housing Minister Reginald Freeson, who has not disguised his aim of completely abolishing the private landlord. When it was proved how the 1974 anti-landlord legislation, for which he was responsible, had aggravated the housing shortage, he bragged that 'he had never denied that the Act would be and was a disincentive to some people to let properties'.[47] The tenor of his speech made it clear that the goal was to punish any still remaining profit-seeking landlords. If this could only be accomplished by less housing being available on the market, then he expected society to pay this price for cleansing Britain of the venomous private landlord.

* At one point during his office as Housing Minister, Macmillan noted that 'millions of houses [are] falling down because the landlords cannot do the repairs'. He, therefore, arranged for a small increase in statutory rents which was devised to induce landlords to spend the incremental receipts on repairs. The increases were modest and did not suffice to more than temporarily patch up leaking roofs and carry out similar urgent repairs. The Conservative administration nevertheless felt it necessary to apologize for this puny relaxation. Churchill, the Prime Minister, told Macmillan that this 'legislation to amend the Rent Restriction Acts must be so designed as to bring no financial benefits to landlords'. Profit-making in housing was clearly wicked. The socialists said so and the Conservative, Macmillan, of course agreed.

Tenants of private landlords

A government estimate in 1976 appraised that only 3,000 privately-rented dwellings in Great Britain were then not subject to the provisions of the Rent Acts. The government, and/or special tribunals established for this purpose, set the 'fair rents' which are the statutory ceilings on rents that a landlord may charge. They are not calculated to allow for a return on the invested capital and frequently are so low that the landlord, out of the proceeds of the 'fair rents', cannot carry out the maintenance needed to avoid the premature obsolescence of the properties. Sometimes they do not even suffice for urgent repairs and consequently poorer landlords have literally abandoned their houses. In 1974 the Wilson administration made things worse by extending rent controls to furnished accomodation.

Apart from cheap rents, politicians – proud of their humanity at the expense of the parasitical property owners – have accorded security of tenure to tenants of private landlords. When tenants misbehave or do not pay the 'fair rents' regularly, landlords are obliged to have recourse to protracted and expensive litigation. On occasions, unsympathetic courts do not order the eviction even of such tenants as these.

Council tenants

The Treasury supplies 'cheap' loan funds for the construction of council houses. Nevertheless, the rents charged by the municipalities do not suffice to repay these loans, with interest, over sixty years. Hence mammoth subsidies are given by the Exchequer. In 1977 the rents collected by the Greater London Council were just enough to cover management and maintenance costs.

Owner-occupier

Until 1963 it was held that they had an imputed annual income from the ownership of their dwelling which was taxed like any other return on a capital asset; to catch votes, the Conservatives changed the law and exempted owner-occupiers from paying tax on such an income. When capital gains taxes were introduced, profits from the sale of an owner-occupied house were specifically excluded. Owner-occupiers are given tax relief on mortgage interest.

Most owner-occupiers obtain their mortgages from building societies (the UK equivalent of mortgage banks), which receive some government favours to enable them to charge relatively lower interest. Building societies lend somewhat cheaper than other (non-state) institutions because they borrow funds on the interest of which income tax is due at a reduced rate compared with all other forms of investment income. For example, when in 1975/6 the standard rate of income tax on interest from bank deposits and bonds, and on dividends, was 35%, building society depositors were charged only 27.75%.*

THE BILL OF DAMAGES
The UK housing package enables the subsidized and tax-favoured tenants and owner-occupiers to spend less on housing than it costs to provide it. For once economists are entitled to feel superior. They know what few of the voters appreciate, namely that in fact the British public defrays the full price for its housing. The shortfall, arising from not paying proper rents and mortgages, is covered by the tenants and owner-occupiers in the guise of taxpayers and consumers. The government's housing expenditure in 1976 amounted to £5.2 billion to which must be added at least £1 billion in relinquished tax revenue. (The cost of the state's housing intervention was bigger than the whole of the defence budget.) If the government had not provided 'cheap' housing, then in 1976 income tax could have been cut by 35%. Alternatively, the rates of *all* expenditure taxes (including motor vehicle duties, VAT, customs and excise duties, gambling levies, etc.) could have been lowered by more than 50%.

The above figures merely quantify the fiscal conjuring tricks which politicians play with subsidies and taxes. The other afflictions of their lunatic housing policy are more calamitous.

---

* In order that building societies should be in a position to supply owner-occupiers with relatively cheap mortgage funds, the government has assisted them also in other ways. The clearing banks, in 1974, were about to raise the interest on their small deposits which would have attracted funds away from the building societies despite the latter's tax privileges. The government realized that, if this were to happen, it would impel the building societies to put up their deposit rates which would bring in its wake higher mortgage charges. To keep owner-occupiers electorally happy at the expense of the country's savers, the Bank of England issued an edict to the clearing banks forbidding them to put up their interest on small deposits, thus ensuring that funds earning relatively low interest would remain in the building societies.

First, note must be taken of the engendered illegalities and corruption. 'Rachmanism' has recently been added to the English vocabulary; it commemorates a foul gangster, the landlord Rachman, who hired ruffians with dogs to drive out tenants whose security of tenure was guaranteed by the law. A less violent illegality, which is also directly attributable to rent controls, is (untaxed) 'key money'. Some of the officials determining 'fair rents' have been accused of bias against landlords; others are said to have accepted corrupt favours from them. Municipalities have wide discretionary powers in the apportionment of council dwellings; charges have been laid against some councillors for discriminating on grounds of politics, religion or ethnic origin. For the sake of a curious egalitarianism, the rent structure of municipal houses allows for no, or only minor, variations between good and bad accommodation; some housing officers have corruptly accepted gifts for allocating the better houses. More than just a few municipal councillors and employees (e.g. city architects) have been found guilty of receiving bribes from construction firms.

Malcolm Clarke,[51] a specialist in housing economics, has shown that in the UK the 'problem now is not a general shortage of dwellings but a distorted market structure which uses the stock wastefully'. 'Fair rents' and heavily subsidized municipal rents have created overcrowding and specific housing shortages at a time when *millions* of rooms stand empty. Property owners have preferred to leave houses empty, sometimes for years, rather than let them because their sole interest is in an outright sale. Quantitatively more significant is the reluctance of households in under-occupied dwellings to accept lodgers. There are also millions of houses and apartments, once occupied by families of five persons or more, which are now inhabited by only one or two elderly individuals whose children have moved away and/or whose spouses have died. In the state sector, the municipalities rarely make use of their legal powers to transfer such people from large to smaller housing units. As rents are low – and for indigent* people

---

* The Conservatives introduced housing grants ('rent allowances') for tenants with less than a certain income. These vary in accordance with the income of the recipient and the size of the rent. Thus an old-age pensioner living in a big apartment receives a larger grant than one who

made even lower through 'rent allowances' – there are no strong economic incentives for them to move voluntarily. In the private sector they have security of tenure at 'fair rents' only when they remain sitting tenants; most would find it beyond their means to acquire on the open market a two-room flat – they are thus pressured by the rent controls to stay in a five-room one.

Nineteen months after the enactment in 1974 of a Bill, which extended the rent controls to furnished accomodation, 15% of the furnished dwellings in London had been withdrawn from the market by their owners. A detailed study of the effects of this legislation on furnished rental housing in the City of Glasgow documents the immediate contraction in the supply of private rental accommodation; the author adds laconically that if this law 'was intended to discourage private renting further, then it can be said to have been an unequivocal success'. [161]

Geographical labour mobility in the UK is amongst the lowest of industrial countries. Outsiders, who are unacquainted with the idiocy of the British housing policy, often describe unjustly as work-shy unemployed men with families who reject well-remunerated job offers in another town. A family living in a council flat or enjoying security of tenure at a 'fair rent', can frequently not afford to move if it thereby loses its existing housing privileges and does not immediately gain a subsidized tenancy in the area where employment is attainable.

The biggest mischief caused by Britain's (and many other countries') housing policies is not transparent to the layman. There is no reason why non-economists should be conversant with the difference between the gross national product and the net national product. The public hears almost exclusively of the former, the GNP. This, however, overstates the accretion of a country's wealth between year 1 and 2. Let us assume that a given yearly GNP incorporates the completion of five power stations; if in that period three power stations are destroyed, society has gained only the net wealth represented by two power stations. The size of the net national product is a more valuable economic criterion because it is

---

resides in a small one. In November 1975 Camden Borough Council paid a single person with a weekly income of £25 a 'rent allowance' of £0.36 when his rent was £2 and £3.32 when his rent was £6.

a measure of annual output after allowance has been made for the decrease in the value of the existing capital assets (during that year). To arrive at the net national product, statisticians do not, however, 'shrink' the GNP each year by only the physical retirement of capital goods. They attach an arbitrary life-tag to each investment, say twenty years for a grinding machine, and then go on to assume that in each year society consumes 5% of this asset. The net national product equals the GNP less the consumption (the depreciation) of the store of fixed investments. Politicians understand this vital technicality. When they boast of the completion of x houses in a given year, they do not announce simultaneously how many dwellings have become uninhabitable during that same period. They omit to state a vital figure though it is only the data on *net* new housing which genuinely gauge the progress made in the alleviation of the housing shortage. Each year some houses are pulled down to clear slums and build roads or because they are in a dangerous, irreparable state. Politicians need take only a small blame for such housing 'losses'. However, the striking, undisclosed and unquantified destruction of the housing stock, for which politicians ought to assume responsibility, relates to the accelerated shortening of the life of still habitable dwellings. Statisticians assume that houses ordinarily last for eighty years but this assumption is based on the premise that the dwellings are kept in good condition. When only urgent repairs are carried out, such as patching up the roof to keep out the rain, and permanent long-term maintenance is neglected, then a theoretical useful life of eighty years is shortened to between twenty and forty years. If money is not periodically expended on the preservation of a capital asset, part of the value of the investment good is wantonly destroyed. Three politically-inspired policies have induced such an economic housing misdemeanour in the post-war period.

(a) When Housing Minister Harold Macmillan was in charge of building-materials rationing, he could allocate his limited resources either to repairs and conversions or to new buildings – he chose to lay the emphasis on the latter.

(b) The obnoxious rent controls destroyed the profit motivation of the private landlord and, thanks to 'fair rents', he was also left with no liquid surplus out of which to keep his properties in a durable state.

(c) In all the years since the end of the war the Treasury has been
    more liberal in handing out state funds for the acquisition of
    building land and the construction of new dwellings than in
    making cash grants for the upkeep of the existing housing
    stock. In some years the effect of these three evils has been to
    produce *net* national housing values of less than zero, i.e.
    more housing assets were destroyed (through avoidable decay)
    than were created through the building of new houses.

ON THE POLITICAL SIDELINES

The social obligation placed upon the state to provide some shelter
for every homeless citizen, so that nobody is compelled to sleep on
the street, is widely cheered – and rightly so. However, this is but a
minor aspect of the state's housing intervention. In the ethos of our
society, housing is treated as a basic government function akin to
the supply of unpolluted drinking water. The kernel of the
currently most acceptable housing philosophy is not the provision
of a roof over everyone's head but the offer of below-cost housing
to *all* households irrespective of their incomes. I see nothing
morally uplifting in the selection of housing expenditure as an item
to be subsidized by the state whilst umbrellas, Majorca holidays
and television sets are left to the vagaries of the free market. One
can readily understand the logic of an income redistribution which
raises the material well-being of the poor at the expense of the rich,
subsidizes the old by taxing the young and aids immigrants by
lowering the living standards of the indigenous population. But
why should a family with sufficient earnings to pay an economic
rent or mortgage benefit from 'cheap' housing when the same
family will be bearing the burden of the housing subsidies through
additional taxes and/or the effects of newly-printed money?
Demagogues would have it that only the system of 'fair rents' has
prevented British families from either sleeping on the street or
having to spend such a high proportion of their earnings on a fixed
abode as to be left with no means to buy basic essentials. The truth
is that this consideration applies to 5-10% of the population. To
help them – and they should be helped – it is surely unnecessary to
inflict a set of comprehensive, damaging, housing controls upon the
whole of British society.

When the state takes upon itself to be the country's largest landlord and the controller of all private landlords, the level of rents becomes a current political issue. Some (national, municipal, constituency) election is always lurking round the corner which makes the timing of 'politically permissive' rent increases an electorally sensitive factor. When Macmillan had decided upon a relatively unimportant amendment to the Rent Act (see p.222), which might however prove slightly unpopular, municipal elections were about to be held throughout the country. The public announcement, needless to say, was to be postponed till after the votes were counted. Macmillan heard that Churchill wanted to make a pre-election speech on housing and briefed him accordingly. His parting admonition to the aged Prime Minister is reproduced in the autobiography: 'I warned him not on any account to talk about rents . . . until the Local Elections were over.'

British socialists were right to find it preposterous (and to say so) that in a caring society the rich are given a subsidy - in the form of an important tax-exemption - the cost of which is borne by all taxpayers. So long as owner-occupiers were only a small minority of the population, the tax relief on mortgage interest was denounced in thundering speeches by the chiefs of the Labour Party and the trade unions. Now that they constitute 55% of all UK households, they are no longer decried as unworthy capitalists who receive undeserving subsidies from the state - they have too many votes. In 1970-74, whilst the Labour Party was in opposition, C.A.R. Crosland (the outstanding social-democratic theoretician of the UK) proposed that Labour, once it was returned to office, should legislate to abrogate the tax relief on mortgage interest. The leader of his party, Harold Wilson, (privately) approved of the intrinsic merit of Crosland's proposal but, being an astute politician, he had no time for the airing of such high-minded suggestions in public. He told his senior colleague to shut up on this subject for if it became widely known that the British socialists were thinking such dangerous thoughts, they would be certain to lose the next general election. Jimmy Carter, like Crosland, also recognized the inequitable character of state subsidies to owner-occupiers. In an impromptu speech in Boston on the night before the New Hampshire primary vote, he said that his administration would probably eliminate the tax deductions allowed to home owners on their mortgage interest. Carter's democratic rivals highlighted the *faux pas,* but as luck would have it his Republican opponents later failed to exploit this gaffe. [165]

BEVAN AND MACMILLAN

Aneurin Bevan held the housing portfolio between 1945 and 1950 when he was succeeded by his party colleague Hugh Dalton. Macmillan held the reins between 1951 and 1954. Though all three Housing Ministers of the immediate post-war years operated physical building controls, Bevan's task was the most arduous because he had to make available a large part of the scarce building materials for war-damage repairs. If, instead, he had allocated relatively more resources for the construction of new dwellings, as some urged him to do, the 'magic total' of new houses built under his auspices would have been more impressive.

Bevan's real 'failing', which by default paved the way for Macmillan's success, was his obsession with the long-term character of housing investments. It made economic sense but, as critics later rightly pointed out, was hardly politically expedient: 'I believe if we scamp our work at present we shall never be forgiven. . . . People will have to live in and amongst these houses for many years. . . . If we have to wait a little longer, that will be far better than doing ugly things now and regretting them for the rest of our lives. . . . While we shall be judged for a year or two by the *number* of houses we build, we shall be judged in ten years' time by the *type* of house we build.' [141] This philosophy was translated into his departmental instruction to raise the Ministry of Housing's minimum standard for a three-bedroom house from 750 to 900 square feet (plus 50 square feet of storage space). Bevan also improved other standards and laid down that a substantial proportion of government-financed dwellings must be houses with at least three bedrooms. Despite the material shortages, the war-damage programme, and the ameliorated building standards, Bevan completed 200,000 dwellings per annum. Such a seemingly meagre number easily became a political football. A resolution was passed at a Conservative conference (when the party was still in opposition) promising the electorate that 300,000 houses would be built annually by a Conservative government. When Macmillan was given the ministerial opportunity to carry out this promise, he easily topped the target; in the year in which he left his post as

Housing Minister, to become Minister of Defence, 354,000 new dwellings were completed.

Macmillan played two numbers-games: he built new homes at the expense of repairing existing houses, and he lowered the quality standards of government-financed dwellings. The first thing one notices about Macmillan's biographical references to his housing record is the reiterated analogy to weapons production during wartime. We are told that his wife pressed him to accept the housing portfolio with the plea, 'Surely we could build the houses in the same way that we built the tanks and the guns?' A few pages later Macmillan gratefully acknowledges that his housing effort was aided by the lessons he had learned during the war, especially in his ministerial procurement function for Beaverbrook: 'As in the old Ministry of Supply, improvisation and a certain ruthlessness is necessary.' By what criterion did he expect the performance of his housing ministry to be judged? 'There would be a simple test – the figures of houses and flats actually completed.' His civil servants were soon imbued with the proper martial spirit and he could record happily: 'I really think they were beginning to enjoy the sort of modified "Beaverbrookism".'

One of Macmillan's first steps as Housing Minister was to reverse the Bevan policy of constructing high-quality homes.* In his autobiography, Macmillan says explicitly that his aim had been to build smaller houses and flats and to lower the proportion of three-bedroom dwellings in the housing total. He praised Dalton for having already lowered minimum standards, a policy which he upheld with relish. (Macmillan's 'People's House' needed only nine-tenths of the materials required by the average Bevan-built dwelling with its higher standards.) Macmillan also effected many other 'savings' by, for example, having houses designed with minimum passages.

* Many years later another Minister of Housing, Crossman, became enamoured of the numbers-game and strove to earn political kudos by building, during his tenure of office, a record number of dwellings. The Labour-controlled municipality of London proved an obstacle because it had laid down certain minimum standards which Crossman was now determined to whittle away. He persuaded the socialist leader of the Council 'to reduce their minimum floor-to-ceiling height from eight feet to seven feet six inches. I know it sounds trivial but is a matter of the very

On p.158 I described the Beaverbrook-Kaiser production techniques as eminently suitable when the time-durability of the ouput is of little significance. Readers of Macmillan's autobiography, who come across references to 'Beaverbrookism' which appear to cast a glamour over his peace-time housing strategy, must be forgiven for thinking that he was manufacturing shells to be used in a war with an anticipated duration of two-three years. In war-time it is indeed proper not to consider long-term effects, but what possible justification was there *except political expediency* to build ten low-quality houses instead of nine with a relatively higher standard? It is foolish to suggest that Macmillan had not thought this through – I believe that he was a magnificent connoisseur of time in politics.

Macmillan's other numbers-game was to increase the quotas of building materials for the construction of new dwellings by commensurately reducing the allocations for repairs. To some extent this was made possible by the completion of the war-damage programme but basically, as Macmillan has himself admitted, it was done to build more new houses rather than maintain the old housing stock. Is it only obvious now, with hindsight, how damaging this proved to be? Can apologists for Macmillan not aver that he was at the time unaware how his economically disastrous strategy was actually accelerating the decay of the existing housing stock? Were it not for his autobiography, he might have benefited from the presumption of innocence but he tells us himself that under his regime 'a great many houses whose life might have been prolonged by seasonable repairs were continually falling below standard'. Macmillan conceded that when he was Housing Minister he received a sensational warning (from experts) on this subject. He has not challenged the following veiled accusation that, at a time when he basked in his fabulous housing glory, he was in practice responsible for the destruction of wealth: ' . . . the Sanitary Inspectors' Association has pointed out that the annual wastage of houses was equal to and perhaps even exceeded the new accommodation likely to be made available. This was due partly to the deterioration

---

greatest importance in terms of speedy house building in London . . . . After a time he made it clear that if I would give him orders he would be quite happy to bring his colleagues into line.' [105]

into slums of some of the older houses, but even more to the lack of repairs. This in turn arose from the system of rent controls.'

If Macmillan had allotted a given quantity of scarce building materials to lengthen the life of 40,000 existing buildings by thirty years rather than to construct 10,000 new houses with a life expectancy of eighty years he would have done more good *in the long run*. This is not a profound wisdom first discovered by housing ministers in the seventies.* I am sure Macmillan had appreciated it already in the fifties. However, he also knew that a niggardly approach to keeping houses in proper repair, and thus helping to shorten the life of the existing housing stock, has no *immediate* inimical political consequences. The owner of a car who does not give his engine oil regularly will soon find that the vehicle does not move. A housing asset, however, does not usually become uninhabitable at once even if the owner parsimoniously – or through government-induced circumstances – invests nothing in its maintenance for several years. The cumulative damage will only become apparent after a long period of neglect. Macmillan had no reason to fear that his rent controls would bring about the total dereliction of millions of houses whilst he was still the responsible minister. The indirect impact of his housing strategy, i.e. the premature decay of many dwellings, has been felt gradually in the quarter of a century since his retirement as Minister of Housing.

The biographies of Bevan, Dalton and Macmillan all stress the political aspects of their housing policies. Bevan was pressed to abandon his idealistic stance: 'Could not more houses be built if ... minor adjustments were permitted? The answer was plain;

* Some of the more recent housing ministers seem to take a sardonic delight in knocking Macmillan's deliberate neglect of repairs. (They appear to imply that it was not done deliberately but was due to ignorance.) Crossman writes, 'It is far better to give thirty years' more life to some of this existing central property than to let it become slum and then have to pull it down. In Salford I found that for £200 they were making people happy.'[105] In his 1977-published memoirs, Peter Walker, the former Conservative Minister of Housing, described with pride his efforts to step up the improvement of old houses, an endeavour which he compares favourably with Macmillan's policy: 'In 1973 we improved a total of 453,000 houses (as against only 180,000 in 1970) ... the campaign was a success and made an even greater impact on Britain's housing than the famous Harold Macmillan campaign to build 300,000 houses a year.'[97]

they could. But from 1945 to 1950 Bevan, the alleged demagogue, refused to increase the number of houses he could claim to have built by yielding to the demand. To cut standards, he insisted, was the coward's way out.' Though Foot writes this passage with a warm adulation for his hero, his duty as a biographer compels him nevertheless to elucidate why 'numbers mattered so much' for Bevan's personal political prestige – and the standing of the Labour Party amongst the electorate. Foot allows his readers to deduce that Bevan, as Housing Minister, harmed himself and the government of which he was a part by pursuing a strategy, which would be validated only after many years. Macmillan naturally had no compunction about denigrating Bevan's housing policy. More remarkable is Hugh Dalton's attack on his predecessor and cabinet colleague Bevan. (He called him offensively 'a tremendous Tory'.) In his autobiography,[48] Dalton blames Bevan for having insisted on too high standards and rubs in his disdain for him by praising Macmillan. Dalton concedes, but brushes aside as relatively unimportant, the decline in the quality of houses built by the Conservatives: 'This, I am afraid, was only a secondary debating point. It was the total of new houses which counted with public opinion and public comfort, and led the way towards the "affluent society".' As even Foot seems to admit, Dalton was right in implying that Bevan had hurt the Labour Party electorally by not playing the numbers-game. The Conservatives' housing promises helped them to win the elections of 1951. Macmillan, the man of action, who could point to his actual achievement of constructing more new dwellings than the preceding Labour administration, thereby became one of the architects of his party's victory at the 1955 general election.

Economists ought to be grateful to Macmillan for having written a personal account of how he built houses on the way to 10 Downing Street. He admits that he would have liked to see rent controls abolished but – and here I quote – he was in no doubt that this was 'politically' impossible. Macmillan, the political genius, had no hesitation in abandoning policy measures which he thought were good for the country when he believed that the majority of the electors did not like them. The post-war housing strategies of successive British governments caused billions of pounds of damage. Economists know it – the public does not but, unknowingly, has paid for it.

Chapter XIV

SOME SOMBRE CONCLUSIONS

It is natural enough for the practical man to complain that he asks for bread and the economist gives him a stone.

Joan Robinson

THEIR NUMBERS RISE

Economics has become a growth industry. Anglo-Saxon surveys show that in the post-war years the remuneration of economists has risen faster than that of many other professional groups. There has been an explosive expansion in the teaching of economics at universities and, contrary to pre-war practice, it is now also studied extensively by pupils still at school. The sales of books on economic subjects, particularly textbooks, are flourishing. A new function, 'the in-house economist', has provided jobs for thousands in the private and public sectors. Michael Stewart found that whilst in 1964 only twenty economists were employed by the British government, mostly at the Treasury, by 1970 their number had swelled to 200. [104] In 1978 more than 400 economists had posts in the Government Economic Service but vacancies remained to be filled – the recruitment drive is still in full swing. Nowadays no department of the state is respectable unless it has on its staff civil servants who can construct an Indifference Curve and lecture on the mystery of Pareto. Some years ago an Oxford scholar was appointed as Whitehall's economic specialist on police efficiency – no doubt the job needed to be done and the person chosen was highly competent, but senior police officers were startled that a young man should be invited to bring his wisdom to bear on their functional activities by virtue of having attained a good degree in economics. I am not sure whether readers who reside in countries where the writ of Her Majesty does not run will be impressed by the statistics which show that more economists are now being knighted and elevated to the peerage than in the days of Keynes. Worswick has calculated that whilst in 1938 only one in seven of the council members of the Royal Economic Society was so honoured, by 1971 the proportion had gone up to one in four [57] – and is still rising.

Has there been a parallel growth in the general acceptance of economists' analyses and recommendations? The answer must be a resounding 'no'. Wailing like an Old Testament prophet whose words were not heeded, Samuelson has bemoaned the fate of his American academic brethren: 'The economist has consoled himself for his barren results with the thought that he was forging tools which would eventually yield fruit. The promise is always in the future ....' [117] Why are economists reputed to be ineffectual creatures? A widely disseminated explanation attributes this to the noisy clashes in the economic discipline when solutions are sought to current problems. Star-economists are said to spend much time throwing mud at each other and thus turning their craft into a combative branch of show business. Milton Friedman has made a virtue out of this accusation, he maintains that 'nobody wants to hear economists talk about subjects on which they are agreeing'. [143] This may be true when the television network needs a high audience-rating for a gladiatorial contest between Nobel prizewinners in economics; the producer then has a vested interest in ventilating differences of opinion and stifling the expression of jointly held views. Outside the television studios, and unknown to the general public, there are areas in which the economic discipline speaks with one voice. (For two such examples, relating to the damaging distortions caused by artificially stimulated exports and rent controls, see Chapters X and XIII.) But even if it were true that economists disagree on most subject matters within their orbit, this would still not explain the public's low regard for their discipline. Fundamental professional disputes among doctors, lawyers and architects do not seem to shake the layman's faith in their professional qualifications.

The main reason why the increase in the number of economists has not been accompanied by a rise in the discipline's influence must be sought in the socio-political transformation of Western society during the last forty years. Keynes, the intellectual

Brahmin, chided businessmen and politicians who, as practical men-of-action, were disdainful of theories ' . . . the ideas of economists and political philosophers, both when they are right and when they are wrong, are more powerful than is commonly understood.* Indeed the world is ruled by little else.' [24] Keynes lived in a world where the man-in-the-street did not take an active part in political decision-making. To have his ideas tested, Keynes only submitted them to a select circle where they were indeed hotly debated – all the participants came from narrow political and academic coteries. Keynes and other economists of his generation, who had solutions to offer for the ills of mankind, were happy once they had gained the approval of the readers of *The Times* (of London and New York). Today's economists must find favour with the readers of the tabloids in order to have their economic recommendations implemented – a truly hazardous task!

JOBS FOR ECONOMISTS

There are now more persons than ever before whose passports describe them as economists but, I am sorry to report, Adam Smith and Keynes – watching from above – are not very proud of what most of them are doing. There are also living luminaries of the economic discipline who are deeply shocked at what people, trained in economics, have to do in order to earn their living. Applying a very restricted standard, there are (outside the academic field) few job opportunities for those who seek to do *genuine* professional economic work.

It sounds both sanctimonious and priggish, but the hallmark of a professional, in all disciplines, is that he separates personal inclinations and hopes from his clinical analyses. He is also enjoined not to tailor his pronouncements to what his paymasters would like to hear. A prominent public figure once approached an economist to engage him, on financially attractive terms, as his consultant. The economist was told bluntly that he was not needed to advise him on economic policy: 'I shall determine what I want to advocate – you

* This is often cited to support the contention that the ideas of economists have an immediate impact on current government policies. Actually Keynes went on to say that economic ideas will not be influential 'immediately but after a certain interval'. What is a 'certain interval'? Keynes gives no explicit answer but hints at 'twenty-five or thirty years'.

are to provide me with its economic rationale and justifications.'
Usually arranged with less boorishness, such things happen more
frequently than is generally admitted. Alan Peacock was the Chief
Economic Adviser of the (UK) Department of Trade and Industry
before he returned to his university chair; he has revealed the
following: 'To retain influence with Ministers ... senior economists in individual Ministries may be under considerable pressure
to produce economic argument and statistical backup which
supports their position on economic policy. . . . A situation could
arise in which a Minister may be so committed to his own view of
what policies are "right" that he will instruct his officials to prepare
for him a persuasive case whatever doubt there may be about the
support these policies receive from economic analysis and the
related empirical evidence.' [103]

Joan Robinson pities the economist who is gripped by an
agonizing sense of shame when asked for a 'practical' solution. If
he were to reply as a pure professional economist, employing only
the tools of his discipline, he could frequently not come up with
any 'practical' answer – at best, his bread-giver would then mock
him. Joan Robinson exhorts economists in such a dilemma to
derive 'sardonic pleasure [from] shocking the practical man' [58] by
confining themselves to answers that are not practical in the
conventional sense but sound by the canons of economic theory.
That, she says, is intellectually honest conduct and she herself
publicly promises 'to live up to this standard'. Well might she
preach! Joan Robinson is fulfilling her promise in the university
cathedrals where she has spent the whole of her distinguished
academic life lecturing and penning theoretical treatises. I am
sympathetic to her message but must add the sour note that if
economists, in most non-academic pursuits, followed her prescription they would soon be condemned as ineffectual creatures and
dismissed from their posts. (Joan Robinson's obedient followers
would also be deprived of their chance to appear on television.)
Perhaps it is human frailty that makes many economists ward off
the threat of unemployment by opting to be practical men-
of-action. They then flavour their economic advice with all sorts of
non-academic considerations. Joan Robinson, who laments such
conduct, is told by her former students that economic theory must
adapt itself to the real world. This stance guarantees fat pay

cheques but of course frequently entails the abandonment of economic professionalism.

Not everyone subscribes to the restricted Joan Robinson view on what economists may or may not do if they wish to remain honest professionals. Susan Strange, for example, has argued brilliantly that the compartmentalization of politics and economics is to be deplored as 'academic astigmatism'. She makes a virtue out of blending the two disciplines and consequently finds it misleading when contemporary events are treated 'as if the economist and political scientist were standing back to back ... as though each operated in a totally different and quite separate world and not with the same cast of players ... '. [69] Susan Strange or Joan Robinson? It is especially the 'visiting economists' who ought to make it clear with whom their allegiance lies. The post-war years have opened up a new job opportunity for economists: to advise the governments of developing countries. (These rarely pay for such services; they are ordinarily funded by international agencies or foreign governments). Dudley Seers, despite his support for the aid-lobby, launched at Yale a devastating attack on 'visiting economists' whose activities do 'not seem very useful to those who are being advised'. [60] He has discovered that the cupboards of under-developed countries are full of reports by famous, and not so famous, economists which have been put away and forgotten. Seers is critical mainly of the professional economists who accept such assignments but says also some harsh words about the motivations of the governments which are supposed to benefit from them. Some countries do not really want the economists to come but are bullied into accepting them by foreign do-gooders. There are cases where invitations are extended as a contrived manoeuvre by the host government to distract attention from domestic critics or to pacify foreign donors who suspect that their aid funds are not utilized properly. The height of cynicism is reached when a government has already decided upon some unpalatable measures and merely invites prominent foreign experts to whitewash them in their published recommendations.

In his extensive survey Seers found some 'visiting economists' who interpret their task in the spirit of Joan Robinson. These confine themselves to the preparation of professional diagnoses, the setting out of appropriate recommendations (without taking into account the abilities of the authorities to implement them*) and telling the politicians to act on them if and when they are so inclined. Seers suggests that such a state of mind is not conducive to fulfilling the role of an effective adviser: if 'visiting economists' want to be effective, they must concern themselves with mundane matters of the host environment. The consultants are exhorted to remember that the politicians' first consideration is to stay in office and consequently will want to spend public money in politically sensitive areas; their hosts are interested in an industrial strategy which pleases those industrialists who support them. Economists must choose between offering advice which does not take politics into account, and is therefore ignored, or behaving as meaningful counsellors by ceasing to act as professional economists. Seers sums up the dilemma: 'The foreign adviser may well find that there is no role that is professionally reputable and at the same time politically satisfactory to the host government.'

What happens to an economist who is prepared to snub Joan Robinson and answer an advertisement for 'economist' in the private sector? If he wishes to keep his job, he will not produce orthodox cost-benefit analyses for his bosses; he will also refrain from discussing the intrinsic economic merits of investment proposals and the viability of long-term export propositions. Instead, he will research the political externalities that are likely to affect his company's profits. Will the exchange rate go up? Can the government be made to give an investment subsidy? How will the shop stewards organize a demonstration to urge a ban on competing Korean imports?

The saddest place of work for an economist is probably with a nationalized corporation. What purpose is served if he recommends that the state-owned company should raise or lower prices when its political masters practise index-cheating (see p. 115) or strive to exploit this monopoly as a collector of surreptitious taxes (see p. 128)? The in-house economist's sanity would be questioned if he suggested that the unit costs of his state octopus

---

* Seers warns of ingenuous economists who are on assignments in developing countries where they propose policies which are meritorious *per se* but, in the specific conditions of the country, may have dire consequences: 'to attempt strict import controls may only increase smuggling or corruption and demoralize the whole public service'. [60]

'ought' to be lowered by closing inefficient plants and concentrating output in the more efficient ones when the resultant unemployment would occur in his minister's constituency. An economist was once asked to prepare a detailed exposition of the financial consequences which would result from a certain nationalized corporation agreeing to a steep rise in wages. It is still classified as a secret document but I am convinced that it was a brilliant piece of work of which Joan Robinson would have been proud. (He had been one of her star pupils.) What the good lady professor had not taught is how to react when a serious document full of facts and logical arguments is derided by shop stewards without a Ph. D. The union spokesman was quite adamant that nobody cared whether the state-owned firm had enough earnings or not to pay for the bigger wage bill; he said that state corporations never go bankrupt and the Treasury would help out if there were really a problem with cash flow. The young economist gave up. He resigned from the civil service and emigrated to the United States where he is now teaching economics. I am sure he is a good teacher.

In an attempt to recruit more university-trained youngsters to the Government Economic Service, the UK Treasury issued a touching description of what is expected of them: 'Above all they must be competent applied economists and have a thorough grasp of the principles and tools of their trade.' [162] The boys and girls, who think that by following these precepts they will receive quick promotion or at least wield influence with the mighty, are in for a shock. Their political masters are more interested to learn of the irrationalities of the voters and would also like to know how far illegalities might impinge on new edicts, taxes and regulations which are on the drawing board. They will certainly not wish to hear that rent controls are an economic misdemeanour and should be abolished forthwith.

Economists can meaningfully and beneficially influence politicians in power when they are certain that their recommended policies are either incomprehensible or appear unimportant to the public at large. At the end of 1974 the socialist Chancellor of the Exchequer received advice from the Treasury economists that the liquid resources of the private company sector had been seriously eroded. He was warned that if the current 52% corporation tax was collected in full, massive insolvencies would occur followed by

large-scale redundancies. A stratagem was proposed and immediately implemented. The conventional profit-base on which corporation tax liability had hitherto been calculated was shrunk by an
amount which nearly equalled the – mainly inflationary – rise in
the value of the companies' inventories. It was a fiscal measure with
tremendous implications but the popular press hardly mentioned it
although the economists' advice meant that many UK companies
had their tax payments halved and some escaped altogether from
the tax net. The camouflaged purport of this seeming technicality
was not understood by the average voter and was also beyond the
comprehension of many members of parliament. Had the Chancellor of the Exchequer suggested openly a halving of the corporation
tax rate, or merely proposed lowering it from 52% to 50%, he
would have been crucified for helping the rich and betraying the
cause of socialism. By radically reducing company taxes through an
esoteric technique, the Chancellor's public reputation as a friend
of the poor and an enemy of the rich remained untarnished.
This example shows that there are still fields – albeit very few
– in which economists can successfully counsel their political
bosses.

THERE ARE FREE LUNCHES

Economists have a trump card up their sleeve which they pull out
to put non-economists in their place and bring 'faint ridicule to
bear on simple-minded thinking'.[144] It is said to be easily demonstrated that 'there ain't no such thing as a free lunch'. (This
aphorism was coined by E. G. Dolan of Dartmouth College,
Vermont.) Formulated as if it were akin to a physical law, it is
supposed to convey the message that society can never avoid
paying for the full costs of all goods and services even when these
are offered free or at below-cost prices. Let it first be noted that
this was certainly not true in ancient times. We know from Exodus
16 that the Israelites ate free manna lunches for forty years and,
according to the evidence of Mark 8 and Matthew 15, thousands
enjoyed free bread-and-fish lunches in the mountains of Galilee.
But in the absence of divine intervention, is this aphorism wholly
true today? Though the formal answer must be in the affirmative, it
is however only one of those many true-but-not-very-meaningful
macro-economic generalizations with which economists dazzle the

layman. It sheds no light on the ample opportunities which politicians seize to disburse both real and illusory free lunches. An economic truism is not necessarily a self-evident political truth.

The luckiest politicians are those who can bring goodies to their citizens without their ever having to pay for them. This is indeed possible when foreigners provide charitable aid. Of course somebody in the world is paying for the goodies but to the people of the aid-receiving country it is a genuine free lunch.

By playing around with time, politicians can also serve free lunches. In Chapter XIII the point was made that the British public's cheap rents and mortgages were not free lunches because these benefits were clawed back simultaneously through higher taxes. One important element in the UK housing package, however, veritably reduces the country's housing costs without it being offset by current, countervailing taxes: it is the failure to spend enough resources on the maintenance of the existing housing stock. Since the war many British tenants have occupied houses at a lower cost (to themselves and the state) than would have had to be incurred *currently* had politicians not induced the pernicious consumption of the housing capital by skimping on repairs. As a result of this short-term political expediency, the people of Britain received a free lunch worth £10 which makes later generations poorer by £30. If economists say that this again proves how ultimately (maybe after thirty or forty years) somebody is somehow paying for the lunch, they are of course right. Politicians, however, will note – and economists do not challenge the accuracy of the fact – that the present generation has received a genuine free lunch.

Politicians do not care whether a lunch is free or not for their concern is with the people who eat it; if the eaters believe it to be free – this is all that matters to politicians. Inflation is very helpful in this respect. President Johnson was told by prominent US economists to raise taxes in order to finance the current costs of the Vietnam war, but Johnson did not like economists. He was a superb strategist of the present and had no patience for admonitions that *in the long run* 'there ain't no such thing as a free lunch'. So long as he resided in the White House, the Vietnam war was half-free; Johnson saw to it by printing money. The illusory free lunches which people then enjoyed served Johnson's purpose as well as if they had eaten genuine free lunches.

THE FUTURE OF ECONOMICS

The idea never caught on properly in the United States but
elsewhere, until the Second World War, the leaders of the socialist
movements saw in the re-distribution of wealth the means of
ushering in the millenium. They paid little attention to 'growth' as
a way of raising living standards. The emphasis was placed on the
transfer of wealth from the opulent to the poor – by making the
wealthy less prosperous, the lot of the exploited was to be bettered.
Few intelligent socialists today believe that the pauperization of the
rich would make any substantial material difference to those who
are considered poor. As these lines are written, the UK government
collects 98% income tax from the investment proceeds of the few
remaining rich. When things were not going well after the Yom
Kippur war, some socialist parliamentarians hinted that, to aid the
poor, the rate might have to be raised to 99%. A renowned chief of
one of Britain's most powerful trade unions went on television to
demand a 100% tax on all earnings above £8,000 (which at the
time, when this profound proposal was made, equalled $18,000). It
may be that the ritual of broadcasting such holy messages is good
for the soul but it is to be doubted whether even the proponent of
the 100% tax believed that enacting it would be helpful to the trade
unionists whose welfare he set out to promote.

Apart from a few doctrinaires, most socialists and non-socialists
have agreed since the war that it is not the distribution of the
national cake but its size which is the main determinant of living
standards. For economists the last thirty or forty years have been
marvellous. They were constantly called in to advise on 'optimization' and 'maximization' and on how to feed efficiently the sacred
cow of the GNP so that it might become fatter and fatter. Material
growth, measured by the annual rise in the volume of the GNP,
was given a place of honour in the endeavours of the Western
world. This era is now coming to an end and consequently the
demand will be fading for the services of economists – those
efficiency experts who know how to make the GNP grow fast.

'Economism' is a pejorative word in the dictionary of the
Chinese communists; they use it to abuse Western trade union
leaders who place material gains for their members above the
correct ideological conduct of orthodox marxism. The charge of
'economism' has been flung by the supporters of Mao Tse Tung

even at the reformist leaders of the USSR. Not only the comrades from Peking but capitalists in the West too are asking now whether a continued growth of the GNP is possible and, if possible, desirable. It has been estimated that in the year 2000 the productive *capacity* of the Western industrialized countries will be three times that which it was in 1970. Is that likely to come true? The answer to the question is not very important, for what does it matter whether the capacity is twice or four times as large? More significant is the prognosis that production in the future will not be organized according to our present concepts of efficiency. The Swedish automobile manufacturer, who introduced an assembly line which intentionally did not maximize physical output per man-hour, was pointing to the prospective 'uneconomic' mode of behaviour of big corporations. President Ford's economic adviser found that such thinking has already affected corporate planning and has created a bias against long-term investments. He has spoken of the 'uncertainty that plagues the investment commitment process today ... '.[159] If – perhaps in a decade? – labour-saving production processes are no longer to be venerated in the United States, what is the purpose of investing now in capital-intensive projects? The fact that such heretical questions are being asked is enough to make many economists wonder how long they will be' able to stay in their present jobs.

On p. 18 I conjured up a hypothetical situation in a besieged city where the lives of economists would be amongst the first to be sacrificed in order to ensure the survival of the more useful citizens. In normal times, however, as I have attempted to illustrate throughout the book, economists can make some modest but valuable contributions. If only more of their prescriptions had been followed, our society would be materially richer and – I add this with diffidence – our fellow-citizens might consequently be a little happier. Certainly in my lifetime it will still matter whether there are rent controls or not, whether oil producers charge $15 or $25 per barrel, whether the multis are treated as the saviours or the scourges of mankind, whether price curbs are imposed, etc. But what scope will there be to practise the craft of economics in the twenty-first century? When every household has two dishwashers, three cars and four television sets (all of which are replaced annually), no useful purpose is served by studying techniques to optimize and maximize the output of most of the things that make up the GNP. The veins of economics will be progressively clotted as traditional scarcities disappear from many human endeavours. A new type of scarcity will be engendered: whilst leisure will be a calamity, people will strive (and perhaps offer bribes) to attain the privilege of working – not to earn money but in order to have something to do. This is bad news for today's youngsters who would like to follow in the footsteps of Adam Smith and Milton Friedman. Humanity may not survive the threat of a nuclear holocaust and thus will never enter upon the twenty-first century. If such a disaster is avoided, it can be of little comfort to the economic discipline, because it will be a world with shrinking job opportunities for economists.

BIBLIOGRAPHY OF CITED SOURCES

1   G.C. Allen, 'Advice from Economists', *The Three Banks Review*, Edinburgh, June 1975.
2   L. Robbins, *An Essay on the Nature and Significance of Economic Science*, Macmillan, London, 1932.
3   P. Ormerod, *The Limits to Economic Forecasting*, Labour Economic Finance and Taxation Association, London, 1978.
4   S. Talbott (edited), *Khrushchev Remembers*, André Deutsch, London, 1974.
5   A. Rubner, *Three Sacred Cows of Economics*, MacGibbon & Kee, London, 1970.
6   J. Jewkes, 'Long Range Planning', *The Times*, London, 10 November 1970.
7   I.M.D. Little, *A Critique of Welfare Economics*, Oxford University Press, London, 1965.
8   *38th Annual Report*, Gilbert Corporate Democracy, New York, 1978.
9   'The Day the Experts Tore up their Forecasts', *Evening Standard*, London, 5 December 1967.
10 R.L. Carter, *Theft in the Market*, The Institute of Economic Affairs, London, 1974.
11 J.N. Bhagwati (edited), *Illegal Transactions in International Trade*, North-Holland, Amsterdam, 1974.
12 *The Wall Street Journal*, New York, 20 September 1977.
13 A. Rubner, *Fringe Benefits*, Putnam, London, 1962.
14 F.H. Knight, *Risk, Uncertainty and Profit*, London School of Economics, London, 1933.

15 R. Vernon (edited), *Big Business and the State,* Macmillan, London, 1974.

16 J.K. Galbraith, *Economics and the Public Purpose,* André Deutsch, London, 1974.

17 D. MacDougall, 'In Praise of Economics', *Economic Journal,* London, December 1974.

18 R. Harrod, 'Economic Anaemia', *Financial Times,* London, 24 January 1968.

19 *Ninth Report of the Expenditure Committee,* HMSO, London, 1974.

20 *Office of Public Information,* Columbia University, New York, 15 December 1967.

21 *Hansard,* House of Commons, London, 14 February 1967.

22 F. Catherwood, *The Diseconomies of Size and the High Cost of Discontinuity,* Council of Engineering Institutions, London, 1975.

23 H. Unger, 'Is GM too Big to be Trusted?', *Sunday Times,* London, 5 November 1967.

24 J.M. Keynes, *The General Theory of Employment, Interest and Money,* Macmillan, London, 1936.

25 A.C. Pigou, *The Economics of Welfare,* Macmillan, London, 1932.

26 M.S. Feldstein, 'The Social Time Preference Discount Rate in Cost Benefit Analysis, *Economic Journal,* London, June 1964.

27 A.K. Sen, 'On Optimising the Rate of Saving', *Economic Journal,* London, September 1961.

28 J. Tinbergen, 'Optimum Savings and Utility Maximisation over Time', *Econometrica,* Amsterdam, April 1962.

29 *Hansard,* House of Commons, London, 15 June 1965.

30 I.M.D. Little and J.M. Clifford, *International Aid,* Allen & Unwin, London, 1965.

31 B. Horvat, 'The Optimum Rate of Investment Considered', *Economic Journal,* London, September 1965.

32 J. Tinbergen, 'The Optimum Rate of Saving', *Economic Journal,* London, December 1956.

33 *Sixth Report of the Expenditure Committee,* HMSO, London, 1972.

34 R.F. Harrod, *Towards a Dynamic Economics,* Macmillan, London, 1948.

35 G. Meeks and G. Whittington, 'Giant Companies in the United Kingdom', *Economic Journal,* London, December 1975.

36 A. Bambridge, 'Kindest Cut of All', *The Observer,* London, 31 July 1966.

37 'Multinational Enterprises', *Bank of England Quarterly Bulletin,* London, June 1973.

38 *Financial Times,* London, 7 May 1973.

39 *Financial Times,* London, 1 June 1972.

40 D. Palmer, 'The Thoughts of Chairman Drucker', *Financial Times,* London, 3 December 1971.

41 E. Haynes, 'Collective Action by Multinational Corporations', *Address at Trinidad Hilton Hotel,* 15 January 1972.

42 R.J. Barnet and R.E. Mueller, *Global Reach*, Simon & Schuster, New York, 1974.

43 G.D. Newbould and G.A. Luffman, *Successful Business Policies*, Gower Press, London, 1978.

44 W.J. Reader, *Business and Society*, Unilever, London, 1975.

45 M. Wilkins, *The Emergence of Multinational Enterprise*, Harvard University Press, Cambridge, 1970.

46 H. Macmillan, *Tides of Fortune*, Macmillan, London, 1969.

47 *Hansard*, House of Commons, London, 17 March 1976.

48 H. Dalton, *High Tide and After*, Frederick Muller, London, 1962.

49 J.C.K. Ash and D.J. Smyth, *Forecasting the United Kingdom Economy*, Saxon House, Farnborough, 1973.

50 'IBM Chief Defends the Multinationals', *Daily Telegraph*, London, 10 November 1972.

51 M. Clarke, 'Too Much Housing?', *Lloyds Bank Review*, London, October 1977.

52 *Policing the Hidden Economy*, The Outer Circle Policy Unit, London, 1978.

53 A. Cairncross, 'Economic Forecasting', *Economic Journal*, London, December 1969.

54 R.G. Kaiser, *Russia*, Secker & Warburg, London, 1976.

55 C.E.V. Lesser, *Can Economists Foretell the Future?*, Leeds University Press, Leeds, 1969.

56 *Hansard*, House of Lords, London, 4 November 1969.

57 G.D.N. Worswick, 'Is Progress in Economic Science Possible?', *Economic Journal*, London, March 1972.

58 J. Robinson, *The Economics of Imperfect Competition*, Macmillan, London, 1945.

59 W. Beckerman (and Associates), *The British Economy in 1975*, Cambridge University Press, London, 1965.

60 D. Seers, 'Why Visiting Economists Fail', *The Journal of Political Economy*, Chicago, August 1962.

61 *New York Times*, New York, 17 and 18 December 1967.

62 R. Klein, 'The Case for Elitism', *Political Quarterly*, London, October 1974.

63 N. Davenport, *Memoirs of a City Radical*, Weidenfeld & Nicolson, London, 1974.

64 R.F. Harrod, *The Life of John Maynard Keynes*, Macmillan, London, 1951.

65 K. Schiller, *Der Oekonom und die Gesellschaft*, Gustav Fischer, Stuttgart, 1964.

66 D. Allen, 'The Developing Structure of UK Government', *National Westminster Quarterly Review*, London, August 1978.

67 *Report of Royal Commission on Standards of Conduct in Public Life*, HMSO, London, 1976.

68 'The Moral Powers of Shareholders', *Business Week*, New York, 1 May 1971.

69 S. Strange, *Sterling and British Policy*, Oxford University Press, London, 1971.
70 'Der Grosse Verbrecher Bleibt Ungeschoren', *Der Spiegel*, Hamburg, 26 November 1976.
71 J. Morrish, 'Customs Concern at True VAT Losses', *The Times*, London, 24 July 1975.
72 *Eastern Europe Report*, Vienna, 30 May 1975.
73 H. Wilson, *The Labour Government*, Weidenfeld & Nicolson, London, 1971.
74 *National Institute Economic Review*, NIESR, London.
75 *The Public Health Engineer*, London, November 1975.
76 *Letter to the Author from Ingersoll Ltd*, London, 22 June 1964.
77 J.K. Galbraith, *Money*, André Deutsch, London, 1975.
78 M. Galatin, 'Optimal Forecasting in Models with Uncertainty when the Outcome is Influenced by the Forecast', *Economic Journal*, London, June 1976.
79 I. Fisher, *The Stock Market Crash – and After*, Macmillan, New York, 1930.
80 'Smoke Rings Across the Alps', *The Economist*, London, 23 May 1964.
81 *Financial Times*, London, 1 November 1972.
82 'Smuggling Upsets Marketing Cart for Firms Operating in Ecuador', *Business Latin America*, New York, 15 June 1967.
83 'Indonesian Government Launches Antismuggling Campaign', *Business Asia*, Hong Kong, 4 June 1971.
84 J.O. Bull, 'Rodents and Food Spoilage', *Chemistry and Industry*, London, 17 November 1973.
85 'Russia's Private Sector', *The Economist*, London, 13 May 1961.
86 D. Floyd, 'Soviet Woman who Fed Pigs on Bread', *Daily Telegraph*, London, 10 September 1975.
87 *Spain*, Business International, Geneva, 1974.
88 'How the Coal Companies are Faring', *Business Week*, New York, 28 November 1977.
89 M. Flack, 'People will be People', *Financial Times*, London, 17 March 1976.
90 'State Industries like Mediaeval Barons', *Daily Telegraph*, London, 22 September 1977.
91 *Financial Times*, London, 18 July 1978.
92 A. Rubner, *The Ensnared Shareholder*, Macmillan, London, 1965.
93 W. Beckerman, 'A Social Science Fiction', *The Times Higher Education Supplement*, London, 6 May 1977.
94 *National Opinion Polls Political Bulletin*, London, June 1974.
95 A. Rubner, *The Economics of Gambling*, Macmillan, London, 1966.
96 *Hansard*, House of Commons, London, 20 February 1975.
97 P. Walker, *The Ascent of Britain*, Sidgwick & Jackson, London, 1977.
98 E.G. Kleinwort, 'Plebiscite on EEC', *The Times*, London, 16 February 1974.

99 *Evidence by NHS Works Officers to the Royal Commission on the National Health Service,* West Thames Regional Health Authority, London, March 1977.

100 P.S. Florence, *The Logic of British and American Industry,* Routledge, London, 1953.

101 E.A. McCreary, 'Those American Managers don't Impress Europe' *Fortune,* Chicago, December 1964.

102 M.L. Mace, 'The President and International Operations', *Harvard Business Review,* Boston, September 1966.

103 A. Peacock, 'Giving Economic Advice in Difficult Times', *The Three Banks Review,* Edinburgh, March 1977.

104 M. Stewart, *The Jekyll and Hyde Years,* Dent, London, 1977.

105 R. Crossman, *The Diaries of a Cabinet Minister,* Hamish Hamilton, London, 1975.

106 'Even New Schools are Becoming Slums', *Daily Telegraph,* London, 15 May 1978.

107 D. Irving, *The Rise and Fall of the Luftwaffe,* Weidenfeld & Nicolson, London, 1973.

108 T.E. Smith (edited), *The Politics of Family Planning in the Third World,* Allen & Unwin, London, 1973.

109 K. Owen, 'Third World Revolution', *The Times,* London, 14 January 1972.

110 C. Clark, *Australian Hopes and Fears,* Hollis & Carter, London, 1958.

111 *Business and the Community,* Economic Intelligence Unit, London, 1957.

112 A. Benn, 'A Dedication to the Idea of Accountability', *The Times,* London, 18 July 1977.

113 J.S. Magruder, *One Man's Road to Watergate,* Hodder & Stoughton, London, 1974.

114 H. Heclo and A. Wildavsky, *The Private Government of Public Money,* Macmillan, London, 1974.

115 R. March, 'Better Times for the Railways?', *Coal and Energy Quarterly,* London, December 1974.

116 V.R. Jackson, *A Practical Approach to Current Pension Problems,* The Association of Superannuation Pension Funds, London, 1958.

117 P.A. Samuelson, *Foundation of Economic Analysis,* Harvard University Press, Cambridge, 1975.

118 W. Rees-Mogg, 'How a 9.4% Excess Money Supply Gave Britain 9.4% Inflation', *The Times,* London, 13 July 1976.

119 S.A. Marglin, 'The Social Rate of Discount and the Optimal Rate of Investment', *Quarterly Journal of Economics,* Harvard University Press, Cambridge, February 1963.

120 A. Nove, *An Economic History of the USSR,* Allen Lane, London, 1969.

121 E. Powell, *Address to the East Cheshire Young Conservatives,* Llandudno, 3 March 1973.

122 A. Benn, *Interviewed by R.T. McKenzie on 'Tonight'*, BBC, London, 17 March 1976.

123 J. Wilczynski, *Socialist Economic Development and Reforms*, Macmillan, London, 1972.

124 P. Hanson, *The Consumer in the Soviet Economy*, Macmillan, London, 1968.

125 *Minutes of Evidence*, Company Law Committee, HMSO, London, 1960.

126 H. Maurer, *Great Enterprise*, Macmillan, New York, 1955.

127 R.M. Blough, *Free Man and The Corporation*, McGraw-Hill, New York, 1959.

128 C. Kennedy and A.P. Thirlwall, 'Technical Progress', *Economic Journal*, London, March 1972.

129 *Beecham Group Limited and Glaxo Group Limited*, Monopolies Commission, HMSO, London, 1972.

130 W.J. Reader, *Imperial Chemical Industries (II)*, Oxford University Press, London, 1975.

131 N. Foy, *The IBM World*, Methuen, London, 1974.

132 H. Pilkington, *Address to the Scottish General Meeting of the Federation of British Industry*, Glasgow, 21 January 1954.

133 A.A. Berle, *The Twentieth-Century Capitalist Revolution*, Macmillan, London, 1955.

134 F.M. Andrews, *A Study of Company-Sponsored Foundations*, Russell Sage Foundation, New York, 1960.

135 *Sunday Times*, London, 25 January 1976.

136 *Hansard*, House of Lords, London, 16 April 1975.

137 *The Times*, London, 6 April 1976.

138 R. Nader, *Summary of the Hearings Before the Group of Eminent Persons to Study the Impact of Multinational Corporations*, United Nations, New York, 1974.

139 'Kellogg's Cornflakes Cause an International Incident', *Daily Telegraph*, London, 8 May 1976.

140 M. Cassell, 'Wates Shuns Middle East', *Financial Times*, London, 6 April 1976.

141 M. Foot, *Aneurin Bevan (II)*, Davis-Poynter, London, 1973.

142 *The Times*, London, 22 December 1970.

143 *The Times*, London, 2 September 1976.

144 R. Harris and A. Seldon, *Not from Benevolence*, Institute of Economic Affairs, London, 1977.

145 P. Collier and D. Horowitz, *The Rockefellers*, Jonathan Cape, London, 1976.

146 T. Balogh, *Letter to E. Lundberg of Royal Academy of Science (Stockholm)*, London, 13 January 1977.

147 *Letter to the Author* (from S. Sherbourne), Private Office of E. Heath, House of Commons, London, 16 July 1976.

148 *Letter to the Author* (from F. Cassavetti), OECD, Paris, 9 August 1976.

149 D. Malbert, 'Six Years that Shook the Pound', *Evening Standard*, London, 15 February 1977.

150 'Poland Curtails Investment', *Business Eastern Europe*, Vienna, 1 October 1976.

151 *Financial Times*, London, 7 July 1977.

152 G.D.E. Philip, 'The Political Economy of Expropriation', *Millenium*, London, Winter 1977.

153 J. Jewkes, *The Sources of Invention*, Macmillan, London, 1969.

154 J. Brooks, *Business Adventures*, Gollancz, London, 1969.

155 C.A. Gerstacker, *The Structure of the Corporation*, Dow Chemical Company, Midland, February 1972.

156 *Hansard*, House of Lords, London, 16 June 1971.

157 J.E. Goldman, *Technology and Multinationalism*, Science Policy Foundation, London, 1973.

158 S. Brittan and P. Lilley, *The Delusion of Incomes Policy*, Temple Smith, London, 1977.

159 A. Greenspan, 'Investment Risk', *The Economist*, London, 6 August 1977.

160 *Report on the Supply of Flat Glass*, Monopolies Commission, HMSO, London, 1968.

161 'The 1974 Rent Act', *Economic Journal*, London, June 1978.

162 'The Government Economic Service', *Economic Progress Report*, London, June 1978.

163 L.J. Guitar, 'Are We Really Worse Off Today?', *Times Herald*, Dallas, 17 September 1978.

164 *The UK Electronic Components Industry*, Mullard, London, June 1978.

165 J. Witcover, *Marathon*, New American Library, New York, 1977.

166 J. Norris, *Inflation, Instability and the World Economy*, Chase Econometric Associates, Bala Cynwyd, Pennsylvania, January 1979.

INDEX

of principle references

ff: and following pages

n: footnote

Agriculture 131
  in EEC countries 132-3; International Harvester Company 202-3; farm subsidies 169
Balance of Payments (UK) 88, 88n, 90, 91, 92
Balogh, Lord 9
Bank of England 34, 57, 134, 155, 157, 209, 224
Barber, Rt. Hon. Anthony, MP 126-7
Benn, Rt. Hon. Anthony Wedgwood, MP 131, 194
Blumenthal, Michael 60-2
Bribery and Corruption
  in business generally 54ff; in Japanese Cabinet 55, 57; as a tax-deductible expense 56
British Leyland Motor Corporation 32, 79, 158, 178
Buying Habits 95-6

Callaghan, Rt. Hon James, MP 167
Carter, President 'Jimmy' 18, 193 administration of 60, 229-30
Chrysler Motor Corporation 55n, 178-194, 199-200, 207-8
'Church' US Senate sub-committee on multinationals 54n, 55, 58, 63, 64, 173, 187
Coal industry 130-1
Computers 28, 30, 206
Concorde Project 148
Confederation of British Industry 106n

Corporations 171-192
Crosland, Rt. Hon. C.A.R., MP 229
Crossman, Rt. Hon. R.H.S., MP 167, 231n-232n, 233n
Decimalization of currency 99-100
Developing Countries 128, 129, 145, 146, 150, 159, 165n, 216, 239
Dividend limitation 101
Economic forecasting 20-1, 25-7, 27n, 28-39, 41
Economists 12ff, 237-46
  as broadcasters 13-14, 93, 236, 238; as investors 30:remuneration of 235
Egg exports from UK 86
Exchange regulations 68
Exporting 76ff, 216
Exxon Corporation 42

Financial Times ('that pink daily paper') 176
Ford Motor Corporation 185, 199-200, 206, 210
'Fringe' benefits 45

Galbraith, J.K. 10, 35, 36, 74-5, 122-3
General Electric Company (UK) 114-5
General Motors Corporation 51, 105-8, 183, 185, 199, 208, 210
Gold as an economic refuge 98-9
Government and bad news 35
Gross National Product (GNP) 19-20, 25-7, 37, 38, 41, 43, 80, 97,

111, 124-5, 127, 138, 141, 149, 150, 152, 154, 169, 226-7, 244-6
Norwegian 110; Swiss 165

Harrod, Sir Roy 7, 29-30, 162-4
Healey, Rt. Hon. Denis, MP 139-40 155, 156, 169
Heath, Rt. Hon. Edward, MP 34-5, 35n;
    administration 89, 126, 166
Housing 220, 243
    and council tenants 223; grants 225n-6n; and lodgers 225; Ministry of 230; private landlords 222, 222n, 223, 226, 227; and rent controls 226, 227, 234, 241, 245

ICI 87, 106, 148, 183, 198n, 203
India Durgapur Steelworks 145; rodent damage in 144; duty on tea in 81
Indonesia, smuggling in 65, 67
Inflation 125, 137, 138, 243
    and decimal currency 100; and the EEC 100; and metrication 99, 103; in the UK 21, 32, 34-5, 41, 100, 127, 156, 157; in the UK household 97-9; in West Germany 102
Inland Revenue 78 (see also Taxation, Taxes)
    and bribery in business 57
International Harvester Company 202-3
Investment 134-6, 141-53, 162-3, 167, 168, 181, 189, 191, 203, 211, 212, 215, 217n, 224, 227, 240, 245:
    analysts 178; and optimum consumption 164; in Polish industry 170:

Japanese industry 143

Keynes, J.M., 7, 12-13, 29, 146-7,

148, 152-3, 236, 237, 237n
    as investor 29-30

Labour administration 139-40, 167
Laski, Professor Harold 105-6
Lockheed Aircraft Corporation:
    bribery involving 54n-55n, 57-8, 60, 201n

Macmillan, Rt. Hon. Harold, MP 136, 220, 227, 229, 230-1, 233, 233n
Marsh, Sir Richard and railway finance 168
'Multinational' companies 193-219
    compensation 211; internal fights within 213; and Jamaica 212; and mineral extraction 216; and Nigeria 212

National Health Service 145, 207
    building and equipping of hospitals 168, 169
Nuclear Power Stations 148, 151

Oil 201:
    bribery in the industry 62-3, 100; North Sea 21, 159-60; prices 32, 81n, 111, 113, 138, 245
Owen, Rt. Hon. Dr David, MP 146

Pilkington Brothers 182, 190-1, 217-8
Powell, J. Enoch, MP 121, 127
Premium Bonds 103, 136
Profitability, the myth of 96-7
Public health 21-4

Ricardo, David 30
Robinson, Joan 238-40, 241
Rockefeller, Nelson 8
Royal Economic Society 35, 236
Russia 150, 202-3, 245 (see also Russian)

British exports to 89; corruption in 59-60; currency policy in 137; government of 142
Russian (*see also* Russia)
    National Plan 44; politicians 72, 134, 146, 146n, 150; taxation 134, taxpayers 145

'Salmon' Report (of the Royal Commission) 55-6, 63
Schmidt, Chancellor 9
Seers, Dudley 239, 240, 240n
Shell Group of Companies
    Chemicals 84; Royal Dutch 91; Shell (Germany) 91; Shell (UK) 91
Shipbuilding 90-91, 143
    in USA 133, 158; in Ulster 121
Smuggling 64ff, 74
Spanish foreign currency earners 83-4
Switzerland 196
    ascendancy of Swiss franc 53-4, 116; when bank confidentiality may be annulled 54; banking in 54, 57; foreign bank accounts and tax-evasion 53-4, 59, 61, 64, 162; government and politicians of 165; smuggling exports out of 65; Social Democratic Party of 54

Taxation (*see also* Taxes) 43-47, 73, 124-140, 209, 244
    on exports 78, 129; frauds involving 158
Taxes (*see also* Taxation) 224, 241, 242
    bribes subject to tax deduction 56; capital gains 223; evasion of

47-54, 74, 209; relief on mortgage interest 229; tax-deductible donations 176; Travel Tax 17; Wealth Tax 138
Thatcher, Rt. Hon. Margaret MP 89-90
Treasury, the 46, 47, 125, 129, 130, 143, 151, 223, 228, 235, 241:
    Bills 137; borrowings 139; forecasts 28, 34, 36-7; officials 101, 169

Unemployment 25, 37, 146, 149, 238, 241
    in Germany 102
Unilever 67, 198n, 212
    pensions 160-1
Unit Trusts 30
US Government
    Congress 150; and rodent damage 144; soya bean exports 81

Value Added Tax (VAT) 47n, 50, 51, 128, 224
Vietnam War 36, 111, 113, 218
    US financing of 243

Wages 43, 50-1
    control of 36, 44, 45
Walker, Rt. Hon. Peter MP 166, 233n
Ward, Barbara 14-16
Welfare State 139
Wigan 21-3
Wilson, Rt. Hon. Harold MP 34, 136, 138, 156, 229
    on Premium Bonds 103; visit to Russia 89-90
World depression in 1929 39-40